D0819516

# BARBRA

A RETROSPECTIVE

# BARBRA

## A RETROSPECTIVE

ALLEGRA ROSSI

STERLING
New York

An Imprint of Sterling Publishing
387 Park Avenue South
New York, NY 10016



Produced for Sterling Publishing by Essential Works
www.essentialworks.co.uk

Publishing Director: Mal Peachey
Managing Director: John Conway
Editors: Lori Paximadis, Nicola Hodgson, Tania Bissell
Designer: Barbara Doherty



ISBN 978-1-4027-8823-9 (hardcover)

Distributed in Canada by Sterling Publishing
c/o Canadian Manda Group, 165 Dufferin Street
Toronto, Ontario, Canada M6K 3H6
Distributed in the United Kingdom by GMC Distribution Services
Castle Place, 166 High Street, Lewes, East Sussex, England BN7 1XU
Distributed in Australia by Capricorn Link (Australia) Pty. Ltd.
P.O. Box 704, Windsor, NSW 2756, Australia

For information about custom editions, special sales, and premium and corporate purchases, please contact Sterling Special Sales at 800-805-5489 or specialsales@sterlingpublishing.com.

Manufactured in China

2 4 6 8 10 9 7 5 3 1

www.sterlingpublising.com

# Contents

SHE was born Barbara Joan Streisand at 5:08 am on April 24, 1942. At 5:09, the world was on its way to changing for the better as this baby was to grow up and change the way we listened to music, the way we thought about beauty and style and the way we thought people could sing. This baby, who changed her name in her late teens to "Barbra" turned out to be a singular force in popular culture, crossing boundaries, pushing aside obstacles and allowing her creativity not to be bound by naysayers.

It is in this way that Barbra Streisand changed our world for the better by singing, making us laugh, writing songs, as well as acting, producing and directing films. Streisand is one of the few celebrities to win Oscar, Emmy, Tony and Grammy awards in areas of entertainment where such longevity is rare—and where a top performer's commercial or popular lifespan is more mayfly than tortoise. Barbra has done what was thought impossible, and she's made it look easy.

Her popularity has engendered a legion of loyal fans, and, thanks to TV shows that emphasize skill in singing such as *Glee* or *American Idol*, her legendary vocal talent has become a landmark in achievement. In a time when mature performers are either recapping their greatest hits or retiring to cameos (or completely), Barbra defies time by continually creating something—a kerfuffle with a presidential imitator at one of her live concerts or a coffee table book on interior design entitled *My Passion for Design,* that takes the reader into exquisite homes, including her own. Barbra is a fire hose of innovative creation, unafraid of making a mistake and always up to the challenge of seeking something new. With that urge to perform and to be perfect, she's also set a standard. Now, you have to win that Oscar before you're thirty, if you want to join the pantheon of gods. You have to have so many number 1 hits. In a time when singers are expected to be—and remain—children, Barbra is the lasting womanly goddess of exquisite musical quality. She started out as a starry-eyed, slightly too clever teenager, but she was always womanly, wise beyond her years and truly a force of nature.

In a career spanning over fifty years, Barbra is one of the most successful modern entertainers both critically and financially. She's sold 140 million LPs worldwide, topping the Recording Industry Association of America's list for best-selling female artist and retaining her title as the only female in the top ten and the only non–rock 'n' roll artist in that rating. She's topped the United States's prestigious *Billboard* Hot 100 chart, keeping the record for the most top ten LPs for any female artist—a record of 31 top tens since 1963, when her rendition of "Happy Days Are Here Again" was voted

Barbra on the set of *On a Clear Day You Can See Forever* in 1970.

Record of the Year. She's also the only artist to accrue a number one LP over five consecutive decades.

It's tempting to think that there is some cosmic connection between Barbra Streisand and the other famous people who share her birthdate: Shakespeare, Shirley MacLaine (a friend with whom she co-hosts a party most years), Jean-Paul Gaultier, and other creative people. It is only as she approached her seventieth birthday that we could truly see that Barbra Streisand is as close to celebrity perfection as humanly possible. If she didn't exist, we'd need to invent her, beginning with the basics: an odd-looking, independent girl whose daddy died before her second birthday, a girl who strives to be an actress but, finding it a long haul, begins to sing, because she can. Of the singers famous for their natural skill alone, Barbra stands above all others in pure vocal gifts, barely trained, barely coddled. Match that with star power and staying power, and even her detractors buckle and say, "Well, there is that one song of hers I really like." Even the hardcore anti-Barbra types secretly sing along with her on the radio. It's just impossible not to.

> "I don't care what you say about me. Just be sure to spell my name wrong."

Distinctive in voice and appearance, Barbra seems to have known from the start that her innate understanding of how things should be done to their absolute best was her greatest strength and surest guide. She has her agents, managers and advisors—and she has the pick of the best musicians, writers and designers whenever she wants, for whatever project she plans, be it film, television or audio recording. But ultimately, she is the one who makes the decisions that affect her life the most. Whether her decisions paid off now or later didn't matter: she knew they would pay off in some way, even if it was not in the way envisaged. When she went against the advice of so-called experts in the field of movie-making or recording, her road often led to an unexpected place, usually a place far better than could have been predicted. For example, she refused to get her famous, long, bumpy nose "fixed." Originally she said she didn't have the money to do it. Later, she said she didn't trust the doctors. Now, it seems, rhinoplasty could have muted the voice of the century.

Barbra, New York, 1970.

Barbra the 1960s
fashion icon.

In essence, Barbra learned very quickly the two greatest lessons of all: how to be herself and how to be happy believing in herself. This didn't mean everyone always agreed with her. Referring to her Oscar-winning debut in 1968 in *Funny Girl*, Barbra quipped that she was too pretty to play the 1930s comedienne Fanny Brice. Brice's daughter quipped just the opposite—that her mother was too pretty to be played by Streisand. In a televised interview recently, Barbra said that there were so many falsehoods said about her, disseminated in the press—for one, that if a musician played a wrong note, she'd have him fired. Sensibly, she said, the same would have applied to her: if she'd sung a wrong note, should she have fired herself? In the world of celebrity, extreme nonsense is rife. Concerning the myths of Barbra, some of which we'll address here, she is a professional, a strong woman, and talented, but she's not ridiculous or tyrannical.

Barbra Streisand is like a kaleidoscope: every time you turn her, you see something different. In her appearance alone—her full mouth, exotic eyes and powerful profile—she is striking and unusual, with a face that transforms itself into a myriad of personas with some makeup, a change of lighting, or choice of hairstyle.

Her wisdom extends to her own ideals—and she knows what she likes. For example, she likes to be photographed from her left side. Like Sophia Loren, she knows what beautiful women with pronounced profiles all over the world know: instead of getting a nose job, make up your eyes and sculpt your hair. Barbra knows that, whether she's on TV or in a film, the audience comes to hear her sing or act, but they also "eat with their eyes." Barbra is a feast of sensations, so she lavishes herself with just the right style that makes her stand out and be admired even more for the risks she takes.

Despite her humble beginnings that seem almost clichéd today—it is hard to believe someone so talented and at ease would have had a hard early life—Barbra's transcendence from front of the camera to behind, winning respect as a filmmaker and as a producer (arguably the hardest profession to crack) has extended to design, reinvention and renewal.

Even more amazing is that Barbra makes this all look easy. How did she get to where she is today? Well, being gifted is one thing. But there are many gifted people who fall by the wayside, fail to live up to their potential, or who are crushed by the vagaries of fame. Barbra Streisand has survived beautifully, almost thriving under the pressure to satisfy her fans,

Barbra as Esther Hoffman in *A Star Is Born*, 1976.

quell her detractors and exist in a world where image fades so fast. In the beginning, Barbra Streisand was a voice and a woman, and now a star who has outshone decades of entertainment alteration and upheaval and who has a fanbase loyal, strong and growing.

In a way, her celebrity is even more remarkable these days when fame seems to be given for all sorts of reasons. Barbra is famous, first, because she can sing like no one else on earth. Second, because she was one of the first megastars to cross from small, smoky nightclubs, to TV, to Broadway, and then to Hollywood. Before Barbra, no one had ever done that before because these were new media and new ways of reaching an audience hungry for quality. When today's singers rely on vocal special effects to get them through a song, Barbra's voice is the stellar example of unadulterated talent. She accepted that she was, in fact, hugely talented, a thing that she embraced and used but that she also took for granted. She is a great singer, yes, but so much more. No matter what you may think she does best, her creativity has a mind and an aesthetic of its own. It kicks like a mule, glides like a porpoise, and then transmutes itself into something else—musical, educational, philanthropical or merely wonderful.

She knows who she is. And because she does, we, her fans, can feel even more assured with ourselves and why we like her. In this age of uncertainty, of a lack of real identity and direction, a star like Barbra Streisand lends us a steadying hand, showing us that some things in life are real and discernable. She is the voice, the talent and the joy of life, all rolled into an accessible song, tune, film, or performance. A photo of her can bring gasps from her admirers. Barbra's physical form sums up all the struggle, perfection and beauty that has made for a lengthy, award-strewn career. People love Barbra in what is, for them, a very real way.

From her earliest days in the 1960s to her seventieth birthday in 2012, Barbra Streisand's career and life are what legends are made of—made even more impressive because she was still recording, acting and creating when others had stopped. Just when Barbra's myth precedes her, she gently sidesteps and surprises us all with, say, a rare live appearance at the Grammy Awards—or an ensemble role in a major Hollywood comedy—or a starring, all singing, all dancing role in a major studio musical. Her style, her tenacity and her talent keep her fans inspired and coming back for more. Because Barbra works for and expects perfection, she calls us to do the same in our own lives. Barbra keeps being herself and because she is multi-faceted, she inspires us to be the same. In a way, Barbra's quest for perfection, meshed with such talent, such a strong personality and such an imposing appearance, shows us

At the 40th Annual Director's Guild of American Awards, 1988.

how we can affect the world ourselves, perhaps in a smaller way but with the same kind of courage and conviction in ourselves, especially when it seems the world says no to our dreams. Does Barbra ever give up? No. She doesn't keep doing the same thing over and over again either; she evolves.

For her those who love her, Barbra is life itself. For those who do not adore her as much, there is usually at least a recognition of her endurance, her talent, and her obstinate belief in herself, right or wrong. Barbra is an achiever, maybe even an overachiever, and an inspiration to us all to

> "I don't like the word 'superstar.' It has ridiculous implications. These words—star, stupor, superstar, stupid star—they're misleading. It's a myth."

have the courage to take a risk, make a mistake and be original. Barbra goes ahead and records with Donna Summer or Il Divo. She'd don an embroidered beret and think nothing of it. As for her amazing fingernails, well, they started out as a statement to say she's not going to be anyone's secretary—as if the "boss" existed who'd be able to dictate to her!

For those of us who feel misunderstood, or who don't have the ultimate courage of our convictions—for those of us who feel our talents are somewhat unappreciated or that we don't know where we truly belong, Barbra's achievements shine like a beacon. She lived it her way, doing what her inner voice told her to do, and while we may not have her talent, we can all appreciate her attitude and energy, attempt to emulate it in our own lives. This book goes a little way to show how she did what she did, why it worked and to celebrate her incredible achievements. Mainly, though, this is a celebration of the way she was, and what she is. The fact that Barbra Streisand exists surely helps us all to be happier people? When she sings, we sing along—she sings for us, and we wish within our hearts that we could sing the way she does. When Barbra creates, she does it for us all. Here, then, is the glory of Barbra Streisand, the one and only.

As Roz Focker in *Meet the Fockers*, 2004.

*One: The Early Years*

# Second Hand Rose

BARBRA fans will know all about her climb from obscurity to fame, and a few know the finer details of how her talent was developed, discovered and then recognized. It's some story, of course, of how a young girl from Brooklyn became Barbra Streisand, "the voice" and the icon.

Born in the Williamsburg part of Brooklyn, Barbra's early years weren't typical of her era. In their six-story brick apartment building at 457 Schenectady Avenue, Barbra's father Emanuel Steisand was an extraordinary man. He had a PhD in education from Columbia University and had been the first of his family to attend college. When his daughter was born he was making a good living teaching delinquent boys and had written an instruction manual on how to instruct troubled kids. Everyone who knew him thought he had a brilliant career ahead of him.

> "We were poor, but not poor poor. We just never had anything."

Barbra's mother, Diana Rosen Streisand, was the daughter of a cantor and a garment cutter. Diana was a high school graduate with straight A's and worked as a secretary in Manhattan. Like her daughter to come, Diana had some theatrical leanings and quite a lovely voice, as we can hear in surviving recordings she made at her piano in the 1950s. Like many women of that era, the minute she was married she stopped dreaming of her own career and turned her energies toward being a wife and mother.

Barbra's brother, Sheldon, was born in 1935. Joyful though the Streisands were about Sheldon, they longed for a girl, to "complete the set." In the middle of the Great Depression of the 1930s, however, that second child took longer than they would have perhaps liked. Barbara Joan Streisand came along seven years later, on April 24, 1942.

By all accounts, Barbra was an unusual baby. She didn't sleep very much and was very curious about the world, but was quite silent about it. She rarely cried, preferring to watch the action that was going on around her. Her head seemed too large for her body and she didn't have an ounce of hair on her head until she was two years old.

The fabulous profile, 1969.

Opposite: Brooklyn in 1943, birthplace of Barbra.

Above: Barbra aged seven, in 1949, as pictured on her album *My Name Is Barbra*.

Before then, however, tragedy struck the family. When Barbra was fifteen months old, her father died of what was believed to be a cerebral hemorrhage. Later, the cause of his death was thought to be respiratory failure due to a dose of morphine administered to stop an epileptic fit. Regardless of whether he was allergic to the morphine or it was an overdose, he died at Flesichmanns Hospital near the Catskills where, known to everyone as Manny, he had been working over the summer of 1943. He was only thirty-four years old.

Her mother, in mourning, moved the family to her parents' home at 365 Pulaski Street in Brooklyn.

If money was tight before, it was even more so after the loss of the family's main breadwinner. Barbra's first toy was a hot water bottle, which took the place of a doll. As Barbra was to say later in life, it wasn't that they were really poor, it was that the Streisands didn't have anything. The family was kept aloft by Diana's brother's army paychecks, which thankfully came in regularly. After he returned from overseas, Diana was emotionally fit enough to go back to work and took a job as a bookkeeper, working as hard as she could to provide for her children.

So it was that Barbra Streisand grew up as the myth and marvel of her amazing father grew, year by year, in her family lore. She never really knew him, but his importance and absence dominated so much of her earliest years. With her mother working, Barbra was often left in the company of grandparents, sometimes playing in front of her grandfather's tailor shop.

Barbra learned to fend for herself. With her father gone and her mother working all hours, she had to be independent. Seeing that horrible things can happen early in life and that sometimes there wasn't a thing you could do to stop them, she became determined to survive and thrive, and not rely on other people to make things happen. She walked herself to and from school at the age of five and looked out for herself at home until her mother returned from work. In conditions under which softer, less self-reliant children would have suffered or become emotionally damaged, Barbra became stoic, certain of herself and of her direction, whatever that was.

Barbra was a smart kid. Hanging around the hallways of her apartment building, she'd find neighbors who'd give her a snack—and not always the kosher kind—and find herself being forced to eat dinner when she was not really hungry. Forcing her soon became the thing that never worked with little Barbra—not then, and not later.

Just when Barbra was settling her life into a routine, the unimaginable happened: Her mother brought home a man who was to become the new "head" of the family. The future star was just seven years old when Louis Kind married her mother Diana in 1949. He sold real estate but tellingly, Barbra always referred to him as a used car salesman. It was clear from the start that she did not take to him, and the feeling was apparently mutual. He certainly never loved her the way her real father would have.

Of course, no man could ever have filled the glorious empty shoes of Emanuel Streisand, and it was almost inevitable that Barbra and her stepfather would clash, even if the family's living standards improved because of his introduction into their lives. They moved into a better apartment on the corner of Nostrand and Newkirk Avenues. About this time, Barbra expressed a desire to perform, to be a ballerina, and in order to keep the strong-willed, restless child happy, Diana took her to Miss Marsh's School of Dance. That lasted until Barbra was diagnosed with anemia and yanked out of dance class to preserve her health. Around then Barbra also began to complain of funny noises in her ears, noises that wouldn't go away. It seems one of the greatest singers of our time had tinnitus from a very early age.

They may have stopped her attending classes, but the grown-ups could not, however, stop Barbra from dancing *en pointe* in the living room at home. Here, perhaps, can be seen the emergence of Barbra the Unstoppable. Her solid self-confidence grew as she slowly began to learn how to fight her mother's restrictions on what she could and couldn't do.

Barbra in 1959, from her Erasmus Hall High School Yearbook.

## A Star Is Almost Born

Barbra's home life changed again when her mother gave birth to a half sister named Roslyn Kind in 1951. A happy, fat, cheerful baby, Roslyn was "perfect" compared to her quiet, analytical half sister. It is little wonder that Barbra began to find a fantasy world at the movie theater. Barbra almost obsessively began attending Loew's Kings Theatre on Flatbush Avenue—that is, when she wasn't able to watch a neighbor's television set. Both television and films began to shape her life, while her passion for dance taught her a love of performance and of getting attention.

Diana hadn't encouraged her eldest daughter to sing, preferring to downplay her emerging talents. Barbra, being a shy and standoffish girl, made few friends in public school, but was befriended by the Bernstein twins, Marilyn and Carolyn. They played at being a singing group called Bernie and the Bernsteins—Barbra was always the lead singer. Sometimes she sang too much for other kids, but her voice, although not as strong as it was to become, was already shaping up into something beautiful.

Diana, badgered by Barbra, took the precocious preteen to an audition at the MGM Records studios, ostensibly to shut her daughter up. Not only was Diana worried about the cost that might be incurred from Barbra's desire to audition and take lessons, but she was also worried that Barbra, with her unusual looks, would be rejected because she wasn't conventionally beautiful.

MGM Records was the home of Joni James, Barbra's idol of the moment, and because they were looking for new child star, they held open audition at the Steve Allen Studio. Mother and daughter went in without an agent or any major preparation, except for the new blue dress that Barbra wore. There, in a glass "case" that was their recording booth, Barbra sang the Joni James tune "Have You Heard," plus "Allegheny Moon," without any backing track.

Expecting to be taken on immediately, she was surprised to be told by her mother that the MGM staff had told her to go home and practice. What Barbra hadn't been told by Diana is that they did like her voice, but that they'd wanted to sign her up for training. Since that would cost money they didn't have, Diana nixed the idea. The same thing would happen the next year, with Barbra being accepted at a child performers' school only to be pulled out after four months. Her mother said it was too far away when actually it was just too expensive. Barbra thought, as a child would, that

this was just another way that her mother tried to control her life and ruin her dreams. The truth was that stepdaddy Louis Kind wasn't holding up his end of the bargain and that the money he was supposed to be supplying the family was becoming less and less reliable. In fact, it seems that most of the time Diana didn't know where he was.

Never minding about her stepfather's inability to be a real father, and side-stepping her mother's careful ways, Barbra became an unstoppable force. Maybe there wasn't money for the things she wanted, and maybe there wasn't an easy way to get where she wanted to go, but by the time Barbra was ten years old, she knew very well what she wanted and, like water seeking its own level, she was absolutely certain of the inevitability of attaining her goal—and doing it her way.

Barbra with brother Sheldon and half-sister Roslyn Kind, 1977.

## Can't Stop Believing

Just after Christmas 1955 Barbra and her mother went to the Nola Recording Studio and recorded four demo tunes, two songs each. Barbra opted for "You'll Never Know" and "Zing! Went the Strings of My Heart," while her mother, bullied by the pianist, didn't really get as many notes in as her daughter did. The same year, the burgeoning singer began attending high school at Eramus Hall in Brooklyn, which was also the alma mater of Mae West and Moe Howard of the Three Stooges. Still determined to sing wherever she could, Barbra tried several times to join the school choral club (which initially didn't want her and then, when it did, stuck her in the back row, giving solos to other girls). There she met Neil Diamond and befriended an awkward boy named Bobby Fischer.

There's some confusion about whether Barbra was a kook or not in high school. She says she was, indicating that she dressed strangely compared to other students. She has also been quoted as saying that she dyed her hair in weird shades of blond and wore way-out eyeshadow and lipstick. According to the documentary *I Remember Barbra* (1981) by Kevin Burns, neighbors, fellow students and others have said that Barbra was not some weird kid wearing clown clothes and tribal makeup, though.

> "I want to be famous. I don't care whether it's by singing or acting or what, I want everyone to know my name, even the cowboys!"

Here, then, are the beginnings of young Barbra's self-mythologizing, which extended as far as her Broadway debut. Barbra wanted to plant the seeds of strangeness about herself because in the 1950s, an ethnic look like hers was clearly not the norm—it wasn't even on the beauty map.

A good student, she was quiet, got good marks, and hung out with the smart kids. She was admitted to PS 89's Intellectually Gifted Opportunity Program, which meant an automatic inclusion to the honors class. Perhaps because she was identified as being academically gifted, she didn't put much

effort into being popular in school. Barbra was not Miss Congeniality or the most sought-after—by either sex, it seems—girl in her class. Not that she appeared bothered by it, especially after she had begun to apply her industrious nature to part-time work at a Chinese restaurant.

Between the ages of twelve and sixteen, Choy's Oriental was Barbra's home away from home. What started as a babysitting job with their upstairs neighbors soon became an adventure in earning money as a maitre d', waitress and cashier at the joint; some say she wore a silk kimono and painted her long nails red. Muriel Choy, one of the owners of the eatery on Nostrand Avenue, answered Barbra's pressing questions about life, love, sex and all that; questions that Barbra could never ask her mother, such as whether the man was on top during sex; Mrs. Chow smartly replied, "Not always."

Barbra in 1963.

## Egg Salad Sandwich

This was the stuff that Barbra's teens were made of: curiosity about sex, success, the world, other cultures, escaping from her dreary, hemmed-in life in which she felt unloved and misunderstood. Not wanting to be "seen" or "known" until she was famous was a theme in Barbra's early days. In

1956, at one of the Choy girls' birthday parties, Jimmy Choy tested out his early 8mm film camera. He swung it through the birthday party and caught Barbra, ducking her head and putting her hands up to shield her face. No, there would be no record of Barbra until things were perfect, or at least more perfect than they were then.

That same year, Barbra saw *The Diary of Anne Frank*, which introduced her to Broadway and awakened her desire to be an actress. It was the first Broadway play she saw and was directed by the legendary Garson Kanin, who would later direct her in 1968's *Funny Girl*. A few days after her theatrical epiphany, Barbra convinced her mother to allow her to try out for Otto Premiger's production of *Saint Joan*. Barbra read for the role at a huge open casting. After being told her reading was excellent, she was sent home and told to wait. If she was chosen, she'd be contacted. Jean Seberg went on to achieve stardom in that film. That a pretty blond girl was chosen as a star further convinced Diana that her daughter could only be a disaster in showbiz, and if not a disaster, then hurt very badly by the whole affair.

The family had moved to the Vanderveer Estates in May 1955, but almost exactly one year later Louis Kind moved his belongings out of the family apartment and left for good. On the one hand, Barbra was happy he was gone; perhaps now her mother would be happier and she wouldn't have to tiptoe around Louis and his bad moods anymore. On the other hand, the family was now extremely impoverished.

In 1957, managing to somehow get away with spending only $150 instead of the quoted $300 normally required for food and lodging, Barbra went out for summer stock, having lied about her age, at the Malden Bridge Playhouse. Those sharing rooms with her said that at the time she seemed like a total "Brooklyn brat," making sure she was in front of the line at lunchtime. But putting herself first meant she also learned everything she could from the Malden Bridge lighting man, who let her light one of the plays that summer. In the winter of 1957–58, she worked at the West Village's Cherry Lane Theatre as an understudy in *Purple Dust* before appearing in *Tobacco Road* at the Clinton Playhouse (1958), and *Driftwood* at the Garret Theatre on 49th Street (little more than an unheated garret, true to its name) and *Separate Tables* at the Cecilwood Theatre upstate, both in 1959. She also met a comedienne called Phyllis Diller and performed with her in *Driftwood*, which spanned six shows and got no reviews. Barbra recalled years later that she suffered terrible stage fright before going on at the Garret: "I remember throwing up my egg salad sandwich before I went on."

Barbra on stage, 1962.

## The Lion Tamer

Despite not wanting to go to college, Barbra managed to graduate high school on January 15, 1959, with a 93 average and an award in Spanish. She then went off—against Diana's will—to fulfill her ambition. In Manhattan, Barbra found a cheap place to share with another girl on 48th Street.

Barbra's certainty was shaken when she realized that she wasn't going to be picked up right away by a theatrical producer who could see her talent. She grew weary of the endless cattle calls, those auditions for actors looking for roles. Instead, she made do with other forms of employment, such as being an usherette at Broadway's Lunt-Fontanne Theater. *The Sound of Music* was playing around then and Barbra heard there was an audition for the role of Leisl, the blond older daughter, in an upcoming production. The fact that Barbra didn't look a bit like Leisl didn't stop her from sending in a photo of herself wearing her Chinese clothing. She looked so odd that agent Eddie Blum had to see her for himself. When he heard her sing, he got in touch with Peter Daniels, a talented pianist. That was the beginning of Barbra's ability to make money by singing, which she learned on a smaller scale in the Catskills as she earned a few dollars singing at weddings.

> "You know, I can't remember my good reviews. I remember negative ones. They stay in my mind."

Now that Barbra was in Manhattan, free of her mother's restrictions, she could meet and get to know anyone. Soon she met a somber-looking actor called Barry Dennen. He became Barbra's friend, confidant, and, he later claimed, lover and took her under his wing. He showed her where the money was in those songs she sang.

The weekly talent contest at the Lion at 62 W. 9th Street gave the winner $50 and a week's booking plus free food. Those three things being items that Barbra could certainly use, what wasn't there to like? She won over the crowd of gay men, arguably the toughest room in town, within seconds of taking the stage—not that she would get carried away with any notion of becoming a mere singer, regardless of how much audiences liked her. Barbra

The young star in 1963.

considered herself an actress, not a singer, and she was only both right now because she had to literally sing for her supper.

After becoming the undisputed champion of the Lion, Barbra decided that she needed a new name, a new look—and a new place to sing. For the new clothes, there was the thrift store; she was always able to find the oddest pieces and put them together to make a striking, if unconventional, outfit. Her new venues were the revelation of 1960, though. Her very first professional gig at the Bon Soir was on September 9, 1960, when she opened for Phyllis Diller. This time, *Variety* noticed her.

By June 1960, she'd decided to do something about the name she never liked. After playing around with various pseudonyms, she decided to simply drop the middle a and keep the rest. Two monumental things happened that month: she dumped her first agent (who couldn't get her gigs because she was too unusual) and she hired another, Martin Erlichman, after meeting him backstage at the Bon Soir. They began a professional relationship that would last for the best part of Barbra's long career.

Barbra's prodigious gifts of acting, singing, and almost perfect comic timing were the backbone of musical theater. During the experimental, high-gloss days of the 1960s, these skills found their natural home—not that anyone, not even the girl who was to become Barbra Streisand, could just waltz into a Broadway role. Broadway has traditions, and one of them is that everyone has to pay his or her dues. Barbra began doing so in earnest around 1957 when she embarked on a smattering of theatrical appearances at a variety of venues, in a variety of roles, including some backstage. There was no way you could keep that girl away from the stage; anything to do with acting, she just ate right up.

In May 1960 Barbra had appeared in *The Insect Comedy* at the Jan Hus Theater on the Upper East Side, and in August she appeared in *The Boyfriend* at the Cecilwood Theater Playhouse as Hortense the French Maid. She spent the rest of the year singing solo in small bars and clubs in New York. In 1961, however, she became a part of an ensemble in the revue *Another Evening with Harry Stoones* at the Gramercy Arts Theater on New York's East 27th Street. It was a small beginning for what would become a great big career on the Broadway (and world) stage.

Smiling superstar, 1964.

*Two: The Sixties*

# Funny Girl

HAVING served her stage "apprenticeship" in summer stock and small New York productions, Barbra had to shift slightly away from more mainstream musical theater. Her first stage success off-Broadway was *Another Evening with Harry Stoones,* a comedy that had nine previews and one performance on October 21, 1961. Its first act was called "The Civil War"; the second was titled "The Roaring Twenties." Starring with Dom DeLuise and Diana Sands, Barbra was given three skits to perform in part one of the revue: "Indian Nuts," in which she plays the part of a Native American at the time of Columbus; "Value"—a song she kept in her nightclub repertoire for years afterward, until the 1970s—in which she professes a love of Harold Mengert, and not just because he has a rich family and a car; and "Jersey," in which she laments a boyfriend's move to New Jersey. In part two of the show Barbra confronts her boyfriend in a locker room to tell him she's "with child" during a number titled "Big Barry."

> "I hated singing. I wanted to be an actress. But I don't think I'd have made it any other way."

Despite the brevity of the show, Barbra received a good notice in the trade magazine *Variety.* The writer remarked on her comedic abilities and her facility with singing, especially in "Jersey." *The New York Times* criticized the bitty nature of the show, though, with its thirty-eight sketches and also its lapse of taste, wandering into territories involving "human functions and homosexuality"—which sound as if, with a tweak or two, *Another Evening with Harry Stoones* would probably be an interesting theatrical curio today, if not a minor hit.

With that one accolade from *Variety* under her belt, Barbra dolled herself up in vintage clothing on the morning of Friday, November 24, 1961—the day after Thanksgiving—to audition for *I Can Get It for You Wholesale,* a new musical about New York's garment district. The title of the show is a phrase that had entered the vernacular as meaning that the same goods can be found elsewhere cheaper; it was also a reference to the rag trade of the period, which was predominately run by the Jewish community.

Premiering at Broadway's Shubert Theatre in late March 1962, the rousing comedic musical was written and scored by Harold Rome; its book was by Jerome Weidman, who also wrote the 1937 source novel, which was made into a feature film called *This Is My Affair* in 1951, starring Susan Hayward. Set in the Great Depression in New York City's garment district, it told of a young businessman who will do anything to be a success, be that lying, cheating or stealing. Of course, there is a moral backlash, and the businessman, named Harry Bogen, is brought back to earth and reminded that his girlfriend and his mother still love him no matter what.

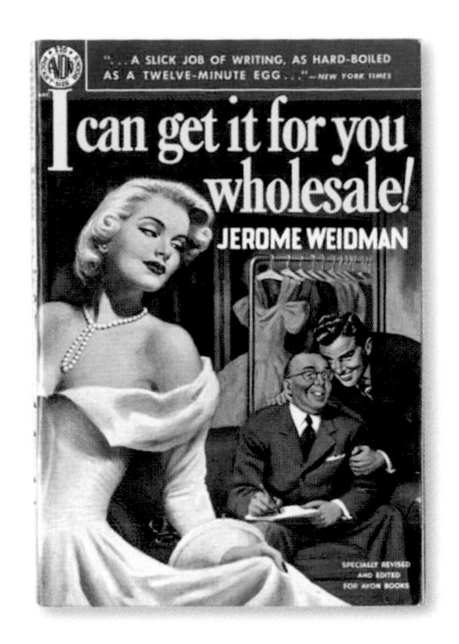

Above: The original paperback book that launched the show that launched Barbra's stage career.

Left: Barbra on stage in *I Can Get It for You Wholesale*, 1962.

Barbra's big hit of the show was named after her character, Miss Marmelstein. The script had been written before she'd been cast, but the young singer was so talented that the role was made larger to accommodate her talent. Barbra ended up carrying *Wholesale* through its previews in Philly. Because she was that good, the show moved to Boston with her role slightly expanded to keep her on stage longer. When it finally opened at the Shubert Theatre on March 22, 1962, Barbra had become a star of the show.

Perhaps it was inevitable that Elliot Gould, the male lead of *I Can Get It for You Wholesale*, would ask Barbra on a date. He had seen her audition and called her (she had just gotten her own phone). He was single, and so was she—why wouldn't Miss Marmelstein, Barbra's character, and Harry Bogen, Gould's character, like each other? So began an offstage relationship that would eventually culminate in marriage and a child—though not immediately. She had to figure him out first. "He wasn't normal," she has said, meaning it as a compliment. Soon enough though, Elliot and Barbra decided to move in together into a tiny apartment on Third Avenue.

> "I knew that with a mouth like mine, I just had to be a star or something."

The production of *Wholesale* not only introduced Barbra to her first husband, but it also landed her a Tony nomination when she was only nineteen. That was an enormous honor, and the first of what would be many nominations—and awards—to follow in her long and productive career on stage and screen.

Barbra's part as Miss Marmelstein in *Wholesale* was as Bogen's secretary, a role she played throughout the original show's run of two previews and three hundred performances. With only one solo ("Miss Marmelstein"), a duet with Mr. Pulvermacher ("I'm Not a Well Man"), and two ensemble songs ("Ballad of the Garment Trade" and "What Are They Doing to Us Now?"), the play wasn't designed to be a platform for Barbra's talent. However, it allowed enough of a glimmer of her skills to shine through to cause Howard Taubman of *The New York Times* to comment that Streisand was a "natural comedienne." It was an auspicious first review.

Barbra in the studio, 1963.

## Happy Days

Through 1961 and 1962 Barbra earned money singing in a club that her agent, Marty Erlichman, booked for her. He organized a tour of sorts in 1961, taking in different clubs throughout the country and into Canada. Barbra performed at New York's famous Village Vanguard, Detroit's Caucus Club, the Crystal Palace in St. Louis, and the Town 'n Country in Winnipeg, Canada, between March and July.

Back in New York Barbra moved between the Bon Soir in the Village and the bigger Blue Angel, uptown at East 55th Street. All the while her new, trusted, and energetic agent pushed to get her a recording contract. She auditioned by tape for RCA, with some success. She even began to make television appearances. On April 5, 1961, she appeared on *The Jack Paar Show* at the behest of its guest host, Orson Bean. He had been in the audience at the Bon Soir to witness an early appearance and really wanted her to perform live on TV. With Marty's help, she wafted easily onto TV with *PM East*, Mike Wallace's late late talk show, to sing and chat later the same year.

Barbra's participation in the cast recordings for *I Can Get It for You Wholesale* and *Pins and Needles* (see pages 56–57 and 58–59) brought her to the attention of Columbia Records president Goddard Lieberson. A noted Broadway expert, he liked her voice and ability, but he thought the girl was too far out there to ever have broad appeal. So, while he was happy with her doing the revue LP, signing her as a solo star was another matter—at first.

Barbra was only just twenty years old and not yet a known quantity. Even being nominated for a Tony award for her role in *Wholesale* didn't mean that she'd be a great recording artist. When *Wholesale* ended, Barbra returned to the Bon Soir, where she met Marilyn and Alan Bergman and began a lifelong relationship with the songwriters. In May 1962, Barbra made another important television appearance, singing "Happy Days Are Here Again" on *The Garry Moore Show.* In August she shared the set with Groucho Marx as guest host on *The Tonight Show*. Later that year, she appeared on the legendary TV chat show again, but with its legendary host Johnny Carson.

The interest in Barbra's voice, combined with her excellent work on TV, brought her to the notice of a lot of influential people. Atlantic Records wanted her, as did Capitol. Barbra's manager, Marty Erlichman, believed that Columbia was Barbra's best shot, though. Despite his misgivings, Goddard Lieberson offered her a contract, which was signed on October 1, 1962. The early contract didn't earn her a great deal of money, but, tellingly, her contract did give her a lot of artistic control, right down to the cover art. That

Mr. and Mrs. Elliot Gould, 1968.

*"Show and Tell . . .
this is Sadie."*

*"Animal Crackers in My Soup . . ."*

*"That Face . . . That Face . . ."*

*"I love your eyes,
your cheeks, your HAIR!"*

*"Were Thine That
Special Face . . ."*

*"I've grown accustomed
to the trace of
something in the air . . ."*

*"What's New Pussycat???"*

*"We have so much
in common!!!"*

*"It's spring again . . ."*

*"Have I Stayed Too Long
at the Fair?"*

may have been what persuaded her and Erlichman to sign with Columbia and why she stayed with them for the rest of her recording career.

She and Columbia set about deciding how best to market her talent and style; she seemed more cabaret than easy listening or pop at the time. Lieberson understood that the theater was a great place for Barbra, but on record, exactly where a distinctive talent such as hers would fit was another question.

Her debut solo Columbia recording session was amazing, with Barbra singing "Happy Days Are Here Again" (which was to become her first single), "Lover Come Back," and others. She took her last bow at the Bon Soir, the final night proving very emotional. She recorded some tracks live from there for her debut LP, although they didn't get released until way in the future.

With an appearance on *The Ed Sullivan Show* Barbra's future began to shape up nicely. Her eponymous debut LP (see pages 60–61) stayed on the *Billboard* charts for 101 weeks and won her Grammys for Best Album and Best Female Vocalist. She appeared on *The Mike Douglas Show* for a week, then went back on *The Tonight Show* and to *Ed Sullivan* for the second time. She seemed to be caught in a TV whirlpool of the same thing over and over again, despite the great reception of her first album. After her single "Happy Days Are Here Again" was released, and aided by her many TV performances, Barbra was invited to perform at the White House. It must have gone well, because she would be invited back many times in the future.

She and Elliott Gould tried to balance their careers as best they could. He ended up having to take off for London when his musical *On the Town* moved there. Barbra joined him very briefly but had to jet back to Las Vegas to open for Liberace.

Busy as she was, Barbra let it be known through Erlichman that she was keen to do more musical theater, and definitely something more challenging than the onstage chair-sliding of Miss Marmelstein. And so it happened. Right in the middle of recording her second LP, Barbra heard she had won the role of Fanny Brice on Broadway. Who knew it would be the role that remains to this day exclusively associated with her?

As 1963 rolled on, Barbra's second LP (see pages 62–63) flew into the charts (where it stayed for seventy-four weeks). She got to sing a duet with the goddess of song, Judy Garland—and then she and Elliott finally married, in Carson City, Nevada, on September 13, 1963.

Opposite: The insert of the *Color Me Barbra* album, taken during the filming of the TV Special of the same name, 1966.

## The Big One That Didn't Get Away

Barbra Streisand was apparently the last choice for lead in the planned musical of the life of Fanny Brice, America's best-loved comedienne and singer of the first half of the twentieth century. She did, however, have half of the songwriters employed to create the show on her side. Jule Styne asked director Jerome Robbins to see Barbra sing at the Bon Soir. When he did, he asked her to audition—and what a shock it proved for the director and crew. Barbra arrived wearing her favorite assemblage of costume: thrift shop clothes. This was long before vintage clothing became fashionable. Nevertheless, Streisand was hired.

Barbra was only twenty-one at the time and, compared to others on Broadway, inexperienced. When her casting was announced, the press called her a nightclub singer who'd appeared on stage only once before, sidestepping the fact that she had accepted the part of *Funny Girl* from Las Vegas, where she was appearing nightly. Instead, reporters focused on her career start, winning a humble yet critical talent show down in Greenwich Village. When confronted about the new spelling of her first name, she replied that she'd know she's made it when everyone spells her name the way she wants it spelled.

Although Barbra admitted that she didn't know much about the now historical entertainment figure that she was to portray onstage, she said that she felt Miss Brice and she were like-minded and somewhat stubborn, and neither of them listened to their mothers or, for that matter, experienced showmen, either. Florenz Ziegfeld couldn't advise Fanny Brice, and, as it turned out, *Funny Girl*'s bosses couldn't control Barbra Streisand. When asked, Barbra said she was preparing for the role of a lifetime by playing herself. After all, this is what the then director Bob Fosse wanted—although he was soon to be replaced by Hollywood film director Garson Kanin.

After numerous rewrites, and with the length of performance curtailed from three to two hours while it was previewing, Barbra found herself remarkably confident in her performance in the show. She experimented with the comedic element of her character in front of live audiences, riffing off their reaction, learning how to "read" an audience as she grew into her role. Barbra said in an early interview that she didn't research Brice's character at all, preferring to take the story from the playbook as it was written, without additional backstory on her part. She also loved one song in particular, "People," despite it not fitting well with the rest of the show. Garson Kanin wanted it out, but Barbra recorded it and planned to release it as a single before the stage show opened. We know who won that argument.

Barbra looking sultry among the palms of the Beverley Hills Hotel, 1965.

## More Variety

Barbra was put to the test physically, emotionally and artistically by *Funny Girl*. Luckily, the tinnitus that had plagued her from her youth doesn't seem to impair her ability to act and sing under extreme duress on a public stage. Not that anyone thought of her as frail; Brice's mother quips in the play that her daughter is "built like a horse," and that applied to Streisand too. She was an energetic twenty-one-year-old performer who loved what she did, but she was singing twelve songs in every show, eight times a week. It was hard work conserving one's energy and still dazzling an audience.

In an interview in 1977, Barbra spoke of the traumas of having to follow the show's demanding schedule. At first, she found the rehearsals exhilarating and challenging, just up her alley, she said. Having grown to love Chinese food because of her job at Choy's Orient when she was a teenager, she would gorge herself on her favorite Chinese dishes before she went out to perform.

> "The first draft of *Funny Girl* was written when I was six. I'm glad it took so long to get it right!"

Stoked with energy, she found that the more variety there was in the show, the happier she was. Unlike other stars who feel secure only when the show is set and everything meticulously timed, with cues set in stone, Barbra loved the fluidity of the changes she was witnessing. Barbra loved the possibility of playing any of the musical's forty-one different final scenes; she loved the huge variety of songs. In fact, the production was only frozen on opening night and until then, the myriad choices of what would be played or could be were a fascinating combination of known elements. The excitement, she admitted, was stimulating to her as an artist and performer.

The minute the show was frozen, however, Barbra said she felt she became locked up herself. Her energy was constrained by knowing what was coming up, and she has said that the difficulty that she felt in getting through a performance in which everything was so confining was what sent her into analysis. Playing *Funny Girl* on stage, she has said, put her on a drug called Donnatal, a medication based on belladonna, which was prescribed for, among other things, stomach cramps.

Barbra was beginning to get enormous publicity and made the cover of *Time* magazine on April 10, 1964. All the publicity and coverage added to the pressure on her, though. That May Barbra won two Grammys for her first LP and became the youngest person to ever win Album of the Year.

## Something Special

Thanks to Marty, Barbra had signed a $5 million contract with CBS to make television music specials. Despite her fame and accolades, CBS was nervous about Barbra's first TV broadcast on April 14, 1965, mainly because she didn't have any guests, which was the format for the time. Of course, the show went on to be an enormous success. It was nominated for five Emmy awards, and won two.

Above: Collecting her first Emmy for a TV special, *My Name Is Barbra*, 1965.

Following pages: Barbra in a feature in *Life* magazine from 1963.

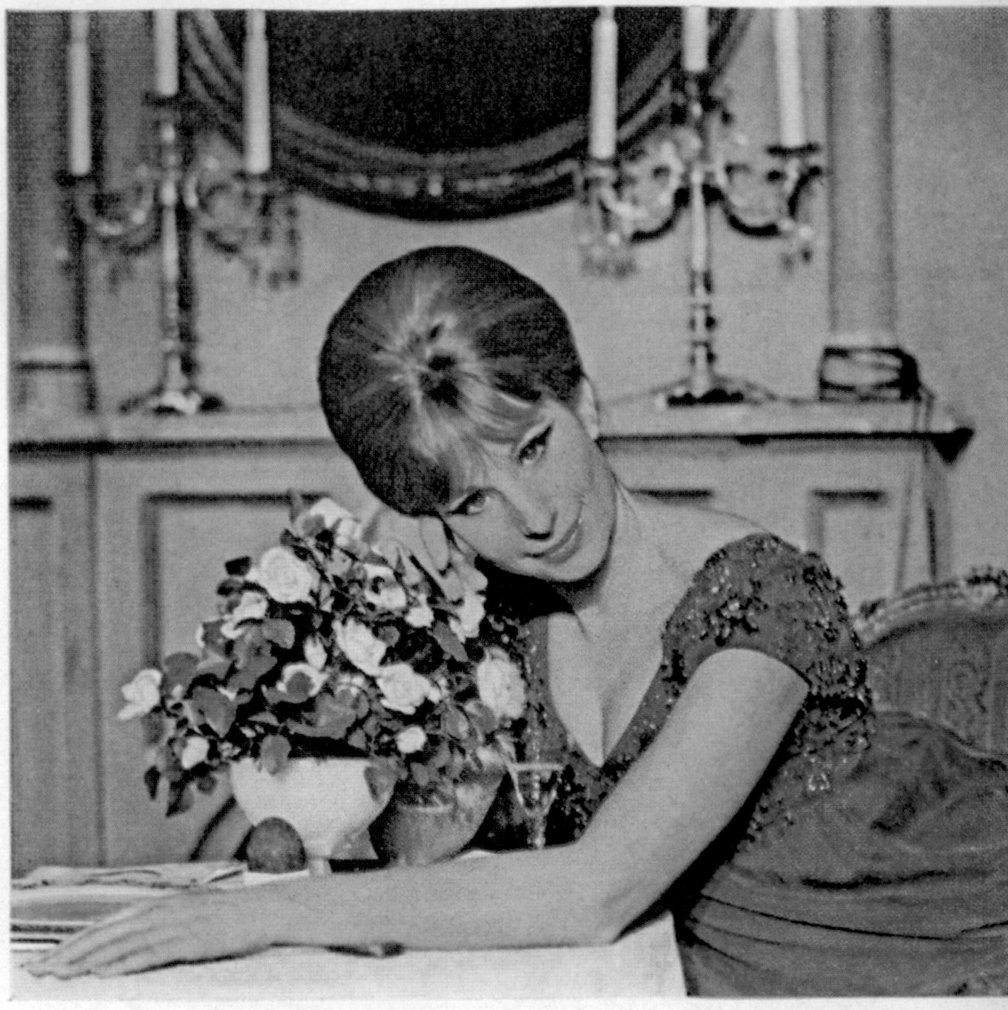

SEDUCTION SCENE is Edwardian farce as she is plied with dry sherry and a blue marble egg. "A bit of *pâté*?" "I drink it all day."

SNAPPING her fan, Streisand is a parody of the vamp. To some, her profile is Nefertiti's; to others, purebred Brooklyn.

SELDOM IN REPOSE, her variable face acquires depth when she stops to contemplate. Then beneath all the laughs, audience discovers—another laugh.

## "Six Expressions More Than All the Barrymores"

BACKSTAGE, Barbra Streisand stares in mirror a long moment as in opening scene when she bubbles forth: "Hello, gorgeous."

PHOTOGRAPHS FOR TIME BY ORMOND GIGLI—RAPHO-GUILLUMETTE

BELTING a number called *Cornet Man*, Barbra re-creates Fanny Brice's no-help invasion of Broadway from the Lower East Side.

BUMPTIOUSLY donning a Ziegfeld headdress, Streisand clowns in same irreverent way that made Fanny Brice a Follies delight.

Barbra and Sadie, the first of her small white dogs, 1965.

Less than six months later, Barbra said goodbye to Fanny—for now. During her final performance in *Funny Girl*, on Sunday, December 26, 1965, Barbra cried while singing "People." She also, for the first and only time, sang Brice's signature number, "My Man." She didn't expect to hear the audience sing "Auld Lang Syne" back to her on that final night after all the cast gave their last bows. The moment was recorded and can be heard on the collection *For the Record*. On it you can hear the emotion in Barbra's voice and her strange reluctance to even say Fanny Brice's name. In 1983, Barbra told critic Gene Shalit that singing "People" for the last time overwhelmed her with emotion, which she said she did not know the origin of but that it was, she thought, from somewhere deep in her subconscious. She was taken aback by the amount of feeling she had when she sang that song and how much it had meant to her.

With all the pressure of the show's success resting on her shoulders, Barbra's *Funny Girl* was a huge hit on Broadway, and it earned her a Tony nomination as Best Actress in a Musical. She didn't win it; the statuette that year went instead to Carol Channing in *Hello, Dolly!* But *Funny Girl* was one of the best musicals of the year, with songs that resonate still, decades after they were penned by Styne and Merrill. After Barbra's run in New York, she was exhausted and fed up with the whole thing, but there was a long road left to go. She was contracted to take the show to London, in the process further delaying her move toward real international stardom: into movies. In fact, Ray Stark had persuaded Barbra to sign her first film contract with him, before she'd even been in front of a movie camera.

## Funny Girl in London

When Barbra landed at London's Heathrow airport with Elliot Gould in 1966, the press was waiting. She was the highest paid singer in the world, having just completed a stellar Broadway show and a top-rated American TV program (the sequel to 1965's *My Name Is Barbra*), titled *Color Me Barbra*, aired in March 1966 and filmed in color, a novelty at the time. Although the UK version of *Funny Girl* was to run for only fourteen weeks, there were rehearsals prior to that at the Prince of Wales Theatre just off Leicester Square, now the center of the city's traditional cinemas. The show opened on April 13, 1966, with Barbra headlining under the direction of Lawrence Kasha with Tony nominee Larry Fuller responsible for the staging.

The show's reputation preceded its arrival in Britain, with celebrities packing the opening night charity performance: David Niven, John Huston, Peter Sellers and Rex Harrison were in attendance. Prince Charles went backstage to meet the star, and his aunt, Princess Margaret, attended the opening night, telling Barbra that she owned all of her records, to which Barbra reportedly replied, "Yeah?" feeling somewhat ill at ease with royalty and unsure of what to say or how to act.

British actor Michael Craig took the role of Nick Arnstein. In his biography he wrote that Barbra could tell when the smallest thing was out of whack in the production. The London production was less than ideal. The British had different theatrical sensibilities: They didn't laugh in the same places, they weren't as excitable as her American audience, and some thought that Craig was miscast. Barbra strived to do her best in the United Kingdom, however, recording her famous *A Christmas Album* there and also singing at the American embassy, where she was given the Anglo American award for Best American Performer of 1966.

Barbra had discovered that she was pregnant just before arriving in the United Kingdom, and that naturally impacted the London production's more physical moments: No more would she be bounding onto a chaise lounge. She gave her final live performance of *Funny Girl* on Saturday, July 16, 1966.

Back in America, Barbra and Elliot set about creating a home for their expected child—and Sadie, a white poodle that her husband had given Barbra for her twenty-third birthday and the first of a long line of small white fluffy dogs to live with her. She gave birth to Jason Gould on December 29, 1966, and naturally was overjoyed, although she was not able to be an at-home mom for long. Returning to work within a year, she taped her third TV special for CBS, "The Belle of 14th Street," which aired on October 11, 1967, although it had been made some months previously. Unlike her other specials, this one included guests and a vaudeville theme. CBS executives didn't like it, so the show was held back. When it was shown, the audience didn't like it either, and it became Barbra's first flop. But, amid her run of huge successes, this was just another TV show, and Barbra had bigger things to do than worry about a failure that had already been put back. She was looking forward to roles in films, namely the lead with the great French star Yves Montand in *On a Clear Day You Can See Forever* (see pages 126–27). She'd also agreed to star in the film version of *Hello, Dolly!* (see pages 100–101) for Paramount, beating the Broadway musical's star, Carol Channing, to the lead role.

## Beginning of the Films

During the filming of *Funny Girl* Barbra made her now landmark free concert recording *A Happening in Central Park* (see pages 88–89) for CBS. Following that, she made another live appearance at the Hollywood Bowl. It was as if she had energy to spare. Being a mother, movie star, singer, performer, and all-around style icon wasn't enough. She was given a copy of Isaac Bashevis-Singer's *Yentl the Yeshiva Boy*. It was a story Barbra fell in love with and never forgot.

By 1968, Barbra was feeling the itch to stretch her musical boundaries a little further. She'd done show tunes already, and in order to get out of that ghetto she recorded a more rock/pop-sounding number, "Our Corner of the Night," with the B-side "He Could Show Me." However, this proved to be the year of Barbra Streisand the actress. *Funny Girl* received a massive eight Academy Award nominations, and although she and Gould were separated (the pressure of them trying to be professional actors and spouses proved too much), he came along to the Oscars with her. His presence proved lucky, and Barbra won Best Actress for *Funny Girl*, tying with Katharine Hepburn

(for *The Lion in Winter*). Barbra was wearing a sparkly pantsuit by designer Arnold Scaasi, and they didn't realize that as the flashbulbs went off, the suit's lining became completely see-through. Photos were shown around the world, of course. Barbra was public property now. She and any new loves became paparazzi material. By 1970 Barbra had started dating the prime minister of Canada, Pierre Trudeau, himself no stranger to gossip pages. She was mobbed at the opening of *Hello, Dolly!* in New York. Only eight years after her first LP was released, Columbia issued her *Greatest Hits* package (the first of many such). Also in 1970, she was awarded a Tony award for Star of the Decade.

The following decade was destined to be one of great change for everyone, and Barbra was to figure enormously in changes being brought about in the movie and music industries.

Barbra looking stunning at the "Broadway for Peace" concert in January 1968. She performed along with many other stars to raise funds for politicians opposing the Vietnam war.

STEREO

MONAURAL-KOL 5780

DAVID MERRICK *presents*

# I CAN GET IT FOR YO WHOLESAL

A New Musical

*Book by* JEROME WEIDMAN *Based on his novel*

*Music and Lyrics by* HAROLD ROME

*Musical Staging by* HERBERT ROSS

*with*

LILLIAN ROTH

JACK KRUSCHEN HAROLD LANG

KEN Le ROY MARILYN COOPER BARBRA STREISAND

BAMBI LINN

*and*

ELLIOTT GOULD

*with*

SHEREE NORTH

*Settings and Lighting by* WILL STEVEN ARMSTRONG

*Costumes by* THEONI V. ALDREDGE

*Musical Direction and Vocal Arrangements by* LEHMAN ENGEL

*Orchestrations by* SID RAMIN

*Dance & Incidental Music Arranged by* PETER HOWARD

*Production Supervisor* NEIL HARTLEY

*Production Directed by* ARTHUR LAURENTS

*Produced for Records by* GODDARD LIEBERSON

# I Can Get It for You Wholesale

**ORIGINAL BROADWAY CAST RECORDING**

**Released**
1962
**Label**
Columbia Records
**Producer**
Goddard Lieberson
**Musical Arrangement**
Lehman Engel and
Sid Ramin

**Tracks**
▪ Overture ▪ I'm Not a Well Man ▪ The Way Things Are ▪ When Gemini Meets Capricorn ▪ Momma, Momma ▪ The Sound of Money ▪ The Family Way ▪ Too Soon ▪ Who Knows? ▪ Have I Told You Lately? ▪ Ballad of the Garment Trade ▪ A Gift Today ▪ Miss Marmelstein ▪ A Funny Thing Happened ▪ What's In it for me? ▪ What Are They Doing to Us Now? ▪ Eat A Little Something

Arguably the first commercial disc that featured Barbra Streisand from her precontract days, this soundtrack recording first brought her into contact with producer Goddard Lieberson, who would sign the young Barbra to Columbia, an arrangement that lasted her whole career. Signing Streisand turned out to be an added bonus for Lieberson, who, it has been claimed, only wanted to sign the soundtrack because he wanted to get its writer, Harold Rome, into the Columbia stable. This was Barbra's first extended session in a recording studio, albeit as a member of a cast and not the star of the show. She appears on only four songs, but among them is "Miss Marmelstein," the number that is most associated with her early days on stage. She can also be heard on "I'm Not a Well Man," "Ballad of the Garment Trade" and the show's big ending number, "What Are They Doing to Us." Remastered in 1993, this is an essential beginning to everyone's collection. The play and its tunes are charming. Barbra's version of "Miss Marmelstein" is lolloping and beguilingly funny and appears on her *Just for the Record* box set, released in the 1990s.

# Pins and Needles

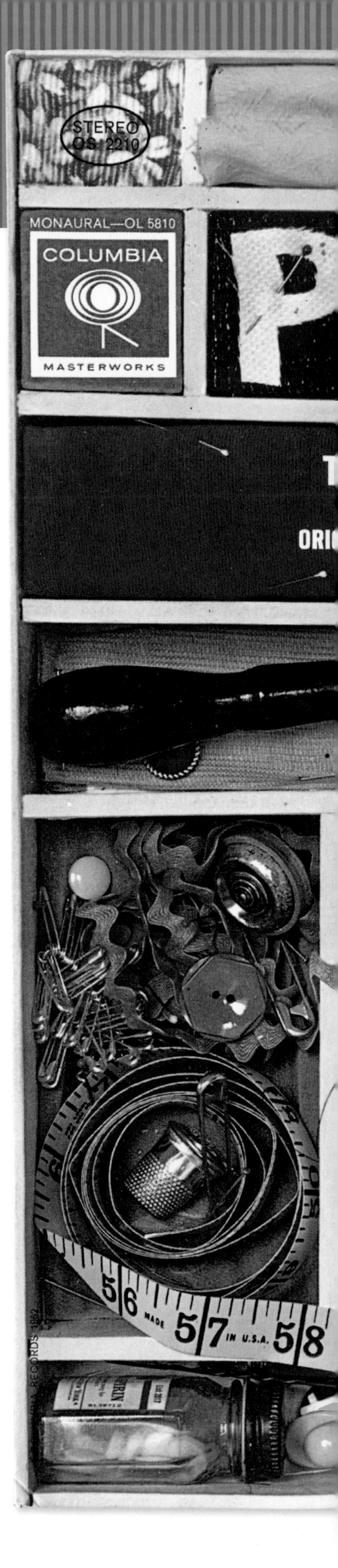


**Released**
1962
**Label**
Columbia Records
**Producer**
Elizabeth Lauer and Charles Burr
**Musical Arrangement**
Harold Rome

**Tracks**
• Sunday in the Park • Sing Me a Song with Social Significance • Doing the Reactionary • Nobody Makes a Pass at Me • Four Little Angels of Peace • Chain Store Daisy • What Good Is Love? • One Big Union for Two • Not Cricket to Picket • I've Got the Nerve To Be in Love • It's Better With a Union Man • When I Grow Up (G Man) • Status Quo • Mene, Mene, Tekel • Back to Work

This was released just a month after *Wholesale*. Besides, Barbra was only nineteen when she stepped in to record the twenty-fifth anniversary LP soundtrack recording of this 1936 show. As with the previous recording, Barbra isn't the star of the show, but at least here she is featured on twice as many songs (six). She sings the rather posh "It's Not Cricket to Picket," and enunciates it extremely well. She's fabulous on "Doin' the Reactionary" and "Status Quo" as well as her best number, "Nobody Makes a Pass at Me," which she sings as if she wrote it herself. The other two tracks on which you can hear the emerging Streisand sound are "Four Little Angels of Peace" and "What Good Is Love." The original 1936 show had been produced by a labor union (the International Ladies Garment Workers Union) and the book positively glows with pro-union sentiment. Composer Harold Rome was quoted as being very impressed with Barbra's contribution to the recording, marveling that "she gets into the songs as if she'd been born to them." A 1993 remastered edition of the soundtrack reveals a very fresh, clean recording chock full of early sixties energy and fabulous songs.

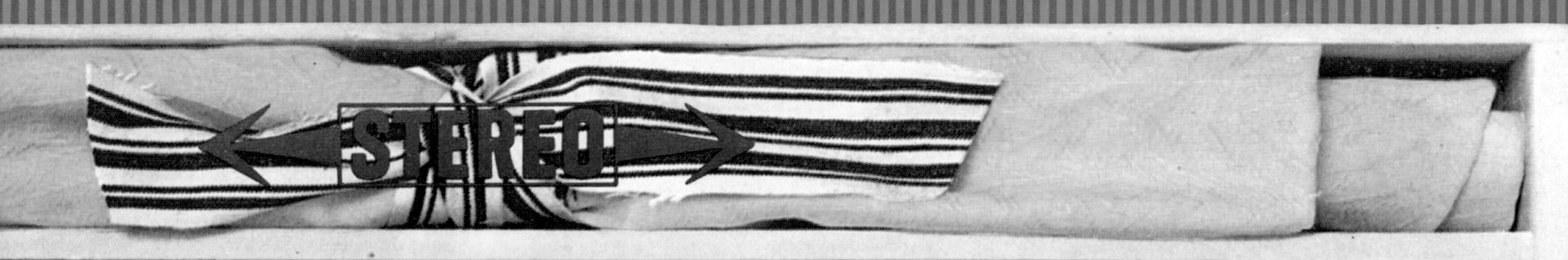


# NS AND NEEDLES

ENTY-FIFTH ANNIVERSARY EDITION OF THE HIT MUSICAL REVUE

MUSIC AND LYRICS BY HAROLD ROME

ALLY PRODUCED BY THE INTERNATIONAL LADIES' GARMENT WORKERS' UNION, NOVEMBER 27, 1937

RECORDING PERSONALLY SUPERVISED BY HAROLD ROME

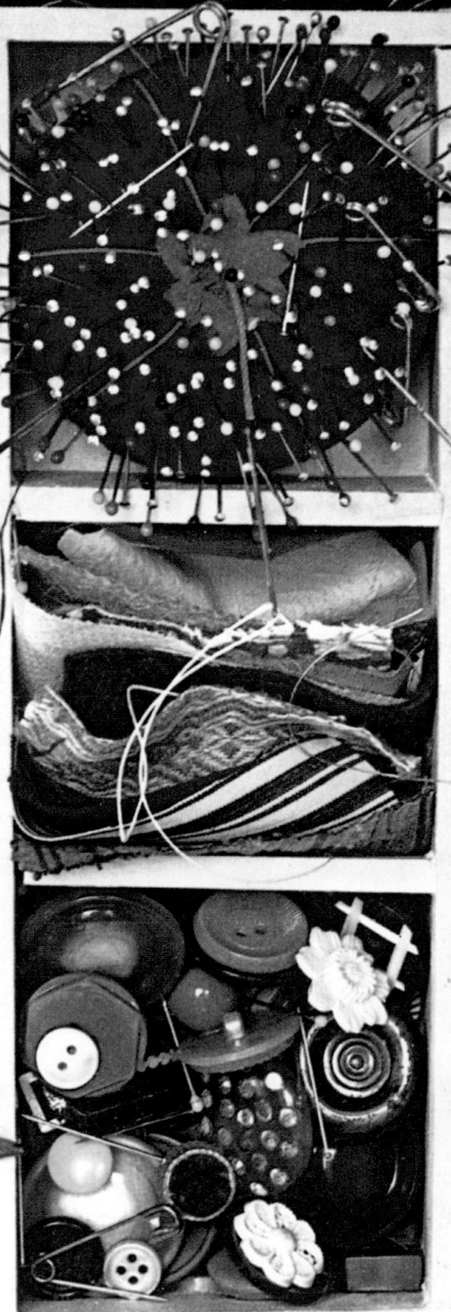

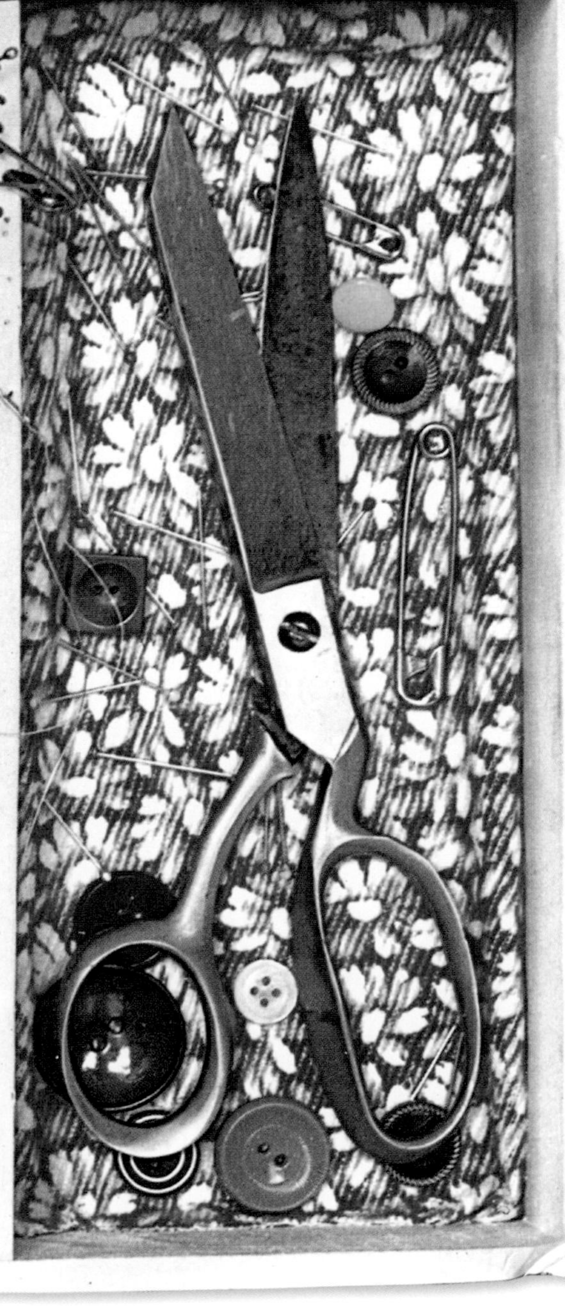

32010
CBS
The Barbra Streisand

Album

Cry Me a River

My Honey's Loving Arms

I'll Tell the Man in the Street

A Taste of Honey

Who's Afraid of the Big Bad Wolf

Soon It's Gonna Rain

Happy Days Are Here Again

Keepin' Out of Mischief Now

Much More

Come to the Supermarket (In Old Peking)

A Sleepin' Bee

Arranged and Conducted by Peter Matz

# The Barbra Streisand Album

**Released**
1963
**Label**
Columbia Records
**Producer**
Mike Berniker
**Musical Arrangement**
Peter Matz

**Tracks**
• Cry Me a River • My Honey's Lovin' Arms • I'll Tell the Man in the Street • A Taste of Honey • Who's Afraid of the Big Bad Wolf • Soon It's Gonna Rain • Happy Days Are Here Again • Keepin' Out of Mischief Now • Much More • Come to the Supermarket (In Old Peking) • A Sleepin' Bee

Streisand's debut album consisted mostly of songs she had been performing at the Bon Soir nightclub in New York's Greenwich Village. Rumor has it she had asked Columbia to have a live segment of her show included on the album, but this idea was shelved at the last minute, apparently due to bad acoustics and a very raucous audience at the club.

"Happy Days Are Here Again" had been released a year earlier, and many felt that that version was far better than the newly recorded one that made the album. Streisand has always sounded best backed by sumptuous string arrangements, and on this track in particular the song sounded stripped, almost like a demo version. The musical arrangements were by Peter Matz, who would continue working with her on many future albums. Barbra got to make the record her way, which was unique for any recording artist of that era, and especially a debutante female. Her personal all-time favorite song, "A Sleepin' Bee," was included, much to the delight of her many admirers, as was her zany version of "Who's Afraid of the Big Bad Wolf?" It was this track, and all the attention it later received, that resulted in her very successful midsixties albums being crammed full of kids' songs. The album's cover photo showed her in performance at the Bon Soir, and it helped firmly establish the classic style of Barbra Streisand in the mind of fans around the world. The set made the U.S. top ten and won her many awards and accolades, notably her first Grammy Award.

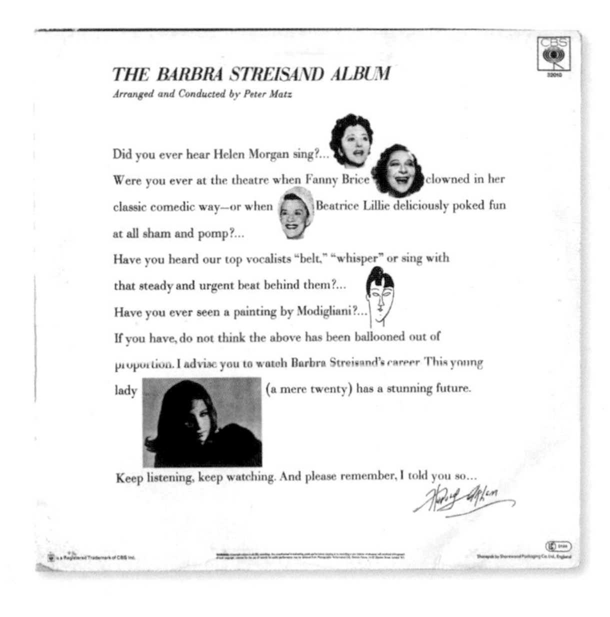
THE BARBRA STREISAND ALBUM

*Arranged and Conducted by Peter Matz*

Did you ever hear Helen Morgan sing?...
Were you ever at the theatre when Fanny Brice clowned in her classic comedic way—or when Beatrice Lillie deliciously poked fun at all sham and pomp?...
Have you heard our top vocalists "belt," "whisper" or sing with that steady and urgent beat behind them?...
Have you ever seen a painting by Modigliani?...
If you have, do not think the above has been ballooned out of proportion. I advise you to watch Barbra Streisand's career. This young lady (a mere twenty) has a stunning future.

Keep listening, keep watching. And please remember, I told you so...

# The Second Barbra Streisand Album

**Released**
1963
**Label**
Columbia Records
**Producer**
Mike Berniker
**Musical Arrangement**
Peter Matz

**Tracks**
• Any Place I Hang My Hat Is Home • Right as the Rain • Down with Love • Who Will Buy? • When the Sun Comes Out • Gotta Move • My Coloring Book • I Don't Care Much • Lover, Come Back to Me • I Stayed Too Long at the Fair • Like a Straw in the Wind

Like her debut, this second set again featured several songs from her live shows. Clearly, these were all favorites and she was determined to have them recorded.

As with "Happy Days" on the first album, she re-recorded another earlier single release, "My Coloring Book," only this time the newer version was a lot better—the arrangements much more tight and her voice soared like a Stradivarius violin.

Writing in the liner notes, musical composer Jule Styne couldn't have been more supportive, concluding that her voice is simply "God given" and that she was the first girl singer who is also a "great actress in each song" she chooses to perform.

The album has much more drama and extremely tender moments, especially on "Have I Stayed Too Long at the Fair?" than we'd previously heard from her. It remains the finest performance ever of this song, bar none.

All arrangements were again by Peter Matz, but with a twist. This time there was a little jazz, a conscious move on Columbia's part (maybe even Streisand's) to elevate her out of the supper club circuit and into a more mainstream appeal. It worked, as the album faired well on the pop charts.

Her rendition of "Lover Come Back to Me" was better even than that of Ella Fitzgerald, although equally fast-paced; no wonder Streisand's live performances of it often brought the house down.

STEREO "360 SOUND"

*The Second Barbra Streisand Album*
*Arranged and Conducted by Peter Matz*
*Additional Material by Peter Daniels*

ANY PLACE I HANG MY HAT IS HOME • RIGHT AS THE RAIN • DOWN WITH LOVE • WHO WILL BUY? • WHEN THE SUN COMES OUT
GOTTA MOVE • MY COLORING BOOK • I DON'T CARE MUCH • LOVER, COME BACK TO ME • I STAYED TOO LONG AT THE FAIR • LIKE A STRAW IN THE WIND

*Produced by Mike Berniker*

*BARBRA STREISAND ...What makes her the unique and ingenious talent that she is? Listening to this album again and again, I have reached one conclusion: besides possessing a God-given singing voice, Barbra is the first girl I have ever heard who is a great actress in each song. Barbra makes every song sound like a well-written three-act play performed stunningly in three minutes. Although the same Barbra Streisand, she takes on an exciting new characterization for each song. At its beginning, she establishes her character; next, she creates a conflict (making all the lyrics mean so much more than they seem to), then she reaches a tremendous conclusion—so that, even after hearing only one song, lasting only a few minutes, one is completely overwhelmed.*

*Barbra knows what she is singing, knows what lyrics mean. I was one of the early, early Barbra Streisand fans and in all my years of writing songs and being associated with top singers, I have never been as thrilled as I was listening to this new album.* JULE STYNE

THE SELECTIONS ARE FOLLOWED BY THEIR PUBLISHERS AND TIMINGS

# econd Barbra Streisand Album

*Any Place I Hang My Hat Is Home*

*Right as the Rain*

*Down With Love*

*Who Will Buy?*

*When the Sun Comes Out*

*Gotta Move*

*My Coloring Book*

*I Don't Care Much*

*Lover, Come Back to Me*

*I Stayed Too Long at the Fair*

*Like a Straw in the Wind*

*Arranged and Conducted by Peter Matz*

THEATER

# Broadway's Funny Girl—
## the Flatbush kid
## who had to make it big

# BARBRA

AN ARTICLE
ON BARBRA STREISAND
STARTS ON NEXT PAGE

Pages from *LIFE* magazine in 1963 showing the young star on the rise.

# A born loser's success and precarious love

## by SHANA ALEXANDER

It is possible to divvy up humanity a lot of ways—rich and poor, black and white, young and old. Another way is winners and losers, and seen from this angle Barbra Streisand started from about as far back as one can get. When, five years ago, 16-year-old Barbra decided to leave Flatbush, invade Broadway and aim for the stars, she had every mark of a loser. She was homely, kooky, friendless, scared and broke. She had a big nose, skinny legs, no boyfriends, a conviction that she was about to die from a mysterious disease, no place to sleep but a portable folding cot and, worst of all, a supersensitive brain which could exquisitely comprehend precisely how much of a loser she actually was. Things being how they were, there was only one possible way out for Barbra: straight through the top of the tent.

*Funny Girl* is the proof that she made it. When Barbra opened on Broadway as the star of the new musical comedy last March, the entire, gorgeous, rattletrap show-business Establishment blew sky high. Overnight critics began raving, photographers flipping, flacks yakking and columnists flocking. Thanks to such massive stimulation the American public has now worked itself into a perfect star-is-born swivet.

Today Barbra Streisand is the drummer boy leading the charge, Cinderella at the ball, every hopeless kid's hopeless dream come true. Having effectively routed the winners, that puny minority of beautiful girls and successful men, she now stands as the fervent heroine of Everybody Else. Her show is a sellout and her albums are a smash. Even more remarkable is the sudden nationwide frenzy to achieve the Streisand "look." Hairdressers are being besieged with requests for Streisand wigs (Beatle, but kempt). Women's magazines are hastily assembling features on the Streisand fashion (threadbare) and the Streisand eye make-up (proto-Cleopatra). And it may be only a matter of time before plastic surgeons begin getting requests for the Streisand nose (long, Semitic and—most of all—like Everest, There).

Like the nose, the girl is unique. For one thing, she reverberates between extremes. She appears to be at once both beautiful and ugly, rough and smooth, graceful and awkward, childlike and of immense age. In the recent journalistic frenzy to commit Barbra's appearance to paper, she has been likened to an amiable anteater, an ancient oracle, a furious hamster and an elegant Babylonian queen. At varying moments she resembles them all. But the surprising, stunning supertruth is that there are times when she does become incredibly beautiful. Stand beside her at her dressing-room mirror backstage, so that you can see simultaneously both the real girl and the reflection in the glass, and the truth about her weird, now-you-see-it-now-you-don't beauty comes clear: a furious Flatbush hamster stares into the mirror, but it is the Babylonian queen, haloed in lightbulbs, who gazes regally back. "I AM GORGEOUS!" she insists. And she is.

But Barbra's talent is no illusion. Her artistry is inborn, and enormous. She has tone, taste, elegance of line, and a sense of what is "right" for Barbra that is close to being flawless. On stage, everything about her is avocado smooth: her voice, her gleaming

CONTINUED

*Barbra met her husband, Elliott Gould, during rehearsals for* I Can Get It for You Wholesale. *He was 23, and a leading man; she 19, and a Broadway novice.*

# The Third Album

MONO—CL 2154

Barbra S

**Released**
1964
**Label**
Columbia Records
**Producer**
Mike Berniker
**Musical Arrangement**
Ray Ellis, Sid Ramin, Peter Daniels and Peter Matz

---

**Tracks**
▪ My Melancholy Baby ▪ Just in Time ▪ Taking a Chance on Love ▪ Bewitched (Bothered and Bewildered) ▪ Never Will I Marry ▪ As Time Goes By ▪ Draw Me a Circle ▪ It Had to Be You ▪ Make Believe ▪ I Had Myself a True Love

A lot of people rate this as the best of Barbra's entire sixties output. She sounds more like an adult contemporary singer than ever here, especially on classics like "It Had to Be You," and "As Time Goes By." The second track on the album, "Just in Time," is a firm favorite with many Streisand admirers. Lasting only two minutes and seventeen seconds, the melody is played mostly on what sounds very much like a harpsichord. When she begins to sing, the vocal continues unabated to the very end, seemingly without taking a breath. This song alone stands as a benchmark of perfectly recorded vocal.

Performances like these are what made Streisand stand out from the rest, and you can hear why her appearances in the clubs of her early career often stopped waiters in their tracks. Much later in her career, an entire tour was called "The Event," a fitting title for a performance by one of the world's all-time greatest singers. This album is a delight throughout; pure, clean, simple arrangements and that sweet, high voice soaring in and around them like no one had before. There was no zaniness here, only assured, late-night-style performances. Sides 1 and 2, as they were in the day, were consistent and, quite simply, perfectly tailored for Barbra's many admirers.

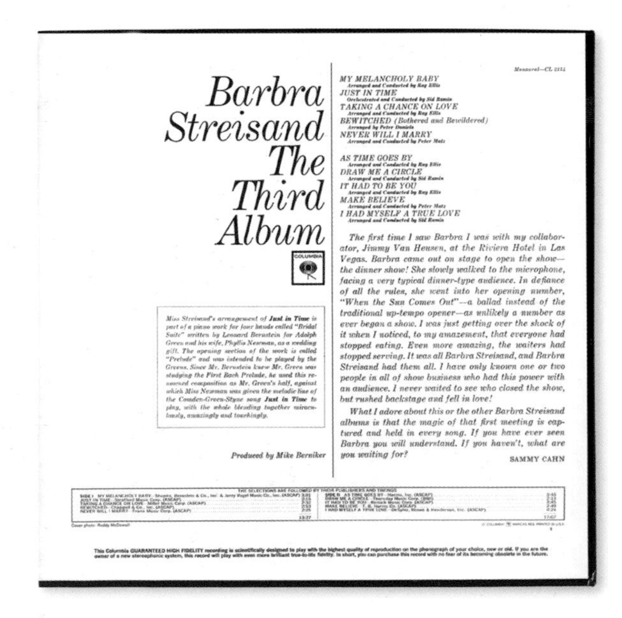

*Streisand/The Third Album*

FUNNY GIRL ★ ORIGINAL BROADWAY CAST

RAY STARK presents

BARBRA STREISAND · SYDNEY C

ORIGINAL B

FUNNY GIRL

A NEW MUSIC

Music by

JULE STYNE · B[illegible]B

Book by

ISOBEL LENNA

from an original story by MISS LE

Musical numbers staged by CAROL H

with DANNY MEEHAN

and

KAY MEDFORD

Scenery and lighting by ROBERT RANDOLPH

Costumes Designed by IRENE SHARAFF

Musical Direc MILTON ROSEN

Vocal arrangements by BUSTER DAVIS

Dance Orchestrations by

Associate Producer AL GOLDIN

Associate Director LAWRENCE KASHA

Presented in association with SEVEN ARTS PROD

Directed by GARS[illegible]N

# Funny Girl

**ORIGINAL SOUNDTRACK RECORDING**

**Released**
1964
**Label**
Capitol Records
**Producer**
Dick Jones
**Musical Arrangement**
Milton Rosenstock
and Ralph Burns

**Tracks**
• Overture • If a Girl Isn't Pretty • I'm the Greatest Star • Cornet Man • Who Taught Her Everything • His Love Makes Me Beautiful • I Want to Be Seen with You Tonight • Henry Street • People • You Are Woman • Don't Rain on My Parade • Sadie, Sadie • Find Yourself a Man • Rat-Tat-Tat-Tat • Who Are You Now? • The Music That Makes Me Dance • Don't Rain on My Parade (Reprise)

This is the Grammy-winning recording of Barbra in the show that put her firmly on track for a fabulous career. Very different from the movie soundtrack, this one features the original song lineup used in the Broadway musical and offers a fascinating contrast to the movie soundtrack. Recorded four years earlier, it sounds like Barbra is experimenting with her voice, sounding stronger and hungrier than she would by mid-decade. She's here to impress and so she does; she's much more Fanny Brice and vaudeville-sounding on these recordings. The orchestra sounds superb—and fans will have a great time comparing the simpler, more intimate sound of a song like "People" with its more familiar film version. Barbra shares the marquee listing with co-star Sydney Chaplin, who played the role of Arnstein which was taken by Omar Sharif in the 1968 movie version.

This original cast recording was made in Manhattan only two weeks after the show had opened in New York, and remarkably the album was in stores less than a month later. It's notable for being one of the rare recordings by Barbra not to be released on Columbia Records. Apparently Capitol had bought into the stage production very early in its development, hence winning the right to release the soundtrack album.

MONO-CL 2215

COLUMBIA

*Barbra*

Streisand
People

GUARANTEED HIGH FIDELITY

# People

**Released**
1964
**Label**
Columbia Records
**Producer**
Robert Mersey
**Musical Arrangement**
Peter Matz
and Ray Ellis

**Tracks**
▪ Absent Minded Me ▪ When in Rome ▪ Fine and Dandy ▪ Supper Time ▪ Will He Like Me? ▪ How Does the Wine Taste? ▪ I'm All Smiles ▪ Autumn ▪ My Lord and Master ▪ Love Is a Bore ▪ Don't Like Goodbyes ▪ People

This was an interesting album for various reasons: First, it featured a photograph on the sleeve of Streisand outdoors, on a beach. She revisited the idea for an album cover much later in her career, *A Love Like Ours* (1999), which showed Barbra, staring out to sea, arm in arm with her newfound love, James Brolin. It almost could have been the same beach and same time of day.

It was also her first album to top the U.S. charts, making her a bona fide pop star. Four albums in and with her first number 1, clearly she was going to be around for some time; Barbra was no flash in the pan. Never before had so much press and public attention come her way.

The songs were in some ways a step backward, but this is no criticism, it was Streisand making a stand in inflecting humor, drama and full color back into her repertoire. In the liner notes, it states that "Miss Streisand is accompanied by Peter Daniels," and this was the first public indication of her taking herself seriously as a star.

The album is largely light, fluffy, almost summer listening, but again this is no criticism. This is Barbra doing what she does best, being herself.

STEREO

# *My Name Is Barb*

## *Barbra Streisan*



Black and white photo courtesy of Sheldon

# My Name Is Barbra

**Released**
1965
**Label**
Columbia Records
**Producer**
Robert Mersey
**Musical Arrangement**
Peter Matz

---

**Tracks**
▪ My Name Is Barbara ▪ A Kid Again ▪ I'm Five ▪ Jenny Rebecca ▪ My Pa ▪ Sweet Zoo ▪ Where Is the Wonder ▪ I Can See It ▪ Someone to Watch over Me ▪ I've Got No Strings ▪ If You Were the Only Boy In the World ▪ Why Did I Choose You ▪ My Man

By 1965 Barbra was more determined than ever to show that she was an actress who sings. This album and its sequel were supported by very expensive and very successful television shows. Perhaps the songs are an odd collection, but many people had a great fondness for them. Columbia spent thousands on Barbra's career during this time; she was on the rise both critically and commercially.

The cover featured a photograph of her at about age six. It was a brave decision for a girl who had spent her entire childhood being told she was ugly. If ever there was a look-at-me-now moment, this was it. It was a conscious move on her part, putting her past right by living out her childhood years and her teens with these albums. She included her version of the Fanny Brice signature song "My Man" on this album, alongside several numbers from Broadway shows *The Yearling* and *The Fantasticks* plus a reworked version of "If You Were the Only Girl in the World" as "Only Boy." "Why Did I Choose You" was released on a blue vinyl 45 rpm single, which was an unusual move for the time.

# My Name Is Barbra, Two . . .

**Released**
1965
**Label**
Columbia Records
**Producer**
Robert Mersey
**Musical Arrangement**
Peter Matz and
Don Costa

---

**Tracks**
• He Touched Me • The Shadow of Your Smile • Quiet Night • I Got Plenty of Nothin' • How Much of the Dream Comes True • Second Hand Rose • The Kind of Man a Woman Needs • All That I Want • Where's That Rainbow? • No More Songs for Me • Medley: Second Hand Rose/ Give Me the Simple Life/I Got Plenty of Nothin'/Brother, Can You Spare a Dime?/ Nobody Knows You When You're Down and Out/The Best Things in Life Are Free

The follow-up album to My Name Is Barbra, My Name Is Barbra, Two . . . was pretty much the same in terms of style, yet equally compelling. Released to coincide with a repeat showing of the televison special of the same name as the first album, this release includes two key songs ("He Touched Me" and "Second Hand Rose") that quickly made it a Streisand classic. The televised performances of her running wild in New York's Bergdorf Goodman store show the performer in her element.

Despite the album containing some new and "difficult" songs, such as "How Much of the Dream Comes True" from Passion Flower Hotel, a British musical about girls planning how to lose their virginity, it made it to number 2 on the *Billboard* 200 charts and stayed on the chart for forty-eight weeks, selling more than half a million copies in its first six months on sale. Not bad for a sequel. The record also includes two songs from a musical that starred her husband at the time, Elliott Gould, *Drat! The Cat!*—"He Touched Me" (which Gould performed in the show as "She Touched Me") and "I Like Him."

ne Is
Barbra, Two...

# Color Me Barbra

**Released**
1966
**Label**
Columbia Records
**Producer**
Robert Mersey
**Musical Arrangement**
Peter Matz, Michel Legrand and Don Costa

**Tracks**
▪ Yesterdays ▪ One Kiss ▪ The Minute Waltz ▪ Gotta Move ▪ Non C'est Rien ▪ Where or When ▪ Medley: Animal Crackers in My Soup, Funny Face, That Face, They Didn't Believe Me, Were Thine That Special Face, I've Grown Accustomed to Her Face, Let's Face the Music and Dance, Sam, You Made the Pants Too Long, What's New Pussycat?, Small World, I Love You, I Stayed Too Long at the Fair, Look at That Face ▪ C'est Si Bon (It's So Good) ▪ Where Am I Going? ▪ Starting Here, Starting Now

Like the earlier *My Name Is* projects, this album was designed to support the television special of the same name. For the first time, though, the entire show was broadcast in color. Although loved by her legions of fans, the critics savaged it. In addition, animal rights groups were up in arms about the many rare and beautiful species having to endure the heat from the studio lights. Tragically a baby penguin died on set, distressing all involved in the show, especially the star.

This album sleeve is particularly memorable; rather than using a photograph of Barbra to sell the product, it uses a vivid pink drawing of a kid's face with enormous eyes and a huge smile from ear to ear. It was, naturally, her most childish album so far. It included a couple of tracks that would eventually lead to her next and most serious album, to be released a year later. Both "Non C'est Rien" and "C'est Si Bon" were sung in true chanson style. "Medley" comprised a variety of numbers, including "Animal Crackers," "Funny Face," and "Sam You Made the Pants Too Long." It was another mixed bag of styles, but again it worked, and the whole project was brilliantly arranged and produced, something the public had come to expect from her by now. The TV special was a runaway ratings success, and the album reached number 3 on the *Billboard* chart and went gold within two weeks of release.

# *Color Me Barbra*

The insert of the *Color Me Barbra* LP.

Gotta Move

*Yesterdays*
*One Kiss*
*The Minute Waltz*
*Gotta Move*
*Where or When*
*Circus Medley*
*Arranged & Conducted by*
*Peter Matz*

*Non C'est Rien*
*C'est Si Bon*
*Arranged & Conducted by*
*Michel Legrand*

*Starting Here, Starting Now*
*Arranged & Conducted by*
*Don Costa*

*Where Am I Going?*
*Arranged & Conducted by*
*Robert Mersey*

*Produced by Robert Mersey*

Non C'est Rien

Where or When

Je m'appelle Barbr

CL 2547
COLUMBIA

What Now My Love
Autumn Leaves
Speak to Me of Love
Once Upon a Summertime
I Wish You Love
Free Again
Martina
Le Mur
I've Been Here
Love and Learn
Clopin Clopant
Ma Première Chanson

# Je m'appelle Barbra

**Released**
1966
**Label**
Columbia Records
**Producer**
Ettore Stratta
**Musical Arrangement**
Michel Legrand

**Tracks**
• Free Again • Autumn Leaves • What Now My Love • Ma Première Chanson • Clopin Clopant • Le Mur • I Wish You Love • Speak to Me of Love • Love and Learn • Once Upon a Summertime • Martina • I've Been Here

Maurice Chevalier wrote in the liner notes of this release, "She sings with the voice of an angel, and gives these French words a poignancy they have never had before." This was strong stuff indeed, coming from one of France's most popular and enduring entertainers at the time.

This album broadened Streisand's success not only in America but overseas. It almost single-handedly made her a huge star in Europe, a place that Barbra has always been fond of, and in Paris in particular.

The final cut, "I've Been Here (Le Mur)," was originally written for Edith Piaf, who unfortunately did not live to record it. Streisand, always canny with her musical career decisions, jumped at the chance to sing it and immediately made it her very own, with an impassioned powerhouse performance. Earl Shuman wrote the English lyrics.

Another notable cut on the album is "Once Upon a Summertime," written back in 1954 by Michel Legrand. Several other songs were recorded at the sessions for *Je m'appelle*, but not included here, though they did appear on an EP titled *En Francais*.

Her French accent here is incredibly convincing, yet she apparently sang the entire album phonetically. That's a true sign of a good ear for music if ever there was one.

*Produced by Ettore Stratta*
*Arranged and Conducted by Michel Legrand*

Stereo—CS 9347
Mono—CL 2547

COLUMBIA

*Je m'appelle Barbra*

*I Wish You Love*
*Speak to Me of Love*
*Love and Learn*
*Once Upon a Summertime*
*Martina*
*Le Mur*

*Free Again*
*Autumn Leaves*
*What Now My Love**
*Ma Première Chanson*
*Clopin Clopant*
*I've Been Here*

*Michel Legrand and Barbra at the recording session*

*Consult label for correct sequence.*

**Arranged and Conducted by Ray Ellis*

*Barbra Streisand is one of those miracles which comes along once in a lifetime, even in America where the sensational apparently never ceases to flourish.*
*She is mad with talent and more gifted than any human being should be permitted to be.*
*She sings* Les Feuilles mortes*—among other songs—with the voice of an angel and gives the French words a poignancy that they have never had before.*
*This very young American girl is enchanting the whole world with an artistry that is new, impulsive and staggering.*
*We bow to you, "grande petite Madame." We embrace you, Barbra Streisand.*

Maurice Chevalier

*When handled with affection, care and respect, superb French songs, like some of the finer French wines, travel well. The flavor, the bouquet and, most important, the afterglow somehow survive the perilous journey between cultures and languages and remain to sharpen our tastes and enrich our lives.*

*In all, the program is a heady, potent mixture of both the old and the new:* Speak to Me of Love (Parlez-moi d'amour) *by Jean Lenoir, with English lyrics by Bruce Sievier, was introduced in France in 1930.* I Wish You Love (Que reste-t-il de nos amours?) *is from the pen of that charming troubadour, Charles Trenet, and the tender English version was written by Albert Beach. One of France's greatest contemporary poets, Jacques Prévert, wrote* Les Feuilles mortes *shortly after World War II to music by Joseph Kosma. As adapted by Johnny Mercer, it became* Autumn Leaves *and turned up in the United States in 1950.* What Now My Love (Et maintenant) *is by Gilbert Becaud who, like Trenet, sings only the songs he composes. The English lyrics are by Carl Sigman.* Clopin Clopant, *with French words by Pierre Dudan and music by Bruno Coquatrix, is presented here in its British rather than its American-lyric version. The English lyrics are by Kermit Goell. Michel Legrand, who conducted and arranged this album, wrote* Once Upon a Summertime (La Valse des lilas) *in 1954 at the age of twenty-two. The French lyrics are by Eddy Marnay, and the adaptation is by Johnny Mercer.*

*Of the new songs,* I've Been Here (Le Mur) *was written for Edith Piaf who did not live to perform it. When informed that Miss Streisand was planning an album of French songs, the composer, Charles Dumont, and the lyricist, Michel Vaucaire, withheld the song from French singers for more than a year in anticipation of her debut on records in France. Following traditional Gallic procedures, the English-language version by Earl Shuman was written specifically for Barbra Streisand.*

Non c'est rien, *which was introduced on the "Color Me Barbra" television show, has words by Michel Jourdan to music by Armand Canfora and Joss Baselli. The French version, along with its English-language counterpart,* Free Again, *by Robert Colby, was also written especially for Barbra Streisand.*

Love and Learn (Qui es-tu) *and* Martina (Les Enfants qui pleurent) *are by the aforementioned Michel Legrand and Eddy Marnay. The English lyrics were written by, respectively, Norman Gimbel and Hal Shaper.*

Ma Première Chanson (My First Song) *was composed by Barbra herself. She asked her friend Eddy Marnay to write the lyric which says:*
*"One finger on a piano, my voice around some words,*
*I played with your name and a song was born.*
*In my hands your heart and mine…*
*That old piano takes me back to the first day of my first love*
*When each second held your name…*
*And then I found…My First Song."*

*The refreshing irreverence that Barbra Streisand has shown toward the moldy concepts of "accepted" popular singing is once more demonstrated in her choice of, and approach to, this group of songs adapted from their French originals. Ever unafraid of open emotionalism and yet wondrously aware of subtleties and characterization, this amazing young woman points the way toward the day when American popular music will reach a new level of intelligence and artistry. May her courage, talent and enormous popularity continue to stimulate and inspire the creation of new songs of beauty, wit and power.*

*Nat Shapiro*

# Simply Streisand

**Released**
1967
**Label**
Columbia Records
**Producer**
Jack Gold and Howard A. Roberts
**Musical Arrangement**
Ray Ellis

**Tracks**
▪ My Funny Valentine from *Babes in Arms* ▪ The Nearness of You ▪ When Sunny Gets Blue ▪ Make the Man Love Me from *A Tree Grows in Brooklyn* ▪ Lover Man (Oh, Where Can You Be?) ▪ More Than You Know ▪ I'll Know from *Guys and Dolls* ▪ All the Things You Are from *Very Warm for May* ▪ The Boy Next Door from *Meet Me in St. Louis* ▪ Stout-Hearted Men from *The New Moon*

Richard Rodgers's sleevenotes are short, succinct, and plastered in enormous type on the reverse of the album sleeve (below). They offer high praise from a legend of the Great American Songbook, and with good reason. If he'd only heard the album's opening track, her version of his and Lorenz Hart's "My Funny Valentine," Rodgers would have been justified in writing such laudatory copy. Yet he must also have been extremely grateful that someone so young and successful was (still) recording his songs. Despite some great performances on standard numbers such as "I'll Know" (from *Guys and Dolls*) and "The Nearness of You" and "The Boy Next Door" (from *Meet Me in St. Louis*), the album was Barbra's first to not make the top ten in the *Billboard* 200 chart, reaching only number 12. However, in truth, the album must have been a bit of an oddity, coming as it did four months after the Beatles' groundbreaking *Sgt. Pepper's Lonely Hearts Club Band* had changed the sound of pop music forever. The old-fashioned sound of this album was something of an anachronism and suggested that her audience were not the kids who'd only months previously made Frank and Nancy Sinatra's "Something Stupid" a big success. Something would have to change, it seemed.

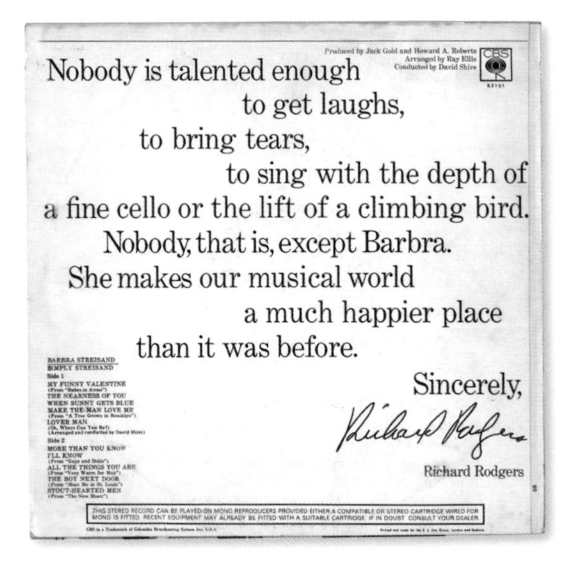

Produced by Jack Gold and Howard A. Roberts
Arranged by Ray Ellis
Conducted by David Shire

CBS

Nobody is talented enough
to get laughs,
to bring tears,
to sing with the depth of
a fine cello or the lift of a climbing bird.
Nobody, that is, except Barbra.
She makes our musical world
a much happier place
than it was before.

Sincerely,

Richard Rodgers

BARBRA STREISAND
SIMPLY STREISAND
Side 1
MY FUNNY VALENTINE
THE NEARNESS OF YOU
WHEN SUNNY GETS BLUE
MAKE THE MAN LOVE ME
LOVER MAN
Side 2
MORE THAN YOU KNOW
I'LL KNOW
ALL THE THINGS YOU ARE
THE BOY NEXT DOOR
STOUT-HEARTED MEN

THIS STEREO RECORD CAN BE PLAYED ON MONO REPRODUCERS PROVIDED EITHER A COMPATIBLE OR STEREO CARTRIDGE WIRED FOR MONO IS FITTED. RECENT EQUIPMENT MAY ALREADY BE FITTED WITH A SUITABLE CARTRIDGE. IF IN DOUBT CONSULT YOUR DEALER.

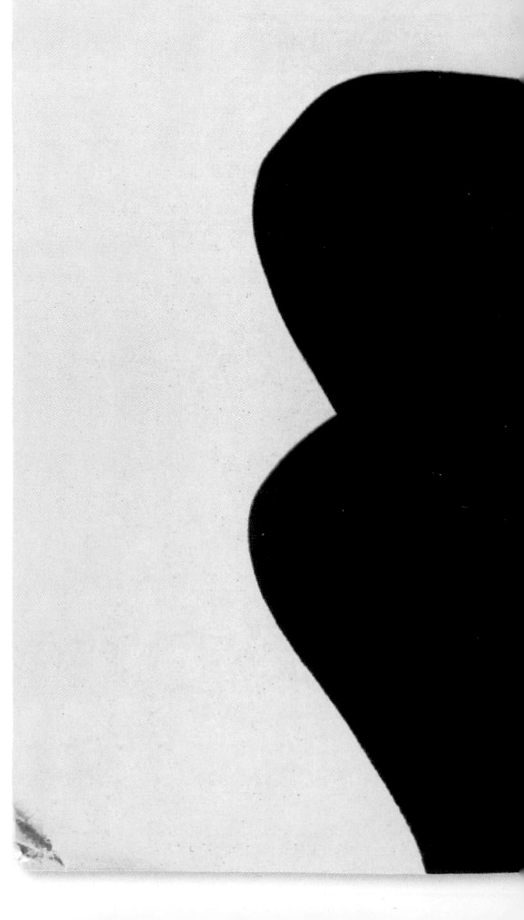

nply Streisand
My Funny Valentine
The Nearness Of You
When Sunny Gets Blue
Make The Man Love Me
Lover Man
More Than You Know
I'll Know
All The Things You Are
The Boy Next Door
Stout-Hearted Men

*Barbra Streisand / A Christmas Alb*

# A Christmas Album

**Released**
1967
**Label**
Columbia Records
**Producer**
Jack Gold
**Musical Arrangement**
Marty Paich

**Tracks**
▪ Jingle Bells? ▪ Have Yourself a Merry Little Christmas ▪ The Christmas Song (Chestnuts Roasting on an Open Fire) ▪ White Christmas ▪ My Favorite Things ▪ The Best Gift ▪ Sleep in Heavenly Peace (Silent Night) ▪ Gounod's Ave Maria ▪ O Little Town of Bethlehem ▪ I Wonder as I Wander ▪ The Lord's Prayer

As seasonal collections go, this album stands as one of the all-time greats, up there with the famous seasonal works by Frank Sinatra, Nat King Cole, and even Phil Spector. Decades after its original release, the album not only still sounds amazing, but it also refuses to age. The sleeve caused some controversy, with people enraged that Barbra had chosen to portray herself as some sort of holy figure shrouded in glowing light as if from the heavens above. That issue faded with time though.

From the first track, an insanely fast, overly camp rendition of "Jingle Bells," you know you're in for something special. She delivers the classic songs with equal fervor and sensitivity, even managing to maintain dignity on an overblown, choir-laden "Lord's Prayer." "My Favorite Things" and "Have Yourself a Merry Little Christmas" stand as Streisand classics, and given that she was only twenty-five at the time of the album's release, you have to take your hat off to her for recording some of the best-known songs of a Christian holiday while maintaining her Jewish identity so fully and proudly.

It topped the *Billboard* album chart, but total sales are not known for this album. Given how many times it has reappeared since 1967, they must be among the highest of her career.

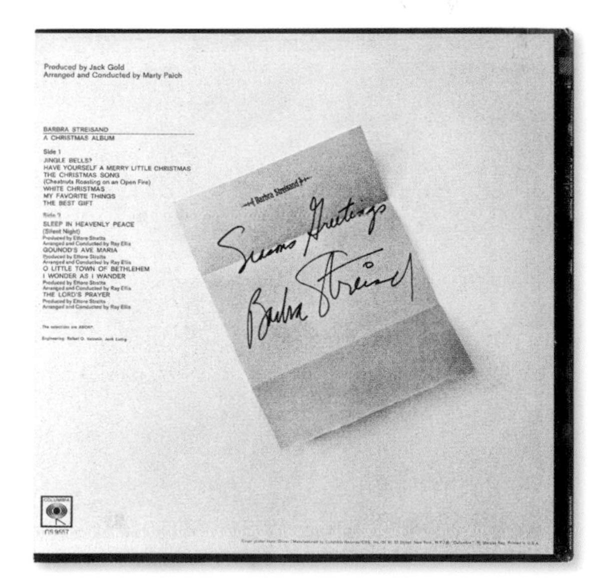

AN OCCASION IN NEWPORT
ONE PERFORMANCE ONLY!
Alan King and Walter A. Hyman
In association with
George Wein
present
An Evening With
Barbra
Streisand
with Peter Matz and his Orchestra
JULY 30
at 8:30 P.M.
FESTIVAL
FIELD
NEWPORT, R.I.


Above: A poster for an appearance at the Newport Jazz Festival in 1966. By the time of the concert Barbra was in the early stages of her pregnancy.

Opposite: A page from *Life* magazine in 1963, featuring the star of *Funny Girl*.

## Show-stopping predicament: should she surrender?

In *Funny Girl*'s funniest scene, Barbra turns an attempted seduction into a riot. Invited to an elegant champagne supper for two by her suitor, suave con man Nicky Arnstein, she permits him to ply her with paté. As she vamps him with a fan, she wonders to herself just what would happen if she should surrender to him ("Would a convent take a Jewish girl?").

63432

CBS

# Barbra Streisand
# A Happening In Central

Second Hand Rose
Happy Days Are Here Again
Cry Me A River
Love Is Like A New Born Child
Folk Monologue/Value
Sleep In Heavenly Peace (Silent Night)
I Can See It
He Touched Me
Marty The Martian
Natural Sounds
People

# A Happening in Central Park

**Released**
1968
**Label**
Columbia Records
**Producer**
Jack Gold

**Tracks**
• Second Hand Rose • Happy Days Are Here Again • Cry Me a River • Love Is Like a New Born Child • Folk Monologue/Value • Sleep in Heavenly Peace • I Can See It • He Touched Me • Marty The Martian • Natural Sounds • People

This album was Columbia Records' idea to bring Streisand live to a mass audience, first by having her perform (for free) to more than 100,000 fans in New York's Central Park, then by editing the show for release on vinyl to further broaden her appeal. The show was a success despite some technical problems and her having received a death threat before the show. Clearly she was responsible for the odd song choice here: "Marty the Martian," "The Sound of Music," and "Second Hand Rose" must have delighted the gay and theatrical members of the audience, while "Silent Night" is performed with her usual consummate ease, though its inclusion was somewhat baffling. Only Streisand could get away with singing a Christmas song on a hot June night.

The album's sleeve is an aerial shot of Central Park taken on the night of the show. It rained very heavily, resulting in thick mud everywhere that the audience seemed to endure most happily. Barbra and the musicians had to risk electrical shorts on stage. The backdrop of New York City's famous skyline includes some incredible buildings now long gone, but at least the music remains.

People who see Funny Girl are the luckiest people in the world!
COLUMBIA PICTURES and RASTAR PRODUCTIONS present
BARBRA STREISAND
TECHNICOLOR® PANAVISION®
THE WILLIAM WYLER-RAY STARK PRODUCTION
OMAR SHARIF
FUNNY GIRL
co-starring
KAY MEDFORD
ANNE FRANCIS
WALTER PIDGEON as Florenz Ziegfeld
Music by JULE STYNE
Lyrics by BOB MERRILL
Musical Numbers Directed by HERBERT ROSS
Production Designed by GENE CALLAHAN
Musical Supervision WALTER SCHARF
Miss Streisand's Costumes by IRENE SHARAFF
Screenplay by ISOBEL LENNART
Produced by RAY STARK
Directed by WILLIAM WYLER
FOR GENERAL EXHIBITION
Based on The Musical Play by ISOBEL LENNART · Music by JULE STYNE · Lyrics by BOB MERRILL

# Funny Girl

Above: Barbra in character as Fanny Brice, being seduced by Omar Sharif.

**Running Time** 151 mins
**Studio** Columbia Pictures
**Year** 1968
**Director** William Wyler
**Screenplay** Isobel Lennart
**Cast** Barbra as Fanny Brice, Omar Sharif and Walter Pidgeon

Her first movie was a cinematic version of the Broadway musical of the same name which had hinged on Barbra's amazing vocals, thrilling acting and uncanny comic timing. She could hardly wait to make the movie. Throughout the Broadway run, she'd said she was marking her calendar until the time came to begin filming.

At first, producer Ray Stark refused to sign her for the movie, saying that she had to sign for a four-picture deal—which she did because she was not prepared for Stark to take the picture elsewhere. Whether the shrewd Hollywood veteran was bluffing or not is anyone's guess.

Stark reportedly asked *Mr. Smith Goes to Washington* scribe Sidney Buchman to have first go on the *Funny Girl* script, with Anne Edwards and other writers brought in to bump up the finished product. It was based on the book of the musical and Isobel Lennart's early first attempt at a screenplay (written before the Broadway musical), plus Brice's autobiographical recordings. Sydney Lumet was considered as director, while other actors suggested for the role of Arnstein (which went to Sharif) were Sam Wanamaker, Sean Connery, David Janssen and Robert Culp. There was rumor that Barbra rejected the suggestion of Frank Sinatra in the role.

Herbert Ross, who came on board to assist Wyler with directing, also took on the task of directing the test footage. He said that they spent many hours getting Barbra into different costumes, trying out different lighting and various makeup and hair coifs, and was surprised at how wonderful she looked. He remarked on her glowing skin which had a radiant, reflective quality to it that the camera adored.

When filming began in August 1967 at a disused railway depot near New York, the first scene shot was the "Don't Rain on My Parade" number, with Barbra posing for pictures and clambering up and down from a train. Although she had always been fascinated by film (and TV), she was, according to Wyler, nervous about her first time in front of the camera. He also said that before he had seen her perform *Funny Girl* onstage, he hadn't been sold on the idea of directing her in a film. Seeing her onstage made all the difference, however. Her star quality and her remarkable confidence persuaded the veteran director. Throughout the shooting, Barbra told critic Charles Champlin in 1967, she surprised the filmmakers who were unused to actresses speaking their minds.

*Funny Girl* was made just before big, stagey musicals were voted out of fashion by diminishing returns at the box office, and just before cynicism began to take hold in cinema. It showcased the talents of the young Broadway star perfectly, though, making all of her hard work—as Army Archerd of *Variety* wrote—worthwhile.

Barbra hadn't realized how hard it was singing numbers over and over again for different camera angles, but when she was done recording the soundtrack, the entire orchestra stood and applauded, and their reaction was soon mirrored by movie audiences across America. *Funny Girl* enjoyed a hugely successful theater run in the fall of 1968.

"To me, being a star is being a movie star."

# The Making of *Funny Girl*

Following a protracted genesis, the story of Fanny Brice (1891–1951), America's beloved actress, comedienne and star-crossed lover of the early twentieth century, became a hot property when producers Ray Stark and David Merrick decided to create a show based on her life. Stark was Brice's son-in-law and knew how popular the deceased entertainer remained with an older audience. He intended to take Brice's as yet unwritten life story and turn it into a musical stage hit.

Stark agreed to an "authorized biography" being written using recordings of reminiscences made by Fanny but never heard by anyone outside of the family. However, the producer was not pleased with the final product, titled *The Fabulous Fanny*, by Norman Katkov. Reportedly, Stark paid $50,000 to get the book's publication stopped. He then approached the great Ben Hecht—the "Shakespeare of Hollywood"—to write the play, followed by a stream of other top scribes, none of whom did the job Stark wanted. Finally, Isobel Lennart's version landed closest to the mark. Titled *My Man* after the title of Brice's famous romantic song, it leaned more toward the performance and personal side of Fanny's life.

Stark spoke to multi–Tony Award winner David Merrick about producing the musical. In turn, Merrick said Stephen Sondheim and Jule Styne should work on the music as he wanted to reunite the powerful team that created the enormous musical hit *Gypsy*. Styne had met and accompanied Fanny Brice for four weeks and had composed a few ditties for her. It didn't hurt either that Merrick came up with the title *Funny Girl*.

Brice had been a hokey comedienne whose material—tart, funny and fast-paced—was drawn from her Jewish roots. Sondheim suggested getting a Jewish performer for the role. Styne had seen Barbra perform at the Bon Soir, thinking that if anyone was going to play Brice, it had to be the girl he saw at that nightclub. Sondheim subsequently excused himself from the project, but luckily Styne then bumped into lyricist Bob Merrill in Palm Beach, and the two hit it off on the subject of Fanny Brice/ *Funny Girl*.

They worked so well together that Merrill wrote lyrics initially on spec—the show's greatest tune, "People," was written in thirty minutes between the two of them (tune first and words second). The many songs the duo wrote in Palm Beach were test driven at parties with pianos all during that winter season. Other singing actresses considered for the role included Anne Bancroft, Eydie Gorme and TV funnywoman Carol Burnett who said she'd like to do the role but that, really, the role called for a Jewish girl—the comedy was complex and particular.

With some productions, things go smoothly from development and casting to fine tuning. Not so with *Funny Girl*. It suffered from a hiatus in its development when everything stopped. Styne left and worked with Burnett. Meanwhile, Merrick hired Bob Fosse for *Funny Girl* only to have the theatrical director-choreographer quit and be replaced by Garson Kanin, one of Hollywood's funniest writers and best directors. After that, Merrick stopped getting involved, turning over the whole shebang to Stark.

Streisand was not enthusiastic about Kanin, mainly because he had wanted her favorite tune, "People," pulled from the score because he thought it didn't fit her character and impeded the flow of the play. Not only a screenwriter but also a playwright and a theatrical director of note, Kanin's play *Born Yesterday* ran for more than 1,500 performances, and he had directed *The Diary of Anne Frank*, so it wasn't as if there was some spring chicken telling Barbra what to do. She was going against the wishes of someone hugely respected and experienced (his direction of *Funny Girl* was to run for 1,348 shows).

But one thing Kanin didn't know so much about was the music industry, and, even at her early age, that was Barbra's world. Unfortunately for Kanin, Barbra had intended to release "People" as a single and had already recorded it. With others saying it was a great track, Kanin left it in because of its amazing connection to the audience. When the show went to Boston and Philadelphia for tryouts before it hit New York, it is reported that people were applauding the song the second they heard its opening bars. Audiences didn't seem to be shocked that a musical about Fanny Brice didn't actually have any of Fanny Brice's famous songs in it.

At the end of 1963, *Funny Girl*'s prep began. The show's first outing was lousy, though, and the producers thought about closing it down. The great music could not offset the fact that it was three hours long—a butt-numbing length of time for even the very best entertainments. The problems with

The original soundtrack album of *Funny Girl*, inside sleeve.

the script and score outweighed the problem of duration, though. Following *Funny Girl*'s Boston opening Lennart continued to tweak the book, deleting one thirty-minute slice and then another. By the time the show moved to Philadelphia, critics thought that it could fly if the plot was sorted out. Everyone, however, adored Streisand's performance in it, saying that without her, the show would be unendurable.

With the shortening of running time and some changing of songs, what could be so wrong with the play? William E. Sarmento, a writer for the *Lowell*

"I don't know what other actresses do. Do they just sorta stand around like mummies, get dressed, get told what to do, move here, move there? That can be pretty boring for the actress and the director."

*Sun*, in an article dated February 3, 1964, comments that after having seen the show twice, he thought the new tunes added in Boston didn't solve the problem of a contained plot—that the story of Fanny Brice was presented as one between the singer and her gambler husband, and that was it. Sarmento goes into lurid detail, using words like "tripe," saying that it was conventional and sentimental and not in a good way. Sarmento did note that Barbra Streisand's following was vast and vociferous though, causing him to compare her to Judy Garland.

Although the feel of the show was sugary schmaltz and cornball, it seemed that Barbra could only grow stronger in the role, relaxing with her knowledge of the songs and experience of the live stage. "People," although it jarred somewhat with the rest of the show, was likened to the greatest tunes in all musical history and often said to be similar to "Some Enchanted Evening," being a ballad that unusually fit into the play and lifted the whole show onto another plane. Styne and Merrill also penned huge, swooping themes for Barbra—songs that were designed to be starmakers for anyone who could sing them well: "Don't Rain on My Parade" and "I'm the Greatest Star," among them.

The New York opening was delayed time and time again while the show was shaped up out of reach of the New York critics. It was only after seventeen previews that the show finally came to Broadway with Kanin at the helm and dancing directed by Carol Haney as Jerome Robbins looked over her shoulder. The day was March 26, 1964, and the theater was the Winter Garden, after which it transferred to the Majestic and the Broadway to finish its prodigious run of almost 1,500 performances.

Reflecting on this time years later, Barbra recalled that she had played *Funny Girl* in almost one thousand performances across the United States and in the United Kingdom. Wanting to keep the standard of the musical high, she would obsessively make notes after each performance on energy levels, music performance, anything that was off or could have been improved, right down to whether the props were clean or not. Her attention to detail was unflagging.

Barbra played Fanny Brice on Broadway until December 26, 1965, and during her time in the role she apparently shortened the songs. Regular attendees (and there was a large group of dedicated fans who went as often as possible) reportedly noticed that the midweek performances were truncated, with the show pared down to a bare-bones version of what it was during the other performance days. This meant, for example, that Barbra didn't sing the second choruses of the more difficult numbers.

Supreme in her triumph, assured of her talent, and unknowingly haughty with her audience, who was increasingly loving everything she did, Barbra was queen of the stage. It sounds egotistical, but, having worked so hard, perhaps harder than the audience could probably understand, she was entitled to feel satisfied with her acclaim. *Time* magazine had called her "a girl for all seasons," and by May, *Life* magazine too had put her on their cover. Barbra was being compared to greats like Sarah Bernhardt. Yet being worshipped isn't that easy when you look at all the hard work that went into being Barbra Streisand. It took grace, certainty and a lot of self-love—which could easily be perceived as egotism—just to keep the show going. After all, the show relied on her for its success—if it folded, everything would go with it.

Above: The first anniversary of the stage play.
Left: Barbra and Elliot at the *Funny Girl* premier, September 18, 1968.

**The Play or the Film?**

Fans will know that in addition to the many photos taken during the musical's long run, there is also a published script available with notes written in it, even the stage directions. There are also amateur films made by a cast member as well as (supposedly) audio soundtracks taken during the performances on closing night in New York and during the London run. They offer proof of the different permutations that the show went through throughout its run.

The differences between the stage production and the movie are many and varied. They are also to be found meticulously pointed out and pored over on numerous Barbra fan websites. Some are small, some much bigger. The endings of the show and the film are very different, for instance. In the play, the last scene has Fanny and Nick in the dressing room. On stage, Fanny has a rage, then begins to sing the middle chorus of "Don't Rain on My Parade." In the film, she watches Nick leave her dressing room, then goes to sing "My Man." The ending with "My Man" was more sentimental, more romantic, and more ruinous to Fanny than it was in the play, where she returned to being the trouper she always was before, during and after meeting Nicky Arnstein.

Whichever you prefer though, what is indisputable is that Barbra *is Funny Girl*.

THE ORIGINAL SOUND TRACK RECORDING

COLUMBIA PICTURES and RASTAR PRODUCTIONS present

the WILLIAM WYLER-RAY STARK Production

# FUNNY GIRL

BARBRA STREISAND

# Funny Girl

**ORIGINAL SOUNDTRACK RECORDING**

**Released**
1968
**Label**
Columbia Records
**Producer**
Jack Gold
**Musical Arrangement**
Walter Scharf

---

**Tracks**
• Overture • I'm the Greatest Star • If a Girl Isn't Pretty • Roller Skate Rag • I'd Rather Be Blue Over You (Than Be Happy with Somebody Else) • His Love Makes Me Beautiful • People • You Are Woman, I Am Man • Don't Rain on My Parade • Sadie, Sadie • The Swan • Funny Girl • My Man • Finale

Highly polished and beautifully performed, the soundtrack to the Oscar-winning movie also contains the haunting heartbreaker "Funny Girl," which was written expressly for the film. This is glossy, upbeat and seamlessly produced—a masterpiece, even if some completists will note that some of the movie's opening credits music is missing. This LP has not aged one bit—and Barbra shows herself to be, as Ethel Merman once put it, "the new belter." Musical director Walter Scharf found Barbra to be exacting and demanding during the recording, but was generous enough to admit that whatever she wanted did make the overall result better. Acknowledging that she was stubborn and temperamental, he said, "She was and is one of the most original and gifted artists I have encountered." Surprisingly, the album didn't make the *Billboard* 200 top ten, although it did stay on the chart for more than three years. It didn't pass the million-seller mark until 1986, either. In 2002, British Barbra fans got to hear a rare, Peter Matz–arranged version of "I'd Rather Be Blue," which had been issued as a single in 1968, on the CD reissue. Why the track wasn't included on the U.S. release is anyone's guess.

# What about Today?

**Released**
1969
**Label**
Columbia Records
**Producer**
Wally Gold
**Musical Arrangement**
Peter Matz, Don Costa and Michel Legrand

**Tracks**
▪ What about Today? ▪ Ask Yourself Why ▪ Honey Pie ▪ Punky's Dilemma ▪ Until It's Time for You to Go ▪ That's a Fine Kind o' Freedom ▪ Little Tin Soldier ▪ With a Little Help from My Friends ▪ Alfie ▪ The Morning After ▪ Goodnight

As if stung by the lack of commercial success for the old-fashioned *Simply Streisand* album, Barbra made her first foray into the adult rock market and her first obvious attempt at making public her political beliefs, at least on vinyl. She might have misjudged her audience, though, and some of her fans were surprised by the change in sound, resulting in the album stalling on the *Billboard* chart at number 31.

She wrote the liner notes herself, another first, dedicating the album to all those people who "push against indifference." The compositions came from a variety of writers such as Lennon/McCartney, Jimmy Webb and Buffy Sainte-Marie. A mixed bag it may be, but it is still very Barbra. The album's great cover shots were taken by Richard Avedon, who styled her in a somewhat bohemian ensemble that was reminiscent of something from the era of vaudeville.

As with some other Streisand albums the sales were not instant, but they were always there. Undeterred by instant success, Barbra discovered that making albums that meant a lot to her personally was what she wanted to do.

20TH CENTURY-FOX PRESENTS ERNEST LEHMAN'S PRODUCTION OF HEL

starring

BARBRA STREISAND · WALTER

MICHAEL C

LOUIS AR

O, DOLLY!
MATTHAU
AWFORD
AND
MSTRONG

Original motion picture soundtrack album.

# Hello, Dolly!

**ORIGINAL SOUNDTRACK RECORDING**

**Released**
1969
**Label**
20th Century Fox Records
**Producer**
Ernest Lehman
**Musical Arrangement**
Lennie Hayton and Lionel Newman

**Tracks**
• Just Leave Everything to Me • It Takes a Woman • It Takes a Woman (reprise) • Put On Your Sunday Clothes • Ribbons Down My Back • Dancing • Before the Parade Passes By • Elegance • Love is Only Love • Hello Dolly! • It Only Takes a Moment • So Long Dearie • Finale

Jerry Herman added a new song—"Love Is Only Love"—to his excellent stage show for its movie adaptation. Naturally, it was a song for Barbra, who performs on eight of the thirteen songs that were issued as the official movie soundtrack. It is not to be confused with the 1964 Broadway cast recording, in which Carol Channing played the lead role. Neither should it be confused with the 1967 cast recording that features Pearl Bailey as Dolly Levi and Cab Calloway as Horace Vandergelder. The movie soundtrack of course features the wonderfully lugubrious vocals of Walter Matthau as Horace and Michael Crawford as Cornelius Hackl. The soundtrack of Barbra's last big musical is wonderful to behold and includes her duet with Louis Armstrong on the title number.

Another rare non-Columbia release, the quality of the pressing was questioned by some critics on original release, but a remixed version released in 1994 and issued on CD is a better sound representation of the movie.

# Hello, Dolly!

**Running Time** 146 mins
**Studio** Twentieth Century Fox
**Year** 1969
**Director** Gene Kelly
**Screenplay** Michael Stewart
(based on a play by Thornton Wilder)
**Cast** Barbra as Dolly Levi, Walter Matthau and Michael Crawford

Left: Director Gene Kelly leads his star from the set.

Barbra's second film was planned as the big release of Christmas 1969. Production studio 20th Century Fox hoped to create another hit like their *Sound of Music* by turning another successful musical into a hopefully equally successful film. At the time, it was the most expensive musical movie ever made, with production costs of $25 million. The money proved to be well spent, and *Hello, Dolly!* became the fifth-highest grossing film of the year, netting $33 million. It went on to eventually accumulate $59.2 million in theatrical returns.

Dancer turned director Gene Kelly was given the task of "opening up" the stage musical, but he was faithful to the play—perhaps too much so, as the production was not without flaws. Producer David Merrick had wanted the play, which had not starred Barbra (Carol Channing had made the role of Dolly her own onstage), to be the longest-running musical on Broadway, and it had been successfully buoyed up by the great title song. The movie naturally made the title number its centerpiece, with Kelly choosing to interpret the lyrics faithfully: Dolly the matchmaker returns to the ornate luxury of Harmonia Gardens to see old friends, who are so happy to see her again (it's been too long!) that they high-kick, smile and sing while waiters perform some great stunt work. Topping it off, the great Louis Armstrong steps in and duets with Barbra—he reportedly filmed for only half a day and made one take for each shot. The song and performance stands out from the rest of the movie so much that it became all that most people could remember about it.

"I guess lots of actors love to be looked at and asked for autographs. I'm totally opposite. I know what is in the fans' heads. They don't want to be disappointed in anyone and reality is always disappointing. I don't like anyone to get too close. You become a celebrity and an image and not a person."

Without succumbing to makeup in order to appear the same age as Dolly Levi (in her sixties), Barbra managed to convey the importance and presence of the lauded matchmaker. She was helped by the spectacular costumes created by Irene Sharaff. However, the gold beaded gown worn in the title number sequence, which reportedly weighed forty pounds and cost (in 1960s dollars) $8,000, kept tripping Barbra and the waiters. So the train was removed during some sequences and put back in others. The result is visually and aurally sumptuous, even if the plot stumbles a bit. It is impossible to take your eyes from Barbra when she's on screen and the movie became her star vehicle, without intending to be.

Almost forty years after its original release, *Hello, Dolly!* enjoyed a renewal of interest with rental and sales of the DVD increasing enormously, thanks to the 2008 hit animated movie *WALL-E*. The Disney feature showed clips of the musical at several pivotal points, all of them featuring Barbra.

## *Three: The Seventies*

# ***Evergreen***

THE sixties had made Barbra an enormous worldwide star of stage, screen and radio. She'd begun the new decade starring in *On a Clear Day You Can See Forever*, which opened in June 1970 to good reviews but moderate box office success. After all the family entertainment movies she'd made, Barbra turned to a film that was more adult in nature—and that was designed to capitalize on the fact that, yes, Barbra Streisand was very, very sexy. *The Owl and the Pussycat* (see pages 128–29) was a shocker, and it opened in November 1970 to shocked reviews. The swearing and the nudity stunned some and delighted many others. More important, perhaps, Barbra didn't sing in the movie. Her now modest-looking lingerie outfit, which featured pink hands over the breast area, was airbrushed for the newspaper ads. They had to take the hands off.

> "A large part of me is pure nebbish —plain, dull, uninteresting. There's a more flamboyant part, too."

The following year she recruited Richard Perry, a noted rock producer, to work with her on the LP *Stoney End* (see pages 130–131), arguably her best rock-oriented album. The title track became a top ten single on the *Billboard* chart, and proved that Barbra had her finger on the pulse of popular music. More than any other album, *Stoney End* proved her talent as a rock-oriented singer, as well as a great selecter of fabulous backing musicians.

Barbra understood that she held an enormous power within show business, and, deciding that she wanted to become a movie producer, she formed a production alliance with two other major stars, the actors Paul Newman and Sidney Poitier. They named the company First Artists. Essentially a vehicle that allowed the actors to participate in the making of movies in which they starred, it allowed them to each share in profits made by the movies, enabling them to earn more than just their fee. In 1971–72 First Artists co-produced two Newman movies (*Pocket Money* and *The Life and Times of Judge Roy Bean*), Barbra's *Up the Sandbox* (see pages 138–39), and Poitier's *A Warm December*. Throughout the rest of the decade First Artist would make more than twenty major movies, including *A Star Is Born* (see pages 164–65) and *The Main Event* (see pages 174–75).

A publicity photo for *The Owl and the Pussycat*, 1970.

Opposite: Smoldering with co-star Robert Redford in *The Way We Were*, 1973.

Above: the fabulous cover art of the "soundtrack" album for *The Owl and the Pussycat*, 1970.

First Artists was not a part of the production team who made Barbra's first big hit movie of seventies, though. *What's Up, Doc?* (see pages 134–35) was produced by director Peter Bogdanovich's Saticoy, in conjunction with the major Warner Brothers studios. It opened at Radio City Music Hall in New York City on March 9, 1972, to good reviews. Being a wholesome comedy, it was a hit that carried through to the summer. But even as it was being made, Barbra's next movie was in development. Another Ray Stark production, it was going to a team Barbra with one of Hollywood's leading men of the day, Robert Redford, and was to be directed by Oscar-winner Sydney Pollack (*They Shoot Horses, Don't They?*). *The Way We Were* was purpose-built for Barbra the actress.

As that movie was being made, however, fans could watch Barbra in the first movie to come from her very own production company, Barwood (see pages 230–31), which co-produced with First Artists. *Up the Sandbox* (see pages 138–39) opened days before Christmas 1972 and didn't do well, mainly because the audience was expecting a comedy and got a semi-comedic fantasy instead. At least Barbra's performances received good reviews. Throughout 1973 Barbra worked on *The Way We Were*, managing to also sign a new contract with Columbia Records for six new albums—as if she wasn't busy enough—the same year.

## Can it Be it Was All So Simple Then?

In September, *The Way We Were* previewed badly in San Francisco, but Pollack ingeniously edited it back into shape; his new edit gained a much better reception from the second preview audience. The film, along with its title song, was released in October 1973 and turned out to be a massive hit that was nominated for six Oscars, including Best Actress. Barbra didn't win—it went to Glenda Jackson for *A Touch of Class*—although she probably should have.

The title song of *The Way We Were* became Barbra's first number 1 single on the *Billboard* charts. On the heels of that, CBS aired the music special she recorded in London, *Barbra Streisand . . . and Other Musical Instruments*. It was—and remains—a strange outing that couldn't be made today. Wild animals, clown suits and talking computers were thrown onstage with the singer, in a strange melange that does, however, have some of the nicest lighting you'll ever see in a TV special.

Meanwhile, after having been contracted for her next film, *For Pete's Sake*, British director Peter Yates (fresh from directing Robert Mitchum's last great movie, *The Friends of Eddie Coyle*) told Barbra that he wanted a new look for her. Unwilling to have her hair cut as short as required, Barbra asked for a wig to be made by Hollywood hairdresser Jon Peters. The two got along so well that they began to date; they found that they had much in common, not least, ambition. Peters would soon make a move into producing movies.

> "I've been called many names like perfectionist, difficult and obsessive. I think it takes obsession, takes searching for the details for any artist to be good."

Around the time *Funny Lady* (see pages 158–59) started shooting in the spring of 1974, Barbra and Ray Stark acknowledged the end of their working relationship. Instead of giving her a nice fluffy poodle, which she would have liked, Stark gave her a horse, a palomino, golden with a white mane and tail. At the end of the film's wrap, Barbra gave him a mirror with PAID IN FULL written on it in lipstick. To be fair, she also sent him a very nice note of thanks.

With the end of *Funny Lady*'s shooting in sight, Barbra prepared for the opening of *For Pete's Sake*, which was another screwball comedy, hoping to cash in on the success of her previous screwball *What's Up, Doc?* The movie, co-starring Michael Sarrazin, opened well in June 1974 and made a nice splash at the summer box office. *Funny Lady* opened in March

1975 and was a huge success, earning five Oscar and six Golden Globe nominations. Barbra was on top again. Unfortunately her success at the box office was not mirrored by success in the charts, since in October 1974 Barbra had seen the disappointing release of a new album. In retrospect it was probably a mistake to allow Jon Peters to act as the record's producer. *ButterFly* (his first music production) ended up being the album she says she liked the least. The cover design of a fly on a stick of butter did not help to sell the record (see pages 148–49).

Barbra on set, *The Way We Were*, 1973.

Following pages: The sumptuous inner sleeve of the *Funny Lady* soundtrack, 1975.

The inside of the *Funny Lady* album.

It is 1930. The country is in a slump and so is Fanny Brice (BARBRA STREISAND), both romantically and financially. Divorced from Nicky Arnstein (OMAR SHARIF), she still carries the torch for him. And, although she is Ziegfeld's star-of-stars, she feels the Depression crunch herself when the great showman has difficulty funding a new show.

Enter Billy Rose (JAMES CAAN), unkempt and uncouth, but full of enthusiasm and theatrical ideas. He and Fanny meet not-so-accidentally at the office of her financial advisor, Bernard Baruch, and after another encounter Billy's wild hope comes true—he convinces her to star in his stage revue.

At first, Fanny and her friend and confidant Bobby (RODDY McDOWALL) don't know what to make of Billy, a champion shorthand writer-turned-nightclub proprietor and songwriter. But Fanny can't discount his ability to get cash for production, even after discovering his method—guaranteeing the financial backer's girlfriend Norma a part in the show.

No matter. The show "Crazy Quilt" hits the road on its way to Broadway. Initially, all is chaos for Fanny and the show's other star, Bert Robbins (BEN VEREEN), because of Billy's over-production and under-experience. But, with Fanny's savvy and help, Billy pulls the show together and brings a hit into New York.

Nicky Arnstein is among the first-nighters and when he comes backstage later Fanny finds out he has married a wealthy older woman.

Arnstein exits from Fanny's life again, a move that's just fine with Billy. After biding his time, he proposes to Fanny. Touched, but not in love, she accepts. They make an unusual pair—the upstart producer and the elegant star—and the marriage has a rocky beginning. The union eventually hits its stride when Fanny travels from Hollywood and the Baby Snooks show to visit Billy in Cleveland where he's producing his spectacular Aquacade. They experience a new and wonderful rapport.

Back on the West Coast, Fanny is decoyed by Norma to a polo game without knowing Nicky is one of the players. When Fanny sees him, she gets that old feeling. They make plans to meet later, and Fanny is compelled to phone Billy and confess that she's going to talk with Nick. When Arnstein offers to leave his wife—wealthily—to return to Fanny, she sees at last that he's not the man for her.

Fanny hurries to surprise Billy in Cleveland and gets surprised herself. Rose, hurt and disheartened by Fanny's seeming liason with Nick, has taken up with his Aquacade star, Eleanor Holm.

Fanny and Billy divorce. However, years later, when Fanny is happily doing her "Snooks" radio show, an important visitor arrives. Billy is back, older, richer, and full of plans to star Fanny on Broadway. Fanny says, "no"! Billy insists. One of their famous tiffs ends with hugs and kisses. Fanny just might take him up on his offer to return to the musical theatre. The old Billy "magic" still weaves its spell.

## At the End of the Rainbow

Sometime during 1974, Barbra turned down a remake movie project called *Rainbow Road.* However, she reconsidered it after Peters read the script and suggested that she give it a go. After its title was restored to *A Star Is Born*, Barbra agreed to go ahead (see pages 164–65), with Peters producing and she executive producing as part of Barwood. First Artists co-produced along with a Hollywood-based TV and film production company called Winters Hollywood Entertainment Holdings Corporation; they had been involved in the hit TV series *The Monkees* in the late sixties, had produced TV specials for Ann-Margret and Raquel Welch, and most recently had filmed Alice Cooper's live show *Welcome to My Nightmare;* these guys knew how to do rock music on film.

Script changes saw writers and the initial choice of director leave the production early on. There were various rumors about who would play the male lead role, with Bob Dylan and Mick Jagger getting mentions as possibilities. However, Barbra apparently wanted Elvis Presley to play opposite her. She flew out to see him, but, being shocked at his bad health, she was relieved when his manager turned her down. So, Kris Kristofferson took over the co-starring role, even though he and Peters argued a great deal. A lot of negative press haunted the movie while it was in production, with bad reports from the set making the film look destined for disaster.

Too busy to attend the unveiling of her own star on the Hollywood Walk of Fame in December 1976, Barbra nevertheless found the time to send little notes out to theaters with all of the prints of *A Star Is Born* for screening from December 17 onward. Clearly she felt she had to tell projectionists how to do their job. Whether they read the notes or not, the film turned out to be a great success. Along with its soundtrack album (see pages 166–67), which features "Evergreen," a song written by Barbra and Paul Williams, it became a huge hit. The soundtrack shot to number 1 and sold one million copies in sixty days. That made up for the moderate success of *Classical Barbra* (see page 163), which had been released in February 1976 and barely made it into the top fifty of the pop charts.

By February 1977, the Golden Globes were enthusiastically heralding *A Star Is Born* as that year's top winner. Peters and Barbra could hardly carry their Globe haul in both hands. They won Best Picture, Best Actress, Best Actor, Best Score and Best Song. Come March and the Academy Awards, Neil Diamond handed Barbra and her lyricist, Paul Williams, an Oscar for Best Song. Her peers in the film industry nominated the film for Best Score, Best Cinematography and Best Sound, but awarded it none of them.

Opposite: From the TV Special *Barbra Streisand and Other Musical Instruments*, 1973.

Above: From *A Star Is Born*, 1976

Opposite: the soundtrack album for *The Main Event*, 1979.

pre-Internet days, the record company didn't hear about it for a while—until several hundred thousand listeners had approved the idea enthusiastically, that is. Having both artists under contract and aware that the duet could only be a hit, Columbia quickly managed to get both Barbra and Neil into the studio to record a "real" version, which by October 1978 had reached the number 1 spot in the singles chart.

*Songbird* (see pages 170–71) was released as Barbra's first album under her new Columbia contract, a little earlier than promised. It capitalized on the success of the duet, rising to number 1 on the *Billboard* album chart.

Following the wrap of Barbra's new comedy *The Main Event* (see pages 174–75), which had Barbra starring again with her old beau Ryan O'Neal, Columbia released a disco song with the same title as the film. It was Barbra's first foray into the then ubiquitous musical genre. While it didn't get great reviews, the frothy gender-clash comedy did boffo box office, as they say in the trade magazine *Variety*. The single release was so successful that Barbra recorded another disco track, apparently at the request of her son, Jason. He was such a fan of Donna Summer that he talked his mother into recording a duet with her in Santa Monica called "No More Tears (Enough Is Enough)." The song had terrific lyrics and a great production. The accompanying album, *Wet* (see pages 172–73), went to the top ten on the *Billboard* chart; the single with Donna Summer went to number 1 and created a mythology of its own—that the long-held note by Barbra was sung while she waited for Donna to pull herself together. Some stories about that long note said that Donna Summer had passed out on the floor, and that Barbra was singing, just waiting for her to recover. It's a great story, but only that. Remarkably, both Barbra's and Donna Summer's record companies (Columbia and Casablanca, respectively) released the single simultaneously, thus sharing the number 1 slot together.

Even after having starred in *The Main Event* braless and wearing short shorts, Barbra still didn't like the idea that the racy man's magazine *High Society* was going to publish the naked shots that Barbra had previously refused to put in the final cut of *The Owl and the Pussycat*. She sued to stop publication, but three thousand copies of the magazine escaped censorship. Although the publication was pulled, the pictures, which seem very tame now, show her breasts in full, and they actually look quite nice.

## Make it Like a Memory

In the final months of 1979, Barbra took her brother to visit their father's grave. Nearby she noticed a headstone with the name Anshel inscribed on it. That was a name Barbra recognized from the book she was reading, which was titled *Yentl*. She took the chance occurrence as a sign to press ahead with making the movie of the book that she'd fallen in love with—but had been forced to abandon due to lack of funding (and time).

As with all of her other endeavors, however, Barbra was mindful of her fans and her first career, the one that paid the bills—singing. So she started work on a new album, titled *Guilty* (see pages 192–93). She had broken off her relationship with Jon Peters, the man whose acquaintance had baffled friends and fans alike over so many years and so many projects. She threw herself into the sudden and extremely lucrative role in *All Night Long* (see pages 194–95)—a delightful comedy written for Gene Hackman that required a sexy woman (Barbra, of course) to be the foil for his midlife crisis. This was to be Barbra's only supporting role, and it was not a film that did much for her career or her profile. It's a difficult film to find. It was a nice comedy vehicle for Hackman though, and provided a hefty paycheck for Barbra, who looks terrific in it.

The world adored hearing about Barbra, and people didn't care that *All Night Long* was not a good film for her. She was the American dream come true. Documentary maker, Kevin Burns, knew this and ended up winning a Student Oscar for his documentary on Barbra. Called *I Remember Barbra*, the naturalistic documentary was made by Burns going around and talking to people who had known Barbra before she left Brooklyn. The attitude of people toward Barbra's persona made for a wonderful documentary—and it made Barbra both a myth and a real woman at the same time.

There was some bad news on the horizon, however. As she pressed to find funding and distribution for her obsession, *Yentl*, she heard that Orion Pictures would get involved only if Barbra agreed to sing in it. She might have agreed to directing and acting in it, but there were forces at work beyond her control. At the time, *Heaven's Gate*, another Orion Pictures film, had tanked badly, and its losses put *Yentl* into turnaround. As the 1980s began, Barbra was in a by now familiar position of having to do everything herself if she wanted to do anything at all—and this movie she really, really wanted to do. Her passion for the project would reap dividends.

Barbra in a serious mood, 1978.

Centerstage in the TV special *Barbra Streisand and Other Musical Instruments*, 1973.

# On a Clear Day You Can See Forever

**Running Time** 129 mins
**Studio** Paramount Pictures
**Year** 1970
**Director** Vincente Minnelli
**Screenplay** Alan Jay Lerner
**Cast** Barbra as Daisy Gamble; co-starring Yves Montand and Bob Newhart

Opposite: Barbra as Daisy in a scene from the movie.

Originally designed as a longer movie featuring the main character Daisy Gamble's many previous lives, accessed through hypnosis, Paramount Studios was at first optimistic about its reception. They even staged a ball with a reincarnation theme before shooting began. However, both the director, Vincente Minnelli, and the studio felt that the original three-hour concept was too long. They might have noticed that musicals were losing favor at the box office at the time, too. The original stage musical had suffered problems, and what had begun as a collaboration between Lerner and Richard Rodgers saw the former writing partner of Oscar Hammerstein II withdraw from the project even before it hit Broadway.

There were problems with the film too: Dr. Marc Chabot, Daisy's admirer and hypnotherapist, was played by Yves Montand, who never really crossed over from being a star in France to one in America or the English-speaking entertainment world as a whole. He was paid $400,000 to co-star here, with an eye to making it more appealing to the European box office (it didn't seem to make a difference).

The film differed hugely from the stage production, most notably with the movie leaving the audience without a doubt that Daisy was the reincarnation of the nineteenth-century Lady Melinda. Bob Newhart appears as a college president in a wonderful if too short supporting cameo role; Jack Nicholson's singing turn as Tad Pringle ended up mostly on the cutting room floor.

Daisy's wardrobe is noteworthy; the legendary Cecil Beaton was brought on board to spruce up her gowns (his last project). His Regency designs for Melinda's flashback sequences look amazing.

Of the many beautiful moments in *On a Clear Day*, one of the final scenes of Barbra walking among blooming flowers is truly memorable. The vivid detail of the visual are testimony to Minnelli's camera work, so well displayed previously in films like *An American In Paris* and *Gigi*. The scenes set in Brighton, England's historic pavilion are memorable: the eight-day shoot produced only fifteen minutes of footage, but it was money well spent. *On a Clear Day* put all its money on the screen and yet, despite its many fine qualities and a terrific title song, it confused audiences, who didn't know if it was a comedy, a musical or a psychological drama.

"It was inspired—and both our ideas, really—to wrap the Streisand features in a glorious white turban to further accent her strong profile."

*—Cecil Beaton on Barbra's outfit in the banquet scene*

# On a Clear Day You Can See Forever

**ORIGINAL SOUNDTRACK RECORDING**

**Released**
1970
**Label**
Columbia Records
**Producer**
Wally Gold
**Musical Arrangement**
Nelson Riddle

**Tracks**
• Hurry! It's Lovely Up Here • On a Clear Day • Love with all the Trimmings • Melinda • Go to Sleep • He Isn't You • What Did I Have That I Don't Have • Come Back to Me • On a Clear Day • On a Clear Day (Reprise)

Barbra's third movie soundtrack release was a much smaller affair than either of the previous two. The orchestrations here, by legendary bandleader Nelson Riddle (who'd famously worked with Frank Sinatra and Ella Fitzgerald in the 1950s) are as gorgeous and inventive as one would expect. The 1993 remastered reissue (on CD) benefited listening greatly. In its remastered version, Barbra's voice is even clearer and more immediate than before. Barbra's voice tinkles on "Hurry! It's Lovely Up Here," she's seductive on "Love with All the Trimmings" and of course, the title track takes lungs aplenty to sing properly. Plus, the clickety-clack of her shoes is a lot less evident on the reisssue. *On A Clear Day* was released at a time when she was between studio album releases, and it's possibly to her benefit that it failed to sell well. The songs are essentially show tunes, and as well orchestrated and cleverly written as they are, their sound was at odds with what pop fans were listening to—and what Barbra was listening to at home too, it seems, as her next studio release would show.

# n A Clear Day You Can See Forever

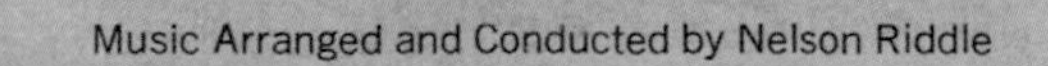

The Owl and the Pussycat
is no longer
a story for children.
COLUMBIA PICTURES AND RASTAR PRODUCTIONS PRESENT
A RAY STARK • HERBERT ROSS Production
Barbra Streisand
George Segal
in
The Owl and the Pussycat
Screenplay by BUCK HENRY
Based on the play by BILL MANHOFF PANAVISION® COLOR
Produced by
RAY STARK
Directed by
HERBERT ROSS
Music from the film by
BLOOD, SWEAT & TEARS
on Columbia Records Soundtrack Album
R
RESTRICTED
Under 17 requires accompanying
Parent or Adult Guardian

# The Owl and the Pussycat

**Running Time** 95 mins
**Studio** Rastar Pictures
**Year** 1970
**Director** Herbert Ross
**Screenplay** Buck Henry
**Cast** Barbra as Doris, George Segal Crawford

This was a bit of an offbeat choice for Barbra, but it came with some wonderful recommendations. The script, written by comedy legend Buck Henry (*The Graduate*), contains some brilliant dialogue. Despite Henry's excellence at comedy, though, the film's ending was problematic, and several different versions were shot as test audiences and producers were not happy with the first shown to them.

Barbra looks luminous, youthful and dewy—but her character, a brash actress/model/callgirl, was shrill, loud and annoying, a kind of stew of neuroses. She was also very sexy, especially when contrasted with George Segal, her neighbor, who is trying to write his novel in the evening when he comes home from his job at a bookstore.

This film has Barbra using the f-word, making her one of the first actresses to do so in a major movie. The emphasis on sex in the film was, perhaps, a way to make up for this being her first nonsinging role. She doesn't even sing the title track, although reportedly one was written for her. She is reported to have quipped, "How many singing prostitutes do you know?"

Her character, rough and uneducated but not dumb, is not the enlightened woman we would see Barbra play in later roles; Doris is homophobic and repeats her tirades against gay men throughout—something Barbra wouldn't dream of doing. She filmed a nude scene—albeit above the waist, quite tastefully done—but ordered it to be cut before release. Stills later showed up in a men's magazine, which Barbra got pulled from circulation via an injunction. Needless to say, her naked form looks beautiful. She apparently thought that the nudity ruined the comedy, even though the producer and director disagreed.

Above: George and Barbra onset, in costume.

The second movie made while under contract to Stark (who really wanted Elizabeth Taylor in the role), it was based on Bill Manhoff's Broadway play that ran in 1964–65 with Alan Alda and Diana Sands.

George Segal gets many of the best lines, and while he's great in the role, apparently he was not Barbra's first choice for Felix. She wanted Sidney Poitier for the role, but sadly was overruled because it was felt that audiences were not ready for an interracial relationship in a major comedy movie.

"The director of 'The Owl and the Pussycat' wanted a topless shot, and I agreed on two conditions—one, there would be nobody in the room but George [Segal]; two, I had the right to kill the shot if I didn't think it would work."

# Stoney End

**Released**
1971
**Label**
Columbia Records
**Producer**
Richard Perry
**Musical Arrangement**
Gene Page, Claus Ogerman, and Perry Botkin Jr.

**Tracks**
▪ I Don't Know Where I Stand ▪ Hands Off the Man ▪ If You Could Read My Mind ▪ Just a Little Lovin' ▪ Let Me Go ▪ Stoney End ▪ No Easy Way Down ▪ Time and Love ▪ Maybe ▪ Free the People ▪ I'll Be Home

In Laura Nyro and Joni Mitchell, Barbra found young female singer-songwriters who, like her, chose to do things their way, without being subjected to the whim and machinations of male managers, producers or record company executives. Young female artists were succeeding in pop and rock on their own terms for the first time, and Barbra admired that. She also loved the songs they wrote. In the two years since her last studio recording Barbra had seen soundtracks and a greatest hits package keep the "old" Streisand in the public eye. With this album she was determined to show the world a "new" Barbra—one who knows a great new protest song when she hears it. More than half of the album's eleven songs are written or co-written by women: There are three Nyro songs ("Hands Off the Man," "Stoney End," "Time and Love"), a Carole King co-write ("No Easy Way Down"), a Cynthia Weil co-write ("Just a Little Lovin'") and Joni Mitchell's "I Don't Know Where I Stand." The other numbers are by such credible rock writer-performers as Randy Newman, Gordon Lightfoot and Harry Nilsson. The horn-flecked, soulful sound is completely contemporary, and the album is arguably the best she'd made for some time. The public appreciated the change in direction, and this album got to the top ten on the album chart and went gold within two months of release.

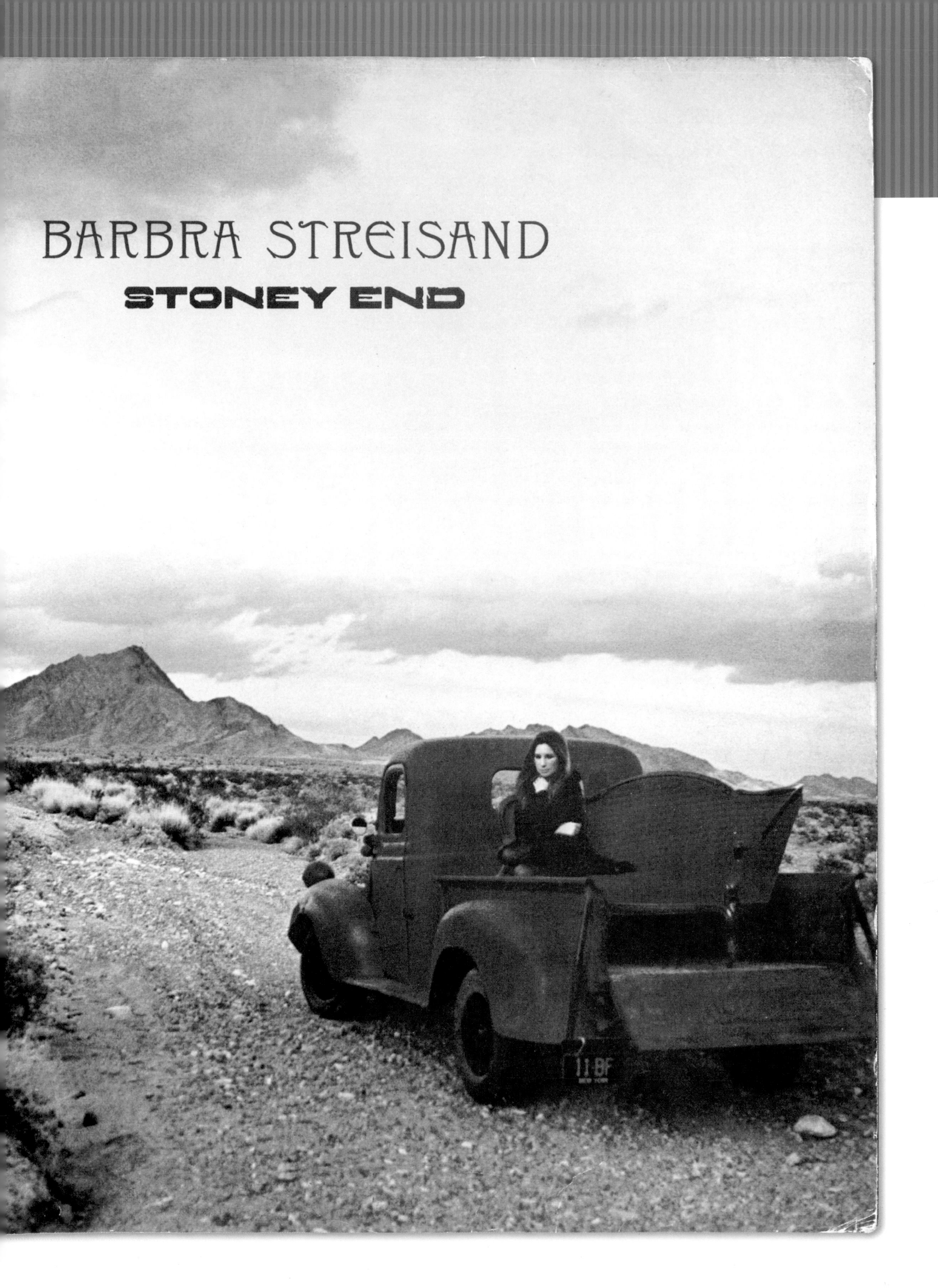
BARBRA STREISAND
STONEY END

# Barbra Joan Streisand

**Released**
1971
**Label**
Columbia Records
**Producer**
Richard Perry
**Musical Arrangement**
Nick DeCaro, Dick Hazard, Kenny Welch, Gene Page, Head and Fanny

---

**Tracks**
▪ Beautiful ▪ Love ▪ Where You Lead ▪ I Never Meant to Hurt You ▪ Medley: One Less Bell to Answer/A House Is Not a Home ▪ Space Captain ▪ Since I Fell for You ▪ Mother ▪ The Summer Knows ▪ I Mean to Shine ▪ You've Got a Friend

With songs again from the likes of Carole King, John Lennon and Laura Nyro, Barbra was clearly trying to perfect her recent new sound. This album showcased not only her choice of a great song, but also her vocal prowess in a rock setting. She chose John Lennon's "Mother" (she also covers his "Love"), but it seems odd that she didn't feel the need to change it to "Father," therefore making it even more perfect for her. She belts out this excruciatingly melancholic song with total abandon, and her voice has rarely sounded better. As it fades it makes you yearn for more, slowly disappearing at the very point you can hardly believe what you're hearing. She's assisted in her rock performances by the all-female rock band Fanny on four tracks, while Rolling Stones keyboard player Billy Preston also guests. Steely Dan founder Donald Fagen and legendary rock drummer Jim Keltner also help out on some tracks.

On the sleeve she's looking her hippie best; the styling is far less formal than on most of her previous covers. With long straight hair and a huge cloth flat cap, she looks very much at ease with herself and her crew, whom she chose to include on the cover for the inner sleeve photos.

Standout cuts are Buddy Johnson's "Since I Fell for You" and the beautiful "The Summer Knows" by Michel Legrand, Alan Bergman and Marilyn Bergman.

BARBRA JOAN STREISAND

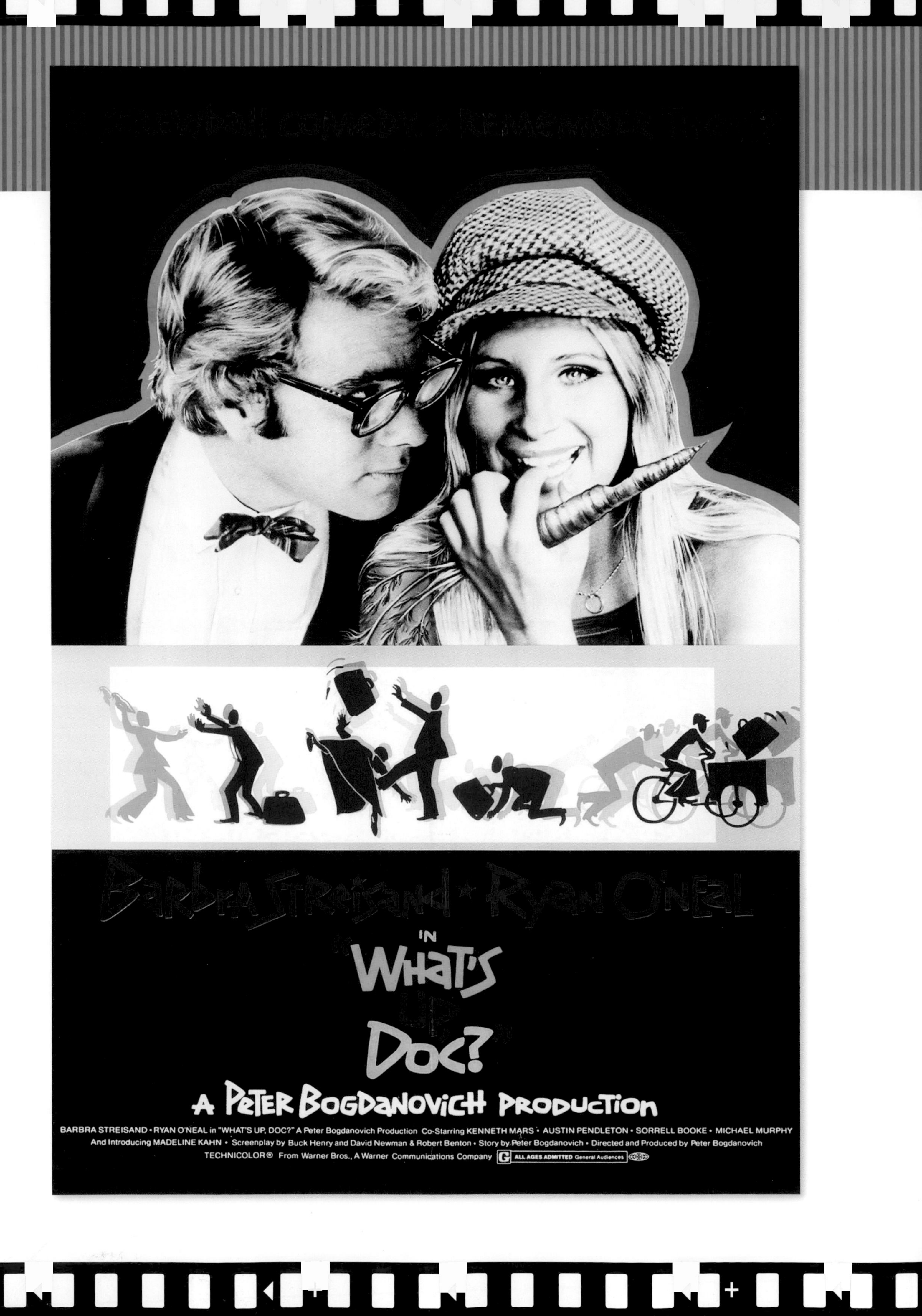
A screwball comedy • Remember them?
Barbra Streisand • Ryan O'Neal
in
"What's Up, Doc?"
A Peter Bogdanovich Production
BARBRA STREISAND • RYAN O'NEAL in "WHAT'S UP, DOC?" A Peter Bogdanovich Production Co-Starring KENNETH MARS • AUSTIN PENDLETON • SORRELL BOOKE • MICHAEL MURPHY
And Introducing MADELINE KAHN • Screenplay by Buck Henry and David Newman & Robert Benton • Story by Peter Bogdanovich • Directed and Produced by Peter Bogdanovich
TECHNICOLOR® From Warner Bros., A Warner Communications Company
G ALL AGES ADMITTED General Audiences

# What's Up, Doc?

Above: A naturally screwball Barbra in action.

**Running Time** 94 mins
**Studio** Warner Bros. Pictures, Saticoy Productions
**Year** 1972
**Director** Peter Bogdanovich
**Screenplay** Buck Henry, David Newman and Robert Benton
**Cast** Barbra as Judy Maxwell, Ryan O'Neal, Madeline Kahn and Kenneth Mars

With *What's Up, Doc?* director Peter Bogdanovich determinedly set out to make what used to be called a screwball comedy. Its clever potshots, risks and slapstick setups mimic the kind of 1930s comedies starring the Marx Brothers (Barbra's dialogue and delivery are very Groucho), or directed by Howard Hawks, such as *His Girl Friday* and, of course, *Bringing Up Baby*, on which this is more than loosely based. The 1938 original starred Cary Grant as the absentminded zoology professor and Katharine Hepburn as the flighty woman who decides she wants to steal him away from a "sensible" fiance. O'Neal does a fair impression of Grant throughout the movie, perhaps because he consulted Grant on how to play his role; Grant said to try silk undergarments. Barbra makes her character all her own, of course.

The film is a rollicking comedy, full of pratfalls and ridiculous chase scenes (including one that aped the famous car pursuit in *Bullitt*). It remains a notable production for other reasons too: It was the first American film to credit its stunt players, of which there were many. Originally, Barbra did not want to make this movie, apparently, saying that she didn't think the script was funny and that it was going to be a major flop. She had every reason for thinking this would be the case. After all, the kooky final chase sequence cost a quarter of the film's entire budget to make, and took a month to complete.

Bogdanovich took cars down the cement steps of San Francisco's Alta Plaza Park without permission, leaving huge dents in the steps that are still visible today—watch the film and you can see it happen. The cars were wrecked, and they didn't have enough cars to re-shoot, so he reportedly authorized the crew to rent some and make sure they got the correct insurance. *What's Up, Doc?* had a lasting effect on San Francisco. It is now very particular about any filming in the city, requiring ironclad, detailed documents about every shoot. It also left a big impression on Madeline Kahn, who said she was petrified of Barbra. She added, though, that she was scared of everything, as it was her first film.

Commenting on Barbra's claim to the American Film Institute in 2001 that she never understood the appeal of the film, Bogdanovich said that she always understood that the film was a screwball comedy, but that she never thought it was particularly funny. Many of the best parts of *What's Up, Doc?* use Barbra singing Cole Porter songs throughout, and to bookend the movie. Reportedly, she didn't want to put "You're the Top" over the opening credits, but thankfully she relented. The version used is made up of different takes spliced together.

"*What's Up, Doc?* is a picture with no socially redeeming value. I've always liked the comedies of the '30s, the kind of pictures that used to be called typically American. The genre went into disuse in the '60s and I wanted to revive it."

—*Peter Bogdanovich, Show Magazine, 1972*

# The Legend of Her Nose

You rarely hear it now, but at the beginning of Barbra's career, the comments about her distinctive look were commonplace. It was not only Barbra's voice that stopped people in their tracks, it was also her striking appearance—and paricularly, her nose. Humorist Mark C. Miller once wrote a comedy article stating that a tribe in Africa worships Streisand's nose, saying, "We did not pick the nose. The nose picked us."

Double entendre aside and as silly as it seems, Barbra and her nose were a real force to be reckoned with. At a time when different kinds of beauty were only just beginning to be appreciated, her glossy, well-styled hair and sleek makeup all served to emphasize her very nontypical Hollywood nose. It subsequently became a focal point for a new kind of beauty for women all over the world to be proud of. By the time Barbra was beginning to appear on television and in magazines in the early 1960s, there was considerable puzzlement expressed about why the young Barbra didn't go ahead and do what so many women had done already: have rhinoplasty surgery. In the 1960s, a symmetrical face and an elegant, dainty profile were still the ideal. Personality in appearance was for men only.

Thankfully, though, experimentation, self-expression and ethnic threads in beauty were coming to the fore everywhere; it a step away from the debutante-style conformity of the 1940s and 1950s. Barbra's nose came along at the right time and made a statement about personality, makeup, self-belief and presentation that was wholly original.

### Looking up

It is probably fair to say that early in her career, Barbra Streisand's nose was her second-most famous attribute. Much has been written and said about it, with press commentators asking whether she did not get it fixed because, as legend has it, it would have affected her voice. Was Barbra making a statement by not bowing to convention when opting for surgery was so fashionable? What really is the truth of Barbra's great asset, everyone wanted to know.

In 1985, the singer talked with Barbara Walters about it and said that she had thought about getting her nose "done" in the early part of her career. It's rather nice to think that Barbra was being stubborn about her looks, insisting that she be loved by the public (and the camera) just the way she is, without surgical attention. However, the truth is that way back then, Barbra couldn't afford to have it done. And by the time she could afford it, although she is a little fuzzy about when exactly she was considering having her nose "fixed," she was worried that the doctors wouldn't have gotten it aesthetically or functionally correct. Barbra has always felt her nose and her face were perfectly matched to each other, and we should be grateful to her for thinking that.

In an interview conducted for *Playboy* magazine in 1977, Barbra said that she believed a nose job would have ruined her singing voice, suggesting that her deviated septum was the reason for her distinctive, clear sound. She also added that she would have had a nose job if she could have designed and operated on her nose herself, straightening the bridge, taking off a little bit from, and changing the angle of, the tip. But she'd never touch the bump, because she loves it.

Barbra grew up when a lot of girls were having their noses "fixed" in high school, many of them unnecessarily so. For a time women were having their noses "bobbed." The goal seemed to be to make all women look nasally identical. Like many of us, Barbra was inspired by the beauty of others, especially European actresses who didn't have to adhere to the American ideal. She admired the looks of French actress Catherine Deneuve and Italian actress Silvana Mangano, saying of the latter that her nose resembled a sculpture—imperfect, shapely and definitely Roman.

In the twenty-first century celebrities are allowed to have remarkable rather than classically beautiful profiles or standard pretty faces. But before Barbra Streisand, that was less acceptable. Her unusual, elongated nose does not stop her from being beautiful; it is part of her beauty, part of what sets her apart and inspires others to be beautiful as themselves. She fought the good fight and changed our and Hollywood's accepted idea of beauty in the process. We can only guess at how many children who weren't tiny-nosed found comfort in Barbra's being so fantastic.

With a profile as individual and immediately identifiable as a trademark, Barbra Streisand's look is as distinctive and strong as her voice. No other nose would do.

Right: The nose that launched a thousand quips.

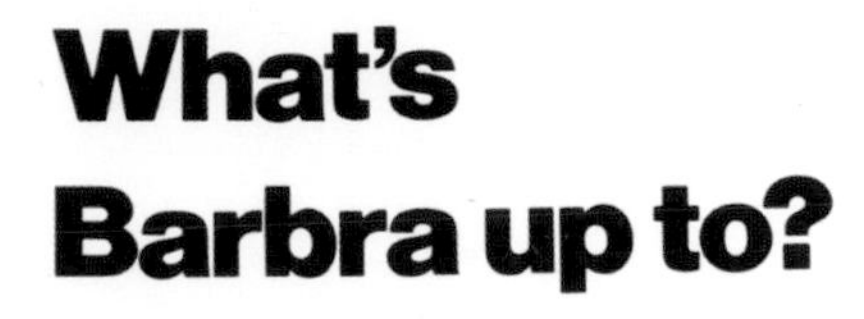


Up the marriage trap.
Up the revolution.
Up the Zambesi River.
And up to something
surprisingly wonderful.

UP THE SAND BOX

BARBRA STREISAND

A FIRST ARTISTS PRESENTATION
A BARWOOD FILM
A ROBERT CHARTOFF-IRWIN WINKLER PRODUCTION

STARRING **BARBRA STREISAND** IN **"UP THE SANDBOX"**
CO-STARRING DAVID SELBY · SCREENPLAY BY PAUL ZINDEL · BASED ON A NOVEL BY ANNE RICHARDSON ROIPHE · DIRECTED BY IRVIN KERSHNER
PRODUCED BY IRWIN WINKLER AND ROBERT CHARTOFF · TECHNICOLOR® · A NATIONAL GENERAL PICTURES RELEASE R RESTRICTED

 STYLE B 73/4

"UP THE SAND BOX"

# Up the Sandbox

Above: Star and producer in a pit; Barbra as a fantasizing American housewife.

**Running Time** 97 mins
**Studio** Barwood Films
**Year** 1972
**Director** Irvin Kershner
**Screenplay** Paul Zindel
**Cast** Barbra as Margaret Reynolds; co-starring David Selby and Ariane Heller

---

Barbra's sixth film was the first with First Artists (her movie-making partnership with Paul Newman, Sidney Poitier and Steve McQueen). It was also the first of many she would make with a socially significant message, without songs. Making significant movies was her reason for taking on a producer's responsibilities. This was also the first film that her own Barwood Films company co-produced and marks the point at which Barbra became actively involved in every part of the filmmaking process. She said when she saw the budget that she was sick to her stomach—it remains unpublished to this day, but speculation has it grossing $4 million.

Director Irvin Kershner was well respected, with a good attitude and some reputable movies already under his belt. (He was to go on to direct *Star Wars: Episode V—The Empire Strikes Back*, and Sean Connery's last film as James Bond, *Never Say Never Again*, among others). Kershner recalled that many photographs were taken of Barbra to determine where she looked best and where she could look bedraggled and worn out—needed for her portrayal of Margaret Reynolds, a young New Yorker who's a mother, a daughter and a wife and under mental stress. Based on Paul Zindel's screenplay, which was itself taken from Anne Roiphe's feminist novel, Margaret disappears into different fantasies with increasing frequency. One of them is to be seduced (or kidnapped, or both) by a Fidel Castro lookalike who turns out to be a woman. Another features a terrorist attack on the Statue of Liberty by a gang of black supremacists. A more satisfying fantasy involves getting even with her snipey mother.

Barbra felt that the fantasies had to be handled in a truthful manner. As she had based her singing career on truth—and every other part of her life, for that matter—she made sure the lapses of reality within the movie were very subtly done, but it was something that the cinematic audience wasn't really ready for. "[That] broke my heart because I thought they were so clever," she said on the 2003 DVD release of the movie.

The quest for reality can be costly. The African fantasy sequences had to be shot on location because despite Kershner telling Streisand that although those sequences would be shot on the MGM backlot that they would look as real as possible, they didn't. The crew ended up going to Kenya to reshoot, with the result that the African sequence is extremely beautiful (and funny). However, it was also extremely costly. Although a favorite with Barbra fans, the film has not enjoyed a wide audience viewing since release.

"One of the aspects of our society is that women's ideas are immediately negated—because they originate from women. That has been the source of my frustrations in motion pictures. I had ideas, and I expressed them. But because I was a woman, I was disregarded."

# Live Concert at the Forum

**Released**
1972
**Label**
Columbia Records
**Producer**
Richard Perry
**Conductor**
David Shire

---

**Tracks**
• Sing/Make Your Own Kind of Music • Starting Here, Starting Now • Don't Rain on My Parade • Monologue • On a Clear Day (You Can See Forever) • Sweet Inspiration/Where You Lead • Didn't We • My Man • Stoney End • Sing/Happy Days Are Here Again • People

Streisand became a publicly political performer with the release of this album, recorded at a fundraiser for 1972 Democrat presidential candidate George McGovern and his stand against the war in Vietnam. It marks the beginning of a trend that she has continued throughout her career. A multi-artist event, the evening included performances by Carly Simon and James Taylor, among others. However, it was Barbra's forty-five-minute segment of the show that Columbia decided to release. She was of course that night's biggest draw, so why not?

In many ways this was a live greatest hits album, and it includes several of her signature tunes: "Second Hand Rose," "People," "Don't Rain on My Parade," and the recent top ten hit single "Stoney End," which went down well with the audience. It was an evening of purpose as well as entertainment, and Barbra was in full control, totally at ease with the eighteen-thousand-strong crowd at the Forum in Los Angeles.

Her son, Jason, six years old at the time, was a big fan of the song "Sing" from TV's *Sesame Street* and a hit on the charts by the Carpenters. Naturally she chose to open her set with it, in medley with "Make Your Own Kind of Music." Midway through the show, while chatting to the audience, she lit up what appeared to most to be a joint, asking the audience, "It's STILL illegal?" to rapturous applause. If ever there was a single moment when Barbra Streisand caught the attention of the rock audience, this was it.

# Barbra Streisand . . . and Other Musical Instruments

**Released**
1973
**Label**
Columbia Records
**Producer**
Martin Erlichman
**Musical Arrangement**
Jack Parnell

**Tracks**
• Piano Practicing • I Got Rhythm • Johnny One Note/ One Note Samba • Glad to Be Unhappy • People • Second Hand Rose • Don't Rain on My Parade • Don't Ever Leave Me • Monologue • By Myself • Come Back to Me • I Never Has Seen Snow • Lied: auf dem Wasser zu Singen • The World Is a Concerto/Make Your wOwn Kind of Music • The Sweetest Sounds

If there were ever a poll for the oddest of Barbra Streisand releases, *Other Musical Instruments* would surely top it. This was all Barbra. However, the album's sheer unadulterated boldness lures you in, and keeps you entertained throughout. Who wouldn't want to hear her belting out "People" with a Turkish/Armenian backing, or "I Got Rhythm" in authentic Japanese style? It's a difficult listen, and perhaps only hardcore fans are prepared to persevere with it, but all should try. Those fond but not fanatical might have preferred the television special, from which this album recording is taken; let's just say that may be because it's a lot easier on the eye than the ear.

In the liner notes Morte Goode expressed what many fans already knew: "Barbra—stylish, fanciful, full of never ending amazement." The great photograph on the sleeve captures her standing atop a grand staircase, with the entire orchestra and rhythm section—plus a camel—behind and below, looking on in either total admiration or utter confusion. Barbra, as ever, seemed to be having the time of her life.

STREISAND
& REDFORD
TOGETHER!

THE WAY WE WERE

Everything seemed so important then... even love!

COLUMBIA PICTURES and RASTAR PRODUCTIONS Present BARBRA STREISAND · ROBERT REDFORD in THE WAY WE WERE · A RAY STARK—SYDNEY POLLACK Production
co-starring BRADFORD DILLMAN · VIVECA LINDFORS · HERB EDELMAN MURRAY HAMILTON and PATRICK O'NEAL and introducing LOIS CHILES
'THE WAY WE WERE' sung by BARBRA STREISAND Music MARVIN HAMLISCH · Written by ARTHUR LAURENTS · Produced by RAY STARK · Directed by SYDNEY POLLACK · PANAVISION®
PG PARENTAL GUIDANCE SUGGESTED

# The Way We Were

Above: Barbra as Harpo and everyone else as Groucho.

**Running Time** 118 mins
**Studio** Columbia Pictures, Rastar Pictures
**Year** 1973
**Director** Sydney Pollack
**Screenplay** Arthur Laurents, Francis Ford Coppola, David Rayfiel and Dalton Trumbo
**Cast** Barbra as Katie Morosky; co-starring Robert Redford

This is arguably Barbra Streisand's best film, for several reasons. First of all, she was perfectly cast as Katie Morosky, the Brooklyn bluestocking in love with Robert Redford's privileged Hubbell Gardiner. The screenplay was based on Arthur Laurents's days at Cornell University as well as his brush with the House Un-American Activities Committee.

Up to this point in Barbra's career, filmically speaking, she'd played funny, sexy, heavy socially dramatic and light musical roles but never a role where she seemed to be a real actress, rather than Barbra Streisand the actress. When producer Ray Stark hired Laurents to write something expressly for Barbra, she jumped at the chance to do it after reading just a few scenes. Working with Pollack, then yet to have a massive hit, suited her because she saw him as a fellow performer-turned-actor. It is possible that Barbra found Pollack's style inspirational for her own directing.

Co-starring with Robert Redford was another strong point for Barbra. Both chose not to over-communicate their roles off-camera, preferring to let the script and their characters unfold in front of the lens. Redford, speaking at the American Film Institute in 2000, said that working with her was a highlight of his career and that Barbra was, simply put, very alive and yet a very harsh self-critic who was always "questioning, doubting, putting forth a huge effort to be the best she could be."

Although Laurents's work was augmented by other writers, then revised by him and reworked in postproduction by Pollack, the story always focused on two people who are at odds and yet in love. The love scene between Katie and Hubbell is probably Streisand's greatest moment on screen—she is strong, loving and showing the audience her feelings. It's a heartbreaker of a romance, a period piece that is timeless. Pollack said that he wanted Barbra to really act, and this is the result: She demonstrates her full power as an actress, unfettered by over-sentimentality, with no over-earnest message-making or her own persona getting in the way of the character. Here, she disappears into the role of Katie and becomes an actress. Sometimes, strong talents and personalities need strong wills to help them find the best within themselves, and in this case, the alchemy of Redford, Pollack, Laurents, and a team of skilled others helped Barbra emerge into the brilliant light she had been aiming for her whole life.

*The Way We Were* was an enormous box office hit, and went on to win two Oscars, one for Best Original Score another for Best Original Song (the title number). The soundtrack sold more than one million copies, and, amazingly, gave Barbra her first number 1 single in America.

"Yeah, it made a fortune and got very mixed reviews. It's one of those pictures that's gotten better treatment as time has gone by. It's funny how pictures get looked at differently as time passes."

*—The late director Sydney Pollack, on* The Way We Were *(The Hollywood Interview)*

# The Way We Were

**Released**
1974
**Label**
Columbia Records
**Producer**
Tommy LiPuma, Marty Paich and Wally Gold
**Musical Arrangement**
Nick DeCaro, Peter Matz, Marty Paich and Claus Ogerman

**Tracks**
• Being at War with Each Other • Something So Right • The Best Thing You've Ever Done • The Way We Were (from The Way We Were) • All in Love Is Fair • What Are You Doing the Rest of Your Life? • Summer Me, Winter Me • Pieces of Dreams • I've Never Been a Woman Before • Medley: My Buddy/ How About Me?

This album is not to be confused with the film soundtrack of the same name, although both were released the same year in order, most likely, to capitalize on the movie's huge success.

This release is one of Barbra's finest albums, and a slight move away from some of the producers, songwriters and engineers we were used to hearing her work with. While Carole King was an obvious Streisand favorite, present here as writer on "Being at War with Each Other," this time there were also writing contributions from significant others, notably Paul Simon and Stevie Wonder. Her interpretation of Wonder's "All in Love Is Fair" is a real treat. Inflecting a little more soul into her work was a smart move and paved the way for future R&B- and disco-based material. She opened herself up to many other musical opportunities and, of course, a far wider audience.

Photography was by Steve Schapiro (front) and David Bailey (back). Barbra for the first time looked very much the Hollywood star here. Greta Garbo would have been proud of this glossy, sophisticated and sexy look.

This album, along with the movie, helped create and mold Streisand for a new generation. The title tune was not only one of her most successful songs, but also one of the most enduring and definitive.

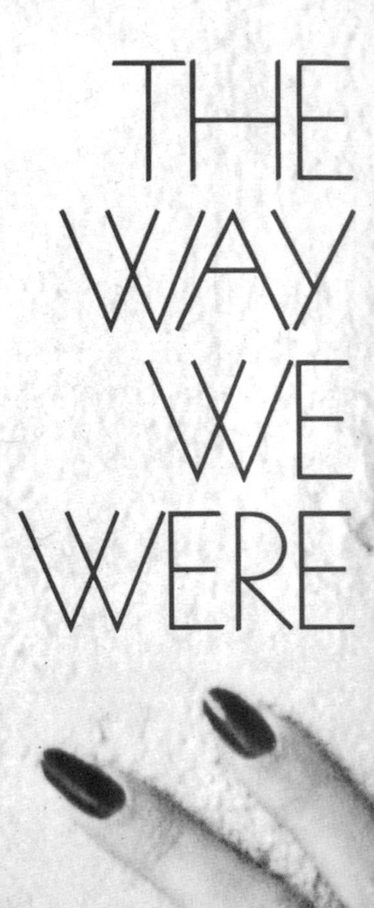

Side One LOVE IN THE AFTERNOON (BMI & ASCAP) Arranged by Tom Scott/Engineered by Hank Cicalo. GUAVA JELLY (ASCAP) Arranged by Tom Scott/Vocal Arrangement by John Bahler/Engineered by Hank Cicalo. GRANDMA'S HANDS (BMI) Arranged by Tom Scott/Vocal Arrangement by John Bahler/Engineered by Hank Cicalo. I WON'T LAST A DAY WITHOUT YOU. (ASCAP) Arranged by Lee Holdridge/Engineered by Michael Lietz/Remixed by Hank Cicalo. JUBILATION (BMI) Arranged by Tom Scott/Vocal Arrangement by John Bahler/Engineered by Hank Cicalo.

Side Two SIMPLE MAN (BMI) Arranged by Tom Scott/Engineered by Hank Cicalo. LIFE ON MARS (BMI) Arranged by Tom Scott/Horns & Vocal Arrangement by John Bahler/Engineered by Hank Cicalo. SINCE I DON'T HAVE YOU (ASCAP) Arranged by Lee Holdridge/Engineered by Michael Lietz. CRYING TIME (BMI & ASCAP) Arranged by Lee Holdridge/Engineered by Michael Lietz. LET THE GOOD TIMES ROLL (BMI) Arranged by Tom Scott/Horns & Vocal Arrangement by John Bahler/Engineered by Hank Cicalo.

Inside the *ButterFly* album cover.

BARBRA STREISAND, Background Vocals / MAX BENNETT Bass / TOM SCOTT, Woodwinds / BEN BENAY, Guitar
CLARENCE McDONALD, Keyboards / LARRY CARLTON, Guitar / JOHN GUERIN, Drums / KING ERRISSON, Congas
GARY COLEMAN, Percussion . All flute & tenor sax solos by TOM SCOTT.
Ben Benay
JUBILATION
Art Direction & Design: Jon Peters
Cover Photo: Carl Furuta
Inside Photos: Steve Schapiro
Back Cover Painting: Bill Shirley

# ButterFly

**Released**
1974
**Label**
Columbia Records
**Producer**
Jon Peters
**Musical Arrangement**
Tom Scott, Lee Holdridge and John Bähler

**Tracks**
• Love in the Afternoon • Guava Jelly • Grandma's Hands • I Won't Last a Day Without You • Jubilation • Simple Man • Life on Mars • Since I Don't Have You • Crying Time • Let the Good Times Roll

This album was produced by Barbra's hairdresser boyfriend Jon Peters, and it's tempting to suggest that perhaps she was blinded by love while making it. The decision to record David Bowie's "Life on Mars" is still considered one of her daftest career moves. Bowie himself denounced her version as "bloody awful," which must have upset her. Bob Marley's "Guava Jelly" isn't much better and is all too obvious in its references to semen. At least it doesn't attempt to be a reggae tune proper; Barbra really doesn't sound sexy singing it. The cover features an appalling pun, which didn't help, either. Who wouldn't prefer another lovely photo of an idol instead of an open packet of butter with a fly on top of it? It's a dumb joke. Columbia might not have approved of the cover either, since their ads for the release displayed the album really small alongside a big photo of Barbra looking naturally elegant, with the headline "Barbra's new beauty," and the copy leading with "*The Way We Were*, with more than one million albums sold . . ." just to remind people of how good she could be. The inner sleeve (previous pages) shows Barbra at work in the studio.

Barbra

Love In The Afternoon • Guava Jelly • Gr

ButterFly

ma's Hands · I Won't Last A Day Without You · Jubilation · Simple Man · Life On Mars · Since I Don't Have You · Crying Time · Let The Good Times Roll

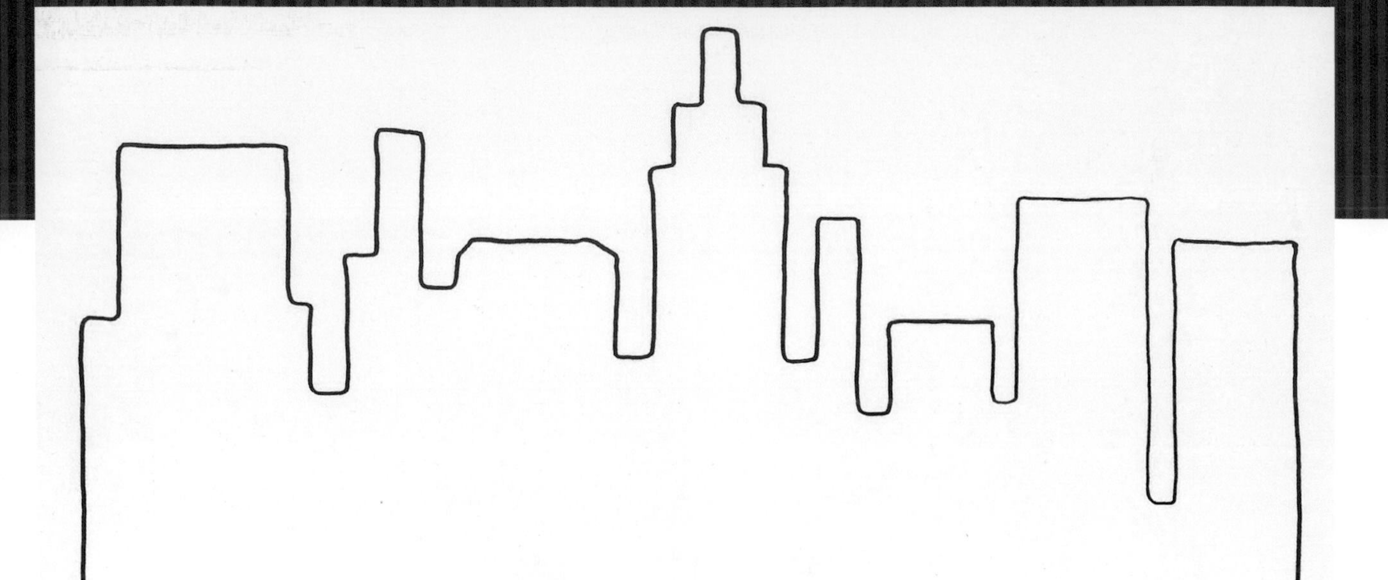

**zanybarbra.**

COLUMBIA PICTURES and RASTAR PICTURES Present

# Barbra Streisand

in

# "For Pete's Sake"

A PETER YATES Film

starring

MICHAEL SARRAZIN · ESTELLE PARSONS

co-starring

MOLLY PICON · WILLIAM REDFIELD

Written by STANLEY SHAPIRO and MAURICE RICHLIN · Music by ARTIE BUTLER

Directed by PETER YATES · Produced by MARTIN ERLICHMAN and STANLEY SHAPIRO

Executive Producer PHIL FELDMAN

PG PARENTAL GUIDANCE SUGGESTED



74/167

# For Pete's Sake

Above: Barbra as Henry, stopping traffic on set.

**Running Time** 90 mins
**Studio** Barclay, Rastar Pictures
**Year** 1974
**Director** Peter Yates
**Screenplay** Stanley Shapiro and Maurice Richlin
**Cast** Barbra as Henrietta "Henry" Robbins, Michael Sarrazin

*For Pete's Sake* was Barbra's return to comedy after the drama of *Up the Sandbox* and *The Way We Were*. Given the enormous success of *What's Up, Doc?,* comedy seemed the best place to go to play on her greatest strength. Director Peter Yates had been a fan of Barbra's role in *What's Up, Doc?* but thought more could be made of who she was and what her strengths were. He wanted to update her look, give her a more focused comedy role to perform, and show off her wonderful figure. In short, Yates wanted to make a film that was fun and that fit Barbra.

So, Barbra went to get her famous long hair cut, choosing Jon Peters, then Hollywood's hairdresser to the stars for the job. When he showed up for the meeting, she kept him waiting and then told him she wanted a wig. Great hairdressers rarely do wigs. But that was what Barbra wore throughout filming. He may not have been allowed to cut her hair, but Peters was soon to shape a large part of her life.

In *For Pete's Sake* she stars as Henrietta "Henry" Robbins who is married to taxi driver Pete (Michael Sarrazin), and they struggle with money. He decides he wants to go back to school, but can't afford the fees. So, being the loving wife she is, she gets the bright idea to borrow money from the Mob in order to buy some futures that are predicted to go high and, of course, when they don't her unpaid debt gets sold to a prostitution ring. Henry's debt grows as she tries various madcap ways to pay it off, including cattle rustling the world's most enormous Brahman bull—which emerges from the back of a motor home to join Barbra in the driver's seat during the getaway. "Zany Barbra" was what was billed on the posters, and so she was, riding the bull, whose breed is famous for its loose slippery hide, through the streets of Brooklyn.

*For Pete's Sake* is a farce, like *What's Up, Doc?*—very old fashioned, very predictable, and often very silly—but it is also often stupidly enjoyable. It doesn't try to do anything particularly new. The plot is all about Barbra's character, not interwoven storylines, and it features a very strong supporting cast. The movie belongs to Barbra alone, and she carries it off impressively.

To add to the mirth, production designer Gene Callahan made an apartment with doors that could open and close at precisely the right times to emphasis the comedic workings of the script and in keeping with traditional stage farces. Of all of her movies, this one best demonstrates Barbra's comic timing, which was always impeccable. Along with singing the title song, she acquitted herself well in this rather old-style comedy.

"You see, it's the kind of part I've always wanted, an intelligent, refined, sophisticated woman of the world."

# Barbra Style

Like Sophia Loren, Barbra's looks can be deceiving. Artful use of makeup and hair styling transforms the singer's distinctive appearance into a multitude of different looks. Being a conventional "beauty" was never Barbra's easiest option: Beauty was something she created herself. Style she developed. Verve and nerve were things she always had.

Barbra was a gawky teenager when she left Brooklyn to seek her fame in Greenwich Village, and her appearance was either makeup-free or at best badly applied. She had skinny legs, far from flawless skin, a large nose and a big chest. Photos from those early years, before her arrival onstage, show a pudgy face, a spotty complexion, flat hair and a big, untamed mouth.

Designer Bob Schulenberg talked about redesigning Barbra's look using different makeup in 1960. He met her when she was starting out, singing in talent contests at small gay bars like the Lion and the Bon Soir in New York, wearing mix-and-match outfits and self-applied makeup. Before she hit it big, Barbra was like many women and just doing the best she could with what makeup she had. Because makeup is expensive, and it is difficult to know what you need and what will work without lengthy experimentation or assistance, Barbra kind of muddled through as the rest of us do, despite the fact that her looks were of very important to her burgeoning career.

Schulenberg says that the young Barbra wasn't ugly, but that she thought she was. Of course, as with all girls her age, she wanted to look beautiful—which she would if only she'd recognize that she had amazing eyes, a memorable face, and a profile that reminded one of the Egyptian pharaohs. Taking it slowly, Schulengberg convinced Barbra that she needed a makeup overhaul. Armed with a case of theatrical makeup, Schulenberg applied eye makeup and false eyelashes—two sets, in fact—explaining at every step what he was doing and why. The heavy greasepaint covered up her less–than–perfect skin. Barbra seemed to be pleased, glancing at herself in the mirror and proclaiming the effects to be quite good. Schulenberg also made a sketch of Barbra's face half made up and half bare, so she could practice and perfect her look, which she did. Sometimes, Schulenberg said, she would do it many times in a row, taking hours before she felt it was done well enough by her own hand.

### America's Cinderella

Further along in her career, when her star was rising, the entire nation—if not the world—became obsessed with getting the Streisand look. Hairdressers were swamped with requests for wigs and hairpieces to emulate her thick, coiffed hair, which was a version of a messed-up Beatles cut or a pageboy. Women's magazines cobbled together editorial beauty pages on how to get that look with makeup, with extra emphasis on extreme eye makeup, Cleopatra-style. Some writers suggested that it was only a matter of time before plastic surgeons were getting demands for a Barbra Streisand nose. Barbra's looks were described in exotic terms by the media; she was called a Babylonian queen, an anteater, an oracle or a hamster. *Encyclopedia Britannica* named her as one of the fashion trendsetters of 1964, the year that she was featured in the pages of *Vogue* three times.

Her unusual eyes—often said to be too close together to be classically beautiful—seem to have come from her father, Emanuel, who also had an unusual gaze that seemed slightly crossed, as if he were looking at something in the distance. Her eyes, along with her long, unique nose, have been as asset to Streisand's public image, giving her a malleability of appearance that other stars dare not attempt. It is precisely because Streisand is not a classical beauty that she has been able to shape her appearance to match her career, her mood, a role or a trend. Unlike those of a more ordinary beauty, Barbra's face and features lend themselves to alteration. If she wants her eyes to appear less close-set, makeup and hair tricks can achieve it, such as styling her hair forward, to the side of her face, to lend balance. Texture in the form of ringlets, waves and curls also take the focus off her unusual eyes.

### Homages

In the 1981 documentary *I Remember Barbra*, filmmaker Kevin Burns went to Brooklyn and talked to people who knew Barbra when she was growing up, before she made it big. The documentary, which is only twenty-three minutes long, carries a lot of insight to the nascent Barbra Streisand's style. People who remembered her say that she was

Opposite: From the beginning, Barbra was a unique fashion model, here she is in the mid sixties.

"unconventional" and that she was "very different, very bright," often chewing masses of gum, wearing unusual clothes, and knowing exactly what she had to do. One young fan, Jacqueline Holmes of Flatbush Avenue in Brooklyn, says that she never tires of looking at photos of Barbra, because her look is never the same. Barbra's face changes from photo to photo. This is, in essence, the key fascination with the looks of Barbra Streisand. Burns won an achievement award at the Student Academy Awards of that year for his efforts.

The September 2010 issue of *Harper's Bazaar* magazine in America featured a style spread with Jennifer Aniston channeling Barbra Streisand's look of the 1960s, particularly in *Funny Girl*, and the 1970s, as in *What's Up, Doc?* Apparently inspired by her own hairdresser, Chris McMillan, the actress, famous for her role in TV's *Friends*, feature films, and as the ex-wife of Brad Pitt, was out to promote her film *The Switch*. Because of her comedy roles, Aniston was deemed the "Funny Girl" of the day, hence the reason for her homage to Barbra across several glossy pages snapped by photographer Mark Seliger. Using pieces from designers such as Moschino, Albertus Swanepoel and Louis Vuitton to recreate Barbra's original part vintage, part designer style, Aniston also sported bobbed hair, heavily lined eyes and extremely long acrylic nails. That, with Chopard earrings and a Gianfranco Ferre dress in gold, recreated the visual verve and thunder that Streisand did so well.

The shoot, which made critics and commentators sit up and take notice, also brought home the fact that Barbra's style is associated with feminine power. As Aniston said in the *Harper's Bazaar* editorial, there isn't anything Barbra Streisand hasn't done. "She's a true renaissance woman," said Aniston, who claims to have met Barbra at a New Year's Eve party and bonded over their mutual love of film direction and interior design. (One critic astutely pointed out that Aniston was Streisand, but as she would have looked with a nose job.)

Barbra's beauty has aged well. In an era where stars often opt for plastic surgery, Barbra appears to be allowing nature to take its course, with the result that she looks relaxed and recognizable, especially in contrast to those in Hollywood who pursue youth at all costs. After six decades, Barbra Streisand

Left: Barbra was voted one of the best dressed women in the world in 1965 by New York fashionistas.
Opposite: Jennifer Aniston as Barbra in *Harper's Bazaar* magazine, 2010.

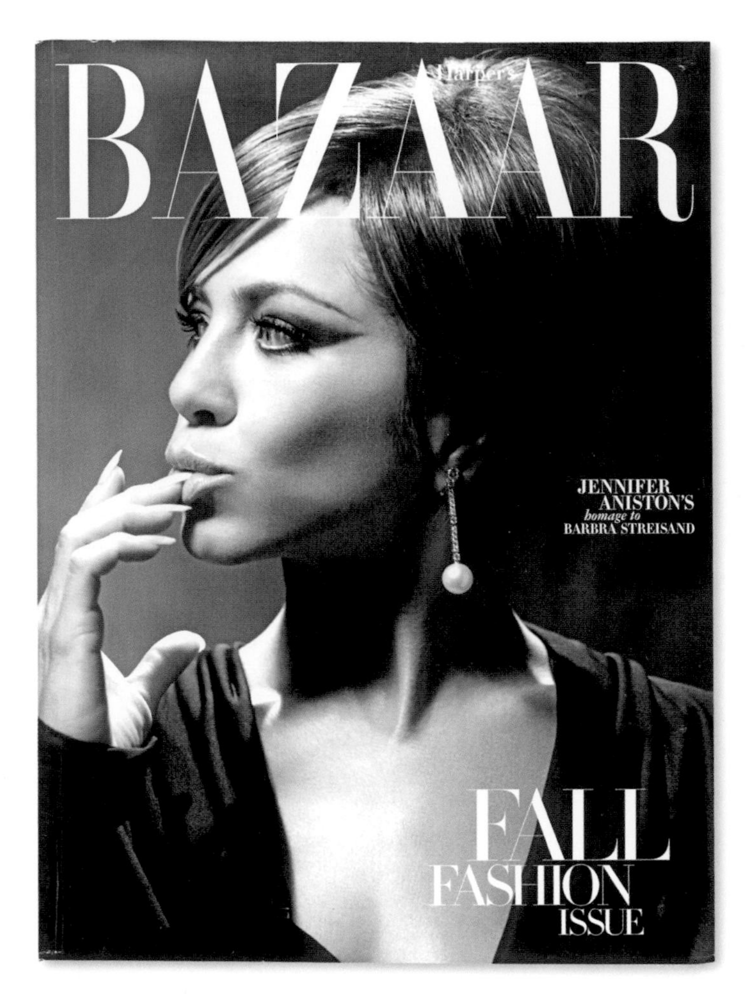

Harper's
BAZAAR
JENNIFER ANISTON'S
*homage to*
BARBRA STREISAND
FALL
FASHION
ISSUE


**EDITOR'S**
LETTER

# WELCOME TO THE ISSUE

*"I was very flattered that Jennifer chose to do this photo tribute to me. I can't wait to see it."*
*—Barbra Streisand*

BARBRA STREISAND FAMOUSLY SANG, "People who need people are the luckiest people in the world." In the case of our September cover story, there are many people to thank.

It started with Jennifer Aniston and her longtime hairstylist and friend, Chris McMillan, who had the brilliant idea to pay homage to Barbra. The two mentioned it to photographer Mark Seliger, who then told me. I thought it was too good to be true—until I ran into Jennifer at the La Mamounia hotel opening in Morocco last Thanksgiving.

After that, we started our collaboration in earnest. Jennifer personally chose the pictures of Barbra she wanted to emulate, storyboarding the shoot like a director. On set, she hit all the right notes, channeling her muse all the way to Barbra's legendary fingernails.

This fall is set to be a Streisand moment in more ways than one. Barbra is releasing her long-anticipated book of interiors, *My Passion for Design*. My good friend Wendy Goldberg made an introduction, and the next thing I knew, it was "Barbra Streisand on line 1."

As it always does, the conversation turned to fashion. Barbra laughed and said she wore her famous newsboy cap from *What's Up, Doc?* recently and was followed by the paparazzi. (Never underestimate the power of a great accessory.) "I was very flattered that Jennifer chose to do this photo tribute to me," Barbra says. "I can't wait to see it."

So, while people need people, it's thanks to Jennifer's passion and Barbra's continued inspiration that this story truly sings. ➤

On Jennifer: **Gianfranco Ferré** dress. **Chopard** earrings.

90

*"People laugh at me. Sometimes I know why, and sometimes I don't. But I can pretty much find humor in anything."*

Swinging in '60s. Dress, $13,500, **Giambattista Valli.** Neiman Marcus; 888-888-4757.

Jennifer Aniston is sitting at home in Los Angeles, musing about singing Barbra Streisand songs in the shower. "Someone said to me, 'If I had Barbra's voice for just one day,' and I said, 'Nah, I don't want to be greedy. If I had her voice for just one shower—just a shower's worth—I would be happy.'" If so, perhaps it's worth forgetting modesty and selling tickets. "Hmm, no," she laughs. "Well, actually, if it was *her* voice..."

Jennifer has long idolized Streisand, patron saint of stage and screen (two Academy Awards, eight Grammys) and the exemplar of times-they-are-a-changing feminism, who is, of course, more than a muse. She's an icon.

Jennifer first met Streisand, 68, at a New Year's party a few years ago. "I've loved her since I was a kid, and all of a sudden there she is, and she's just like someone you've always known," Jennifer says. "You know when you meet people you idolize and then you walk away from the conversation thinking, 'Well, that was a disappointment; they were kinder and more fabulous in my mind'? Well, she was wonderful, and you could talk to her about anything." She starts to laugh. "So, I happened to be talking to her and Jim [Streisand's husband, James Brolin] when it struck midnight. They said, 'Excuse us,' kissed each other, and then, very politely, kissed me."

It was Jennifer's hairstylist and friend of almost 20 years, Chris McMillan, who inspired her to write her own love letter to Streisand's style. "He is, of course, hair obsessed," Jennifer explains, "and I'm a Barbie doll for him. So, whenever we'd see great pictures of Barbra or a movie, he'd be like, 'You *have* to do an homage to Barbra.'" ➤

444

Faux fur for *Funny Girl*. Coat, by special order, **Moschino.** 212-243-8600. Hat, **Albertus Swanepoel.** Pumps, $1,500, **Louis Vuitton.** 866-VUITTON.

has earned the right to wear her face and figure with ease. After all, ordinary beauty can pale and wither with age. Distinctive beauty, especially when enhanced by personality and confidence, defies time and adds to the visual appeal as the years pass. Barbra is a prime example of that old French adage of Coco Chanel's: By the age of forty, we have the face we deserve. Barbra has a face that reflects intelligence, comfort, and knowledge of who she is. We should be so inspired.

Typical of Barbra's early and apparently innate self-possession, she has always had a sure opinion about her looks, and sometimes she thinks she looks beautiful, but at other times, maybe not so much. She always wanted to be unique, however, which is also the reason why she dropped the third *a* from her name. Even as a child, Barbra had to face criticism of her looks—that her mouth was too big, her nose was too big, or her eyes were crossed. She was even teased and bullied by girls at school because of her looks, causing her to take the unique look thing a little too far. Some biographies of Barbra claim that her stepfather refused to buy her an ice cream cone once because she wasn't pretty enough.

A perfectionist, Streisand is said to prefer to be photographed from her left side. Her features are not as symmetrical as they seem, and, as we all know, the camera doesn't lie. Barbra has actually never come out and said that she prefers photographs of the left side of her face, but there are simply more photos of her left side. Iconic shots by famous photographers like Richard Avedon, Irving Penn, Francesco Scavullo and others have usually used that side. The only comment Barbra has made is that the one side of her face is better but the other side isn't actually bad. Like the stars of old Hollywood, Barbra knows how to work with the camera, having spent an entire lifetime in front of it. Even working with cinematographers, Barbra knows how the light plays along her features. Reportedly, great beauties like Marlene Dietrich and Ava Gardner had the same skill.

Like many female stars, Streisand has endured many years of less-than-kind comments about her looks. So, like others who make their living from performing in public and who rely on their image for their career, Barbra admitted in an interview in 2003 that she has an unusual face, one that varies from facet to facet. Sometimes she feels she looks really beautiful, and from another angle, she feels she looks quite ugly. But, she adds, she's not going to shed tears over her looks. She says it is more important to live, love and enjoy life. Beauty is, for Barbra, being in the moment, not worrying about whether she looks beautiful or ugly at that moment. There is nothing uglier than neuroses or worrying about how you look. Beauty is ease, grace and being.

Early on, however, Barbra had very sure ideas about her looks, especially for her debut film role in the 1968 film *Funny Girl*. Playing Fanny Brice, Barbra thought she was actually too good-looking to play the awkward if popular vaudeville performer. Barbra doesn't look like anyone but herself, of course.

Kindly called an "unlikely beauty" by some, Barbra can't compete with the classic good looks of, say, Sharon Stone, but then, she doesn't have to. Her strong profile, exotic eyes, and full mouth combine into a different kind of beauty, one that not everyone can appreciate.

### Beauty evolution

Barbra's beauty timeline begins in the late 1950s, when she experimented with hydrogen peroxide, putting streaks through her mane and using a rinse that turned her hair different and unpredictable colors.

By 1966, Barbra wore a trendy short cut on top of which she'd plunk small hairpieces to give lift and shape. This is around the time of the release of the LP *Color Me Barbra*. Two years later, she appeared as *Funny Girl* with the memorable look of ringlets around her distinctive face. By 1971, however, she'd relaxed into the times by going a little long and hippie-ish, with a swing. For 1976's iconic remake *A Star Is Born*, she opted for a short afro and the natural look. Ten years later, she still liked shoulder-length hair but did her own thing with clothes—not always successfully, but what did she have left to prove by then?

At the 1993 Oscars, she dazzled as she gave out the Oscar for Best Director, the same year she released *Back to Broadway*. In the 2000s, Barbra embraced the earth mother look, as suited her role in *Meet the Fockers*. At 2008's Kennedy Center Honors, she looks confident and comfortable, and quips that awards need to match her dress. Presenting the Best Director Oscar again in 2010, this time to a woman for the first time ever, Kathryn Bigelow—an honor that Barbra herself would have treasured—she looks elegant, confident and happy. Sure, she is a little heavier, but Barbra has earned the right to have whatever figure she wants.

Opposite: Barbra in 1973.

# Funny Lady

Left: Let's hear it for Fanny again. Barbra reprising her role as Ms. Brice.

**Running Time** 136 mins
**Studio** Columbia Pictures, Rastar Pictures, Vista
**Year** 1975
**Director** Herbert Ross
**Screenplay** Arnold Schulman and Jay Presson Allen
**Cast** Barbra as Fanny Brice, Omar Sharif, James Caan and Roddy McDowall

---

If *Funny Lady* seems like a hybrid of *The Way We Were* and *Funny Girl*, two of Barbra's largest hits so far, that's because it is. Barbra's ninth film is, as the title suggests, the sequel to her breakthrough hit *Funny Girl*. She was thirty-two and more wary with her choices of roles by now, and although loath to attempt to repeat past successes, she was obligated to producer Ray Stark for one last film. *Funny Lady* completed a contract she signed in 1967.

Arnold Schulman's plot looked perfect: taking Fanny Brice's career and restarting it in Hollywood. Now Fanny was smarter, less vulnerable, and more worldly. Also, Barbra got to work with director Herbert Ross (*The Owl and the Pussycat*) again.

Because of the nature of the film, Barbra found herself with a script that was written to play to her dramatic strengths and to make her sing again, too. However, the songs were in the style of Fanny Brice, a more mature woman. Although the *Funny Lady* cast LP went to number 6 in the *Billboard* charts, none of its songs became classics in their own right, as "People" and "Don't Rain on My Parade" from *Funny Girl* had. There was no song with the power of "On a Clear Day" or that could emulate the wild popular success of "The Way We Were," despite the new numbers being written by *Cabaret* and *Chicago* soundtrack authors John Kander and Fred Ebb.

Barbra looks amazing in the movie, helped by the legendary (and quite ill at the time) cinematographer James Wong Howe, who, at age seventy-five, came out of retirement only a few days into the production, replacing another legend, Vilmos Zsigmond. Zsigmond recounted that he had wanted the film to look darker, edgier, and more adult and dangerous, while director Ross wanted something lighter and more in the same tone as *Funny Girl*. Howe said that the movie needed to be lighter, to bring out the tones of the music. So he opted for tones in his lighting of pink, blue, gold and pink-purple. Ultimately, Howe's work won him an Oscar—his second—for what was his last movie.

Nicky Arnstein (Omar Sharif) returns fleetingly, as Brice's seductive ex-husband, but introduces James Caan as Fanny's crude and abrupt if sexy new husband. Caan played Billy Rose much in the same vein as he had the hot-headed Sonny in *The Godfather* in 1972. Caan was cast because, as Barbra was quoted as saying, it came down to who the audience wanted to see her kiss—and she's right. The chemistry between her and Caan is much greater than it was with Sharif.

"My Fanny syndrome is ending. I think I'm younger than that now."

ORIGINAL SOU

COLUMBIA PIC

BARBR
STREISAI

FUNI

a RAY
of a H

Co-Starring
BEN VERE

OMA

as

Original So

a

Addition

Direc
JAMES

Cos
RAY AGH

Music Arranged
Production D

Screenplay by
and AR
Story by A

Directed

Produc

# Funny Lady

**ORIGINAL SOUNDTRACK RECORDING**

**Released**
1975
**Label**
Arista
**Producer**
Rick Chertoff
**Musical Arrangement**
Peter Matz

**Tracks**
• How Lucky Can You Get? • So Long, Honey Lamb • I Found a Million Dollar Baby (in a five and ten cent store) • Isn't This Better • Me and My Shadow • If I Love Again • I Got a Code in my Doze • (It's Gonna be a (Great Day) • Blind Date • Am I Blue • It's Only a Paper Moon • More Than You Know • Clap Hands, Here Comes Charlie • Let's Hear it for Me

Former Columbia Records boss Clive Davis had set up the Arista label with distribution through his former employees, and as part of the deal he got to release this soundtrack to the Columbia Studios movie. Barbra had benefited from his advice on song choices for *Stoney End* and liked Davis, so she was happy for this to not be with Columbia Records. Originally containing fifteen tracks, it has some anomalies, as most original soundtracks do. It has been rereleased several times since 1975, so there are a variety of tracks to be found on different editions, depending on which version you purchase. The initial release was as a double LP with original show composers John Kander and Fred Ebb (*Cabaret*, *Chicago*) providing seven of the songs. Others include "It's Only a Paper Moon," "Clap Hands, Here Comes Charlie," and "Me and My Shadow"—as sung by James Caan, despite the number being cut from the movie release. "How Lucky Can You Get" and "Let's Hear It" are standout Barbra performances. The 1998 Arista CD reissue includes an extra song, and presents the lot in order as they are sung in the movie, which the original album release didn't do. The album originally made only number 25 on the *Billboard* album chart, and went gold after six months of release.

# Lazy Afternoon

**Released**
1975
**Label**
Columbia Records
**Producer**
Jeffrey Lesser and Rupert Holmes for Widescreen Productions
**Musical Arrangement**
Rupert Holmes

**Tracks**
• Lazy Afternoon • My Father's Song • By the Way • Shake Me, Wake Me (When It's Over) • I Never Had It So Good • Letters That Cross in the Mail • You and I • Moanin' Low • A Child Is Born • Widescreen

A most fitting title if ever there was one. This album is perfect accompaniment for a long, hot summer afternoon, doing nothing. The title (and opening) track almost sends you to sleep, and that's not a criticism. The arrangements are lush, with Barbra's whispery vocal making for an entirely pleasurable experience, and offer just a taste of what's in store.

Producers Jeffrey Lesser and Rupert Holmes, known for their storytelling songs, are joined on piano by a young David Foster (later to pen the theme for *St. Elmo's Fire*), and songwriting contributions from Paul Williams, Stevie Wonder and Alan and Marilyn Bergman.

"By the Way" was penned by Streisand herself, with lyrics by Holmes. Surprisingly, it was something of a first for Barbra, of which she was very proud. She recorded it several times to perfect it before finally including it here.

The surprising hit single from the album was the disco-styled "Shake Me Wake Me (When It's Over)." The only up–tempo number on the album, it owed a lot to the then hottest label in music, Philadelphia International. There's a classic disco middle eight, which made for a great extended single.

# Classical Barbra

**Released**
1976
**Label**
Columbia Records
**Producer**
Claus Ogerman
**Musical Arrangement**
Claus Ogerman

**Tracks**
• Beau Soir
• Brezairola—Berceuse
• Verschwiegene Liebe
• Pavane (Vocalisé)
• Après un Rêve • In Trutina • Lascia ch'io pianga • Mondnacht
• Dank sei Dir, Her • I Loved You

Apparently, a lot of people hated "the classical album." Personally, I think it's very good. Columbia may have supported her throughout her career, but some of her decisions led to them to refuse her financial advances, for fear of lack of sales. This was such a project, and in some ways they were right to be wary about its commercial potential, as it took years to become financially successful.

Anyone who wasn't a fan disliked the album, so it was almost universally panned. Barbra may be a great singer, but an opera or classical singer she is not. I personally think there are some very fine moments on this album, especially on Fauré's "Pavane," on which she simply hums the melody throughout. The idea might sound dreadful, but the result is quite incredible.

It was all a bit too contrived, though, more so than any other of her albums. It even had a classical music–style label on the sleeve. The decision to turn the original color photo by Francesco Scavullo into black and white was an attempt to make it look more "classy."

# A Star Is Born

Left: Barbra as Esther (with perm).

**Running Time** 139 mins
**Studio** Barwood Films, First Artists, Winters Hollywood Entertainment Holdings Corporation
**Year** 1976
**Director** Frank Pierson
**Screenplay** John Gregory Dunne, Joan Didion, and Frank Pierson
**Cast** Barbra as Esther Hoffman, Kris Kristofferson and Gary Busey

Filmed first in 1937 with Janet Gaynor and Frederic March, then in 1954 with Judy Garland and James Mason, Barbra's version was the third remake of *A Star Is Born*. (It was remade again in 2010, starring Beyoncé Knowles and directed by Clint Eastwood.) The popularity of the story lies in its melodrama. Two stars, one on the way up and one on the way down, in love with each other, struggle to maintain a public and personal life. Everyone knew about *A Star Is Born* except, it seems, Jon Peters, who was Barbra's lover at the time. As she admitted to James Lipton, the host of *Inside the Actors Studio*, she had been shown the script by Peters, who didn't have a clue about its legendary past.

Nevertheless, Barbra gamely took on the role made famous by Judy Garland: She's Esther Hoffman, a singer on the way up, the lead singer of a trio called the Oreos, with Venetta Fields and Clydie King as co-stars. She gets picked up (at breakfast no less–pizza) by drunken druggie rock star Kris Kristofferson, who's fallen in love with her. He gives her a shot at one of his concerts and, despite her music being radically different from what his audience expects, she becomes an enormous hit and soon eclipses his career, with tragic results.

Although it was criticized at the time for portraying the singing sensation who's trying to make it as being too professional or unbelievable (Barbra ruins a commercial opportunity by refusing to sing a certain way—something few struggling amateurs would do), the story is, in part, that of Barbra herself, who also had to pay her dues to "make it". She had to work for peanuts, sing for her supper, and struggle to make a name for herself.

Working with Kristofferson proved uneasy, and there's precious little chemistry between the two on–screen. Barbra had wanted Elvis or Bob Dylan to play her singing husband, but, as with most legends, they brought complications of time, money and schedule clashes. Kritofferson's character, who in previous films had been done in by alcohol, was now addicted to drugs in order to update the story and make it more believable.

Despite swearing she'd never cut her long nails, Barbra did so to be able to strum the guitar. Learning how to play in a rudimentary fashion, she ended up writing (with Paul Williams) "Evergreen," which earned them an Oscar. The duet filmed in the studio between Esther and John was done live: Barbra disliked lip synching and Kristofferson disliked singing live, hence the apparent awkwardness of that pivotal scene. The film came in at number two at the box office that year and earned an Oscar, with three other nominations. It also won five Golden Globes from as many nominations.

"I wanted to explore relationships today . . . the women in the past were very passive. I wanted Esther to want everything."

# A Star Is Born

**Released**
1976
**Label**
Columbia Records
**Producer**
Barbra Streisand and Phil Ramone
**Musical Arrangement**
Roger Kellaway, Jim Pankow, Kenny Ascher, Ian Freebairn-Smith and Pat Williams

**Tracks**
• Watch Closely Now • Queen Bee • Everything • Lost Inside of You • Hellacious Acres • Evergreen (Love Theme from *A Star Is Born*) • The Woman in the Moon • I Believe in Love • Crippled Crow • Finale: With One More Look at You/Watch Closely Now • Reprise: Evergreen (Love Theme from *A Star Is Born*)

This album features Barbra's Oscar-winning "Love Theme from a Star Is Born (Evergreen)," co-writtten with Paul Williams—otherwise known simply as "Evergreen." It also includes some terrific "live" recordings made in the studio with great session musicians, including Booker T (but no MGs). Some of the songs on the album are alternative versions produced by Phil Ramone to those used in the movie. The songs, by Leon Russell, Donna Weiss, Paul Williams, Rupert Holmes and Kenny Loggins, perfectly suit both star performers, even if Kris Kristofferson's vocals sound rough in contrast with Barbra's. "Everything," "The Woman in the Moon", and "I Believe in Love" are terrific tracks for the period—and they really sum up the sense that rock was coming into its own in the mainstream. The reprise at the end has "Evergreen" in a brief duet with Barbra and Kristofferson swapping verses, but it's the "live" improvised opening on the longer track that everyone knows. This, then, is more a collection of songs from the film—plus one that isn't, "Crippled Crow"—than a traditional soundtrack recording. Which is presumably why it doesn't include the words "Original Soundtrack Recording" in the title.

AND
KRISTOFFERSON
A STAR IS BORN

# STREISAND

SUPERMAN • DON'T BELIEVE WHAT YOU READ • BABY ME BABY • I FOUND YOU LOVE • ANSWER ME • MY HEART BELONGS TO ME • CABIN FEVER • LOVE COMES FROM UNEXPECTED PLACES

SUPERMAN

# Streisand Superman

**Released**
1977
**Label**
Columbia Records
**Producer**
Gary Klein
**Musical Arrangement**
Nick DeCaro, Jack Nitzsche, Charlie Calello and Larry Carlton

---

**Tracks**
• Superman • Don't Believe What You Read • Baby Me Baby • I Found You Love • Answer Me • My Heart Belongs to Me • Cabin Fever • Love Comes from Unexpected Places • New York State of Mind • Lullaby for Myself

Only Barbra Streisand could get away with appearing on her album sleeve dressed in a Superman T-shirt, hot pants and white sneakers. At thirty-five she was in her prime professionally, personally, and, judging by this album cover, physically, too. To help promote the album she appeared on the cover of *Playboy* in a similar outfit (the "S" is replaced by the magazine's bunny logo). Being on that cover was proof, if it was ever needed, that Barbra was not just a great singer and actress, but a sex goddess, too.

Musically the album is a mixed bag, and ultimately not one of her greatest. Having said that, there are some gems to be found here. "Lullaby for Myself," the album's closing track, is hauntingly beautiful. Another highlight is her reworking of Billy Joel's "New York State of Mind." "My Heart Belongs to Me" became a hit single. "Don't You Believe What You Read" is Barbra hitting back at the press, whom she felt went beyond the boundaries of intrusion into her private life.

However, it proved to be a successful pop album, making number 3 on the *Billboard* 200. Its success and the press attention it garnered, combined with the huge success of the *A Star Is Born* movie and soundtrack album, all helped to make Barbra one of the world's few superstars worthy of the title.

EW YORK STATE OF MIND • LULLABY FOR MYSELF

# Songbird

**Released**
1978
**Label**
Columbia Records
**Executive Producer**
Charles Koppelman
**Producer**
Gary Klein
**Musical Arrangement**
Gene Page, David Wolfert, Jerry Hey, Larry Williams, Alan Gordon, James Newton Howard, Bill Reichenbach, Jon Tropea, Lee Holdridge, Nick DeCaro and Larry Carlton

**Tracks**
• Tomorrow • A Man I Loved • I Don't Break Easily • Love Breakdown • You Don't Bring Me Flowers • Honey Can I Put On Your Clothes • One More Night • Stay Away • Deep in the Night • Songbird

Look at that list of arrangers—this was a truly epic production. For all that, it failed to make the top ten on the charts, even though it contains the original version of one of Barbra's biggest ever hits: "You Don't Bring Me Flowers." Here she sings it alone, but after going back into the studio later with Neil Diamond to record it as a duet, it was released as a single and became a huge international hit. Diamond and Streisand were hot property in the late seventies, and this pairing was the great idea of a U.S. deejay named Gary Guthrie, who spliced their respective versions together on his radio show. It prompted requests from the public for them to record it as a duet. Columbia saw dollar bills, and the rest, as they say, is history.

No other cuts on this album became significant hits, but there are some great numbers, notably "A Man I Loved," which has Streisand wistfully yearning with such vocal clarity it send shivers up and down the spine. The only oddball cut is a cover of "Tomorrow" from *Annie*. This was a bad choice for an opening track, and "Songbird" would have been more fitting. Cuddling up to her dog on the album's sleeve was an odd choice, but very Barbra. On the rear and inner sleeve there were even more dogs—in fact, her entire canine family.

# Wet

**Released**
1979
**Label**
Columbia Records
**Producer**
Gary Klein for The Entertainment Company, Charles Koppelman
**Musical Arrangement**
Frank DeCaro

**Tracks**
•Wet • Come Rain or Come Shine • Splish Splash • On Rainy Afternoons • After the Rain • No More Tears (Enough Is Enough) • Niagra • I Ain't Gonna Cry Tonight • Kiss Me in the Rain

Released at the peak of disco domination of America's charts and nightclubs, this album contained the worldwide number 1 duet with Donna Summer, "No More Tears (Enough Is Enough)." Taking up almost eight and a half minutes of side two, Barbra was clearly very aware of popular tastes—plus, her son Jason was a big Donna Summer fan. Some felt it was a good move, others were horrified. Barbra had enjoyed a brief disco hit earlier that summer with the title tune from *The Main Event*, and she knew only too well that having Donna Summer on board would almost certainly guarantee a smash.

There was a theme to the album, in that all of the songs were about water, or had water/ wet themes in their titles. "Splish Splash" (originally a hit for Bobby Darin) was a mistake, but her smooth, soulful rendition of "Come Rain or Come Shine" was effortless. "On Rainy Afternoons" is the only Streisand 'classic' here, but without any doubt it was the duet with Summer that drove the album. Curiously, Streisand never thanked Summer in the liner notes, as she did with others.

no swet

# The Main Event

Opposite: Barbra works out some angst on the Kid (Ryan O'Neal).

**Running Time** 112 mins
**Studio** Barwood Films, First Artists
**Year** 1979
**Director** Howard Zieff
**Screenplay** Gail Parent and Andrew Smith
**Cast** Barbra as Hillary Kramer, Ryan O'Neal

Designed as an ensemble comedy featuring two stars who'd jelled before, Barbra was reunited with Ryan O'Neal in her third film for the production company First Artists. With its memorably catchy disco theme song, *The Main Event* sounds and looks great, thanks to cinematographer Mario Tosi (who also worked on *Carrie*). With a funny script by TV writers Gail Parent and Andrew Smith which was completed as the film was shot, the idea was to put Barbra and O'Neal into another *What's Up, Doc?*–style fast-paced comedy. The movie also completed her three-movie contract with First Artists.

The movie's plot involved Barbra's character, Hillary Kramer, a perfume executive, discovering that she's flat broke after one of her employees absconds with her company profits and hightails it to South America. All she has of worth is a contract with a gorgeous young boxer who is, nevertheless, past his sell-by date as a fighter—so much so that he is now a driving instructor. Rather than using his contract as a tax write-off, Hilary needs him to box and earn some money. Roger Ebert, the Pulitzer Prize–winning film critic from Chicago, calls this a modern "meet cute," where the leads are daffy and charming from the very start.

Of course, the premise is silly, but even sillier is that as Eddie "Kid Natural" Scanlon, O'Neal's face looks completely untouched by an opponent's glove. (O'Neal claimed he had to actually box 150 rounds to get in shape for this role.) It is a credit to O'Neal, however, to be the foil for a strong character like Hillary.

The movie was a take on the 1970s gender clashes the audiences knew so well, which also put Barbra in a world full of guys who punch other guys for a living. There is a simmering, if naïve, sexuality to *The Main Event*, with Hillary's character (much like *A Star Is Born*'s Esther Hoffman) not being the kind of girl who's easy to get. As in *What's Up, Doc?* the comic timing is wonderful, with both leads equally stubborn, pig-headed, and idiotic, yet somehow still drawn to each other. What else could you do with a film like that but give it the tagline "A Glove Story"?

The promo photos of Barbra and O'Neal were shot by the legendary fashion photographer Francesco Scavullo, famous for his trademark wind-in-the-hair models. He also created the promo shots for *A Star Is Born* and is responsible for some of the best and sexiest photos of Barbra ever taken. Throughout the movie, fans couldn't help but notice Barbra's long legs (those boxing shorts!) and the lack of a suitable bra, but, given it was the 1970s, she was not exactly being unusual in her dress choice.

This funny, fun, strong, sexy film had a (small) message about gender equality hidden deeply in its gym-bound roots: Hillary may own the Kid, but she also has to rely on him. It's all good clean fun, though. The chemistry between O'Neal and Barbra was strong, and it's a fast-paced, modern screwball comedy. The movie's theme song, the disco-tinged "The Main Event," went to number 3 on the *Billboard* charts for August 1979, and the film was among the top ten earning films at the box office of its year.

"Actually, I wanted to make a film reminiscent of the screwball comedies. They were about relationships."

# The Voice

In the second decade of the twenty-first century, it was recognized by fans and critics alike that only Barbra Streisand remained from the pantheon of great American song stylists. Those she had sung with and competed against for sales—Frank Sinatra, Judy Garland, Dean Martin, Ella Fitzgerald, Liza Minnelli, Tony Bennett—were either gone or semi-retired. Only Barbra remained as a performing artist. She didn't record as often as she had in previous decades, but when she sang, countless numbers of fans wanted to be there to hear it.

As she aged, Barbra's phrasing became more assured, more intelligent, and, if possible, more effective. She had always known how to style a song to suit her perfectly. She reportedly once changed the lyrics of a Stephen Sondheim song ("Send in the Clowns") because it was how she felt it should have been written—and at that moment, it was more fitting for her rendition of the song. Sondheim allowed her to change it. The rewritten version appeared on her hugely successful *Broadway Album* of 1985. She retains great power within the industry and even now, the world's best composers and lyricists clamor for her to sing their material. Ever since Harold Arlen in the early 1960s, great writers and producers have wanted to work with her.

### If You've Got It, Flaunt It

On 1966's *Color Me Barbra* album she sang "The Minute Waltz." It is still an incredibly clever, tight and amazing recording, and it essentially offered her a chance to show off her vocal phrasing at breakneck speed. Never before had she been so overtly over the top, showing off simply because she could.

Barbra continued to demonstrate how differently she could use her voice on a wide range of songs. In 1981 Elaine Paige, the United Kingdom's leading theatrical star, was riding high in the charts with her version of "Memory" from the musical *Cats*. Barbra chose to cover the song in early 1982, and sang it almost note for note the same as Paige had, with a very clipped, perfect English accent. There was no hint of a Brooklyn accent to be heard. The only change she made was at the very end of the song, where she takes a note up instead of down. In some ways the recording was a tribute to Paige, showing how Barbra admired her style. Essentially, though, it proved that the greatest living show songstress didn't come from England.

Another odd and very interesting Barbra recording was "Shake Me Wake Me," a disco version of the Holland-Dozier-Holland hit in 1975. Columbia Records picked up on the fact that this particular cut was being played in clubs on the East Coast of the United States, mostly gay clubs. It was given the disco remix treatment, lengthened from the album cut to more than six minutes, and was on the club charts at the same time as disco queen Donna Summer's first hit "Love to Love You Baby" in the autumn of 1975.

Barbra's disco tunes made her a draw in gay clubs for the first time since those early stints at the Bon Soir and the Lion in Greenwich Village in the very early 1960s. She became a truly contemporary act, credible in the gay bars where club culture was formed.

### Stage Fright

It's a surprise to consider that Barbra appeared in only two shows on Broadway. Choosing not to broaden her live performances following the success of *Funny Girl* on stage was, possibly, an early indication of her much publicized stage fright. The girl from Brooklyn made her name initially almost entirely solely as a result of her nightclub, television, and theater appearances in and around New York City.

Later in her career, she chose to perform concerts in Europe and Australia, adding to her profile as one of the world's most admired (and successful) performers and thrilling people who felt they would never get a chance to see her singing live.

Returning to live performance in 1993 after almost thirty years, Barbra set records for concert tour ticket sales. The 1994 tour, which began at the MGM Grand Garden Las Vegas, raised more than $10 million for charity, with $3 million going to AIDS/HIV and family organizations. A millennium New Year's Eve concert called "Timeless" and held at the Las Vegas MGM Grand set a record for one-day sales of any event. She sold out a twenty-date North American tour in 2006 and a nine-date 2007 European tour in record time. She holds the house attendance record in the twenty-seven venues she played at during that period.

The DVD releases of her concerts have been equally as successful, going triple and quadruple platinum in sales even with a multi-disc set. Clearly, Barbra has a audience around the world who love her live and across multiple media.

A fascinating piece in *The New York Times* by Anthony Tommasini looked at Barbra's voice from a professional singer's point of view. As American recording history's best-selling female singer, Barbra was a prime topic for Tommasini, a classical music critic and opera and Streisand fan, who got the enviable opportunity to talk to her about singing. The results were illuminating. According to Barbra, unlike opera singers and others, she never thought about her diaphragm, that area responsible for "supporting" the voice. Barbra was untrained and natural. Unlike others who sing, Barbra said she found warming up too boring—something she also admitted on a variety of talk shows in the nineties. She said Tony Bennett sent her a recording of warm-ups but that she listened to it only once. She does do-re-mi exercises (called solfege) in the car on the way to the studio, when, really, that's a little too late to be doing such exercises. Barbra says she is an intuitive singer, working unconsciously to produce whatever sound she wants.

Tommasini comments on the aging of Barbra's voice and its range, highlighting the fact that in the sixties she could hit the high notes by focusing a vibrato onto them. Now, these higher notes are, as he puts it, "less available" to her, but she uses the warmth of those tones to full effect. The aging of a well-known singer's voice can be accommodated gracefully, or the singer can opt out completely, preferring not to sing if their voice doesn't sound the way it had many years before.

Barbra always sounded like a grown woman, even on playful ditties like "I Hate Music" or "Miss Marmelstein." Classical pianist Glenn Gould once said that her voice was a "natural wonder of the age." And with her power and range, he is not wrong. Barbra does all the things singers do—vibrato, unique phrasing, interpreting notes and changing emphasis—but without the caution many singers have. She feels her way through a song, passionately and delicately, but also, like most talented people unworried by their own gifts, somewhat carelessly.

Singing came to her during her younger years, when she would pause in the hallway of the family

Above: Barbra sings; *Barbra Streisand and Other Musical Instruments*, TV Special, 1973.

apartment building on Pulaski Street and sing. The hallway had an echoing quality that made her want to sing into it. By then, she says, she was known for having a good voice. But it wasn't so much the singing that she liked, it was the ability to express her passions, her emotions and her feelings, something that she may not have felt she could do otherwise. It may have been the words that moved her more than the sound of her own voice.

Listening to "Second Hand Rose" on *Just for the Record* (1991), on which Barbra and her mother, Diana, sing together in a "home recording," you can hear her mother's lilting vocals clearly enjoying the performance. Wanting to make her daughter's voice stronger, Diana would feed her special eggnog, and she sent her for her one voice lesson—there were no more because Barbra couldn't accept the teacher's appraisal of her rendition of "A Sleepin' Bee." The teacher wanted her to say the word "bee" in an extended fashion. Barbra said she just couldn't do that. The word had to be taken from how she spoke it—how she spoke it, and not anybody else. This quirk, this definite feeling about how a song should be sung, would later emerge again and again in her work. She once told an eminent director that the lines he wanted her to read, which were supposed to make her cry, just wouldn't work. They weren't natural for her.

It's not that Barbra never had an interest in learning the whys and wherefores of the process of singing. She did. Getting a voice coach when she once panicked and lost her voice, Barbra learned exactly how a sound was made in the human throat and mouth. Her voice coach told her she was singing just fine, but also crucially taught her that singing was partially a matter of mechanics and partially a mental thing.

Barbra developed her ability to sustain long notes because she wanted to. She can mold a tune that others cannot; she's able to sing between song and speech, keeping in tune, carrying rhythm and meaning. A prime example of this can be seen on the clip of her singing "Evergreen" with her *A Star Is Born* co-star Kris Kristofferson horsing around in the studio with her. The look she gives him is pure seduction; you can see it in her eyes and hear it in her voice. When Barbra's singing, she's singing just to you. It is no surprise that she's an admirer of Maria Callas; they both put a different kind of meaning into their songs, more than that spoken by the tune and lyrics.

It seems like hyperbole to call Barbra's voice a force of nature, but the more one delves into her method of singing and how she approaches it, the more the it appears the case. Barbra cannot read music at all. She says, even after answering questions about her technique, that she doesn't really know what she does to get this remarkable sound or phrasing. She hears a melody and takes it in, learning it quickly. Even though she can't read or write music, Barbra hears melodies as completed compositions, in her head. So, as when she wrote the Oscar winner "Evergreen," she sings what she hears and then whichever top-flight composer she's working with at the time writes it down and makes it come to life.

Above: Live on stage, in Zurich, Switzerland in 2007.
Opposite: On stage in *A Star Is Born* in 1976.

## Four: The Eighties

# No Matter What Happens

As had become her way, throughout the 1980s Barbra continued to be a multitasking multimedia force to be reckoned with. Besides her work in movies and the music industry, she busied herself with quite a bit of dating and TV work—in production, as well as starring roles. As the world has seen, Barbra was never one to rest when she could be doing something else, and in that way, she was ahead of her time; the notion of synergy between media companies—merging music, film, TV and stage production under one umbrella company—would not begin to be seriously considered by conglomerates until the decade ended.

But her unwillingness to be pigeonholed as just one thing—whether that be as an actor, a singer, a film director or a producer—meant that she could be denigrated as a gadfly, a jack-of-all-trades by her critics, of which there seemed to be many. One minute Barbra was recording, the next she was filming, and then she was on to something else. Desperate to master everything she did, Barbra tirelessly worked toward her dream of being great at everything until it seemed to be coming true. Yet, "dabbling" in film (as it was first seen) made her attempted move into the movies as a director a

> "Yes, my ego is big, but it's also very small in some areas. My ego is responsible for my doing what I do—bad or good."

lot more difficult than it could have been for someone else. No one likes a meddler, and in a staunchly sexist place like Hollywood, a female meddler was considered particularly bad news, if not downright dangerous.

Plus, Barbra famously often rubbed people the wrong way. In her quest for perfection, she'd tell professionals how to do their jobs, despite having demonstrated little or no apparent firsthand experience of having done that job herself. This is why, perhaps, some in the movie industry seemed wary of her: They all wanted to harness her pulling power and popularity, but they also liked to belittle her as an outsider—she was, claimed her detractors in Hollywood, a singer, fooling around in "their" industry.

Barbra in 1983, showing off skills learned during the making of *A Star Is Born*.

## Papa Can You Hear Me?

Barbra's passion for the novel having burned for years, *Yentl* the movie became her overriding concern and took up most of her time in the first couple of years of the decade. Making a movie is immensely hard work, and *Yentl*'s story called for extensive rewriting for the screen (much to Singer's ultimate dismay), along with numerous scouting trips to foreign locations in London and Czechoslovakia. As Barbra began recording songs for *Yentl* in London's Olympic Studios early in 1982, she was also doing several other

things at once: recording a music video for CBS, taping a contribution to the TV special *I Love Liberty*. Her performance of "America, the Beautiful" was filmed on a London soundstage with her accompanied by the U.S. Air Force marching band. The TV special was designed to show a different kind of American patriotism opposed to the then rising Moral Majority as defined by right-wing evangelist Jerry Falwell. Barbra's contribution fit perfectly with the end of *Yentl*, which has her character moving to the U.S. in order to live openly as an educated woman; America, the land of the free.

Barbra welcomes us into her Hollywood home, 1983.

NOTHING'S IMPOSSIBLE
In a time when the world of study belonged only to men, there lived a girl who dared to ask why?
BARBRA STREISAND
YENTL PG
A film with music.
UNITED ARTISTS Presents A BARWOOD FILM "YENTL"
MANDY PATINKIN AMY IRVING
Screenplay by JACK ROSENTHAL and BARBRA STREISAND
Based on YENTL, THE YESHIVA BOY by ISAAC BASHEVIS SINGER
Music by MICHEL LEGRAND Lyrics by ALAN & MARILYN BERGMAN
Executive Producer LARRY DE WAAY Co-Producer RUSTY LEMORANDE
Produced & Directed by BARBRA STREISAND A LADBROKE FEATURE
Original Soundtrack Album on CBS Records and Tapes Distributed by UIP
MGM/UA


All of her hard work on *Yentl*, editing the film and producing the soundtrack recording, meant that she had to make sacrifices in her personal life; Barbra couldn't make her half sister's wedding.

The sacrifices seemed worth it, though, as the premiere of Yentl rolled around on November 16, 1983. With her boyfriend Jon Peters at her side, Barbra looked glamorous but nervous for the outing of her first major cinematic effort. The film went on to earn six Golden Globe nominations, including an amazing nomination—and win—for Barbra as Best Director, which was a first for a female director. The movie also won for Best Picture, and soon received five Oscar nominations, winning one, for Best Original Score. Perhaps tellingly, however, none were for Barbra's directorial work.

Not everyone involved in the movie was happy with it. The author of the original story, Isaac Bashevis Singer, disagreed with Barbra's take on his work. It was unfortunate, as both were passionate about their shared Jewish heritage. Barbra stood up for herself, saying that he shouldn't have sold the rights to his story if that was his concern.

Opposite: Barbra and Jon Peters, 1982.

## Left in the Dark

In June 1984, Barwood, Barbra's production company, was founded (see page 230). Her longtime friend Cis Corman was named president. Meanwhile, Barbra's first music video, for "Left in the Dark," couldn't push sales of the single past number 50 on the chart before it sunk. The LP from which it was taken, *Emotion* (see page 201), took a lengthy (for her) two months to earn enough sales to make platinum status—but at least it did. With this lack of success on the popular front, Barbra wanted to make her next album a collection of songs made famous on Broadway stages, but Columbia Records said no. As is her way, Barbra carried on with recording what was to become *The Broadway Album* (see page 203) anyway. Steven Sondheim stepped in to help Peter Matz produce some numbers, while other notable names from musical theater also helped out; Columbia couldn't refuse to release it when they saw—and heard—the resultant collection. When it came out, the reviews were excellent. It went to number 1 on the album charts.

Opposite: Barbra and Paul Newman collecting Golden Globes, 1984.

Above: Barbra in 1984.

Around that time, Barwood bought the rights to the film *Nuts* (see pages 205), a project Barbra really wanted to make. She approached the representatives of Dustin Hoffman in an attempt to get him in the movie with her, but that was not to be, sadly. Barwood also purchased the rights to Larry Kramer's landmark play about AIDS, *The Normal Heart*. It was to prove to be the beginning of a long, drawn-out, and heartbreaking relationship between Barbra, Kramer and the play.

Toward the end of 1985, U.S. cable channel HBO filmed a music special with Barbra titled *Putting It Together: The Making of the Broadway Album*. It aired on January 11, 1986, before being released on video (and then DVD). Between clips of the singer at work in the studio, there was a relaxed interview between her and legendary film director William Friedkin (*The Exorcist*). It was short, at only forty minutes, but nonetheless successful—so much so that HBO persuaded Barbra to let them broadcast another special with her as the star later the same year. She agreed to them taping a live performance (her first in six years) as long as she had the final say as to whether it would be broadcast; they agreed. *One Voice* aired on December 27, 1986, and was a lovely late present for fans. Barbra performed in front of an audience packed with her peers in Hollywood and had them entranced from the opening number, "Somewhere." The show was issued on video in April 1987 (and DVD in 2006), with proceeds from sales going to Barbra's charitable foundation.

## Encore

In February 1987, *The Broadway Album* won Best Female Vocalist Grammy, making it Barbra's eighth award, the first having been given to her twenty-four years before. Barbra got a standing ovation on that auspicious night.

She sandwiched film and music with her other promotional duties throughout the year, and scored an amazing feat by appearing on *Life* magazine's cover as one of the most powerful women in Hollywood. By the end of 1987, *Nuts* opened in America but failed to get noticed by the Academy, earning no Oscar nominations. Barbra had found some solace in the arms of then hot actor Don Johnson. He was one of the best-looking and most popular stars during that time, and was quite obviously Barbra's main squeeze. The couple were seen out together a great deal. It was made even clearer to the world when Barbra got a walk-on part in Don's hit show *Miami Vice* (in the "Badge of Dishonor" episode, which aired March 18, 1988). Fans felt, however, that Barbra had had her head turned a little too much, and they were not too happy when he appeared on her single in a duet called "Till I

Loved You," released around the same time in 1988. Johnson couldn't really sing—but he sure looked great.

Most of the last year of the decade was spent working on getting her next movie made. Despite being an award-winning director and a box office draw of some stature, Barbra still had to struggle to be accepted as a female director and star of her movies. It took until well into 1990 before Barbra could get down to work steadily on *The Prince of Tides* (see page 225). She did so with the full support of author Pat Conroy, who co-wrote the screenplay with Becky Johnston. By 1991, the film was held back in order to release it during for the holiday season. When it opened, the reviews were terrific.

Barbra was interviewed by Mike Wallace, whose show she had done years before, in order to promote the film. Wallace turned out to be pretty rough on her, and, unusually for Barbra, who was so in control, soon he had her in tears. Wallace looked like a jerk and later admitted he was too hard on her. In a way, Wallace's harshness showed that a strong, talented woman could bring on people's anger, simply because she dared to do what men took for granted as their right. She might have been upset by the interview, but it wouldn't stop Barbra from continuing as she wanted—thankfully.

Barbra out on the town with Don Johnson in 1988.

STREISAND

# Guilty

**Released**
1980
**Label**
Columbia Records
**Executive Producer**
Charles Koppelman
**Producer**
Barry Gibb, Albhy Galuten, and Karl Richardson

**Tracks**
• Guilty (duet with Barry Gibb) • Woman in Love • Run Wild • Promises • The Love Inside • What Kind of Fool (duet with Barry Gibb) • Life Story • Never Give Up • Make It Like a Memory

The Bee Gees were one of the hottest acts in the world thanks to the huge success of the *Saturday Night Fever* soundtrack. They had subsequently scored a run of number 1 hits in the United States, turning them into household names. Barbra had scored two recent number 1 hit singles, both duets (with Neil Diamond and Donna Summer). With a Bee Gee co-producing and dueting, how could she fail? She didn't; this album remains her most successful, reportedly having sold more than 20 million copies since its release. As good as the album is, there are far better Streisand albums that preceded it, but they were not as tuned in to the mainstream pop vibe as this was. The songs were mostly written by the brothers Gibb, and as good as they are, they rely too much on the Bee Gees' style over substance, with the result that Barbra seems like part of a team, not the star. There are some fine moments, for sure. "The Love Inside" is probably the best vocal performance on this album, yet the music feels too synthesized. Having said all that, no one can deny the success and the appeal of this album. It was number 1 around the world, as was the lead single, "Woman in Love." The duets with Barry Gibb, "What Kind of Fool" and "Guilty," were hit singles, reaching the U.S. top ten.

Gene Hackman
Barbra Streisand
She's got a way with men.
And she's getting away
with it…
All Night
Long
A LEONARD GOLDBERG-JERRY WEINTRAUB Production
A JEAN-CLAUDE TRAMONT Film
GENE HACKMAN BARBRA STREISAND
"ALL NIGHT LONG"
Also starring DIANE LADD DENNIS QUAID KEVIN DOBSON
Written by W.D. RICHTER Director of Cinematography PHILIP LATHROP, A.S.C.
Music by IRA NEWBORN and RICHARD HAZARD Produced by LEONARD GOLDBERG
and JERRY WEINTRAUB Directed by JEAN CLAUDE-TRAMONT
A UNIVERSAL PICTURE Read the JOVE book
R RESTRICTED
1981 UNIVERSAL CITY STUDIOS INC
LAFD
88
PRINTED IN U.S.A.

# All Night Long

Barbra as a blonde, with Gene Hackman

**Running Time** 87 mins
**Studio** Universal Pictures
**Year** 1981
**Director** Jean-Claude Tramont
**Screenplay** W. D. Richter
**Cast** Barbra as Cheryl Gibbons, Gene Hackman, Diane Ladd and Dennis Quaid

*All Night Long* isn't usually considered one of Barbra's greatest triumphs, despite her starring alongside an ensemble of other great talents. Perhaps that's why—because it doesn't focus enough on her, *All Night Long* is less than fabulous.

It was written as a vehicle by the great W. D. Richter (*Stealth*, *Big Trouble in Little China*, *Brubaker*, *Invasion of the Body Snatchers*) for Gene Hackman, who plays a man in a midlife crisis. Director Jean-Claude Tramont wanted to bring out the comedy in the otherwise serious, hard man. After seeing Hackman in *Young Frankenstein* (it is worth getting the film just to see Hackman's role, but the rest is wonderful too), the director pressed Hackman to make a comedy with him.

Figuring that he was going to make a high-powered comedy, Tramont thought that they'd have to get Barbra Streisand. It seems, however, that Barbra was hired to replace another actress when the original cast member was fired. The press reported that Barbra came on board for $4 million, a sum that began the gossip on the production immediately. It didn't help that the director was married to Streisand's agent (Sue Mengers); but Hollywood works like that all the time, and any indications that this film was ruined by working with friends proved unfounded. Even the director claims that personal favors had nothing to do with it, as his wife had known Barbra for years and had never asked the star to join one of his productions before.

What attracted Barbra to the role was not only the chance to work with a highly experienced and respected ensemble cast, but also that the part looked like a natural choice for her—a sexy, strong woman—within a fast-paced, funny setting. The script was rewritten to give Barbra a larger role in order to make it more worthy of her star status. Kevin Dobson (who'd been an extra on *Funny Girl*) plays a firefighter who is the husband of Barbra's character, who has an affair first with George's son (Dennis Quaid) and then George (Gene Hackman). Suburban Cheryl allowed Barbra to lose herself in the role and act once more.

Barbra fired Sue Mengers after this film and terminated their friendship, and she also ended her relationship with Jon Peters. Barbra was having a turbulent time in her life, and this charming if lamentably unremarkable film is a reflection of that. It is an unusual example of her taking on a supporting role with less than spectacular results. More remarkable work was to come.

"I put on a blonde wig and I went to a country-western bar in the Valley. And as soon as I walked in the door, I heard someone say, 'Oh, hi, Barbra!'"

Barbra at home,
Hollywood, 1983.

# Yentl

In a time when the world of study belonged only to men, there lived a girl who dared to ask..."why?"
BARBRA STREISAND
YENTL
A film with music.


Opposite: Barbra in drag, as Yentl.

**Running Time** 132 mins
**Studio** United Artists, Barwood Films
**Year** 1983
**Director** Barbra Streisand
**Screenplay** Jack Rosenthal and Barbra Streisand
**Cast** Barbra as Yentl, Mandy Patinkin and Amy Irving

---

This is aguably Barbra's most personal and most powerful work, and not only because it is her debut as a film director. Critics have said this is an ode to her father, who died when she was young, or that it is a testimony to being a woman who must overcome masculine odds in challenging times. Whatever else it is, *Yentl* was Barbra's attempt to memorialize her own Jewish faith and, in a way, it is her memorial to her people and their struggle. The film was difficult to get made, and came from the same studio—United Artists—as the infamous *Heaven's Gate*, director Michael Cimino's epic that tanked, taking its $40 million budget with it. Given the subject matter, studio heads felt deeply unsure about Yentl.

Following the tradition of Barbra movies, the movie began life as a stage play that opened on Broadway in 1975, which was based on an Isaac Bashevis Singer story called *Yentl the Yeshiva Boy*. Released in November 1983 by United Artists, *Yentl* was not only directed by Barbra but also co-written and co-produced by her. The story is a drama about a Polish Jewess who, after her father dies, dresses as a boy in order to study the Talmud. Barbra also sang in the movie, with the tunes based heavily on Jewish traditional songs. The movie won an Oscar for Best Original Score and a Golden Globe for Best Comedy/Musical, as well as earning Barbra a Golden Globe for best direction, making her the first woman to win a Golden Globe for that role. (Amy Irving, in the rather thankless role as the sexy Jewish girl who marries Yentl, was the first—and so far, only—actress who was nominated in the same role for an Oscar and a Razzie. She didn't win either.)

*Yentl* in many ways is Barbra's way of showing what she could do, that she could make the kind of magic she wanted to make. The fact that the film did as well as it did is testament to her tenacity and her dedication to the story and the production, as well as showing her skill at directing actors and controlling a production.

*Yentl* is an important film within its genre, but, more important, it proved the power of Barbra's accumulated experience in the entertainment industry. Again, its effect was recognized when, at an Academy Awards show many years later, Billy Crystal sings about it to the tune of "Don't Rain on My Parade." It has proven to be a memorable movie and remarkably sits easily alongside *The Way We Were*, *A Star Is Born*, and *Funny Girl* as an abiding key Streisand vehicle. The soundtrack album won an Oscar for Best Original Song Score.

"I remember having to go into an executive's office to play my tapes and tell the story. It was like being eighteen again and auditioning for a Broadway show. Now that I look back on it, I know it was good for me."

# Yentl

**Released**
1983
**Label**
Columbia Records
**Producer**
Barbra Streisand, Alan Bergman, Marilyn Bergman, Phil Ramone and Dave Grusin
**Associate Producer**
Michel Legrand
**Musical Arrangement**
Michel Legrand

**Tracks**
• Where Is It Written? • Papa, Can You Hear Me? • This Is One of Those Moments • No Wonder • Way He Makes Me Feel • No Wonder (Part Two) • Tomorrow Night • Will Someone Ever Look at Me That Way? • No Matter What Happens • No Wonder (Reprise) • A Piece of Sky • Way He Makes Me Feel • No Matter What Happens

Barbra was justifiably proud of *Yentl*, and naturally she wanted the soundtrack to be as good as the movie. It was released and promoted as if it were a new Streisand pop album, not just a soundtrack. Because the film is a musical, the songs, produced and arranged by Michel Legrand and written by husband-and-wife team Alan and Marilyn Bergman, work as an interior monologue to what the character Yentl is feeling in the movie. Because the songs were written for the movie, none were specifically created to be sold as a pop single. Columbia wanted at least one pop song and so Phil Ramone and Dave Grusin were employed to create pop numbers out of "The Way He Makes Me Feel" and "No Matter What Happens." They gave both a contemporary sound. The original orchestral versions are also on the album and make for interesting comparison. The 1994 remastered CD is preferred by fans for pushing Barbra's voice further forward in the mix. As a pop record it did pretty well, making the top ten on the *Billboard* 200 chart.

# Emotion

**Released**
1984
**Label**
Columbia Records
**Executive Producer**
Charles Koppelman for the Entertainment Music Company in association with Barwood Productions
**Producer**
Barbra Streisand, Richard Perry, Bill Cuomo, Kim Carnes, Maurice White, Jim Steinman, Albhy Galuten and Richard Baskin

**Tracks**
• Emotion • Make no Mistake, He's Mine • Time Machine • Best I Could • Left in the Dark • Heart Don't Change My Mind • When I Dream • You're a Step in the Right Direction • Clear Sailing • Here We Are at Last

*Emotion* was Barbra's first full studio album in four years, following the hugely successful compilation *Memories*, and the *Yentl* film and soundtrack. She'd also starred in the movie *All Night Long* with Gene Hackman since the enormous success of *Guilty*. The process of making this album was very different than it was for her last studio recording. Instead of a small team, Barbra worked with eight different producers and twelve writers and in a variety of studios. A usual, however, she manages to shine in several places, particularly on "Here We Are at Last," co-written with her new love, Richard Baskin (of the ice cream family). Other notable songs are "Best I Could," "Clear Sailing" and "Time Machine," which ironically is the only dated cut on the album. Now in her early forties, Barbra still sounds incredible, even on a typically overblown track such as Jim Steinman's "Left in the Dark." An expensive video was made for the album's title track; filmed partly in London, it featured Roger Daltrey as the leading man and Mikhail Baryshnikov (a big admirer). Suprisingly, both that single and a duet with Kim Carnes, "Make No Mistake He's Mine," had little chart success.

Barbra Streisand

The Broa

# The Broadway Album

**Released**
1985
**Label**
Columbia Records
**Executive Producer**
Barbra Streisand and Peter Matz
**Producer**
Barbra Streisand, Peter Matz, Richard Baskin, Randy Waldman, Bob Esty and Paul Jabara
**Musical Arrangement**
Peter Matz, Jeremy Lubbock, Paul Jabara, Sid Ramin, Alexander Courage and David Foster

**Tracks**
• Putting It Together (from *Sunday in the Park with George*) • If I Loved You (from *Carousel*) • Something's Coming (from *West Side Story*) • Not While I'm Around (from *Sweeney Todd*) • Being Alive (from *Company*) • I Have Dreamed/We Kiss in a Shadow/Something Wonderful" (from *The King and I*) • Adelaide's Lament (from *Guys and Dolls*) • Send in the Clowns (from *A Little Night Music*) • Pretty Women/The Ladies Who Lunch (from *Sweeney Todd/ Company*) • Can't Help Lovin' That Man (from *Show Boat*) • I Loves You Porgy/Porgy, I's Your Woman Now (from *Porgy and Bess*) • Somewhere (from *West Side Story*)

By the time of this album's release, it was as if either Columbia Records or Streisand had realized their previous mistakes and begun a quest to rectify them. Ardent fans will of course support anything she ever releases, but it is clear that *The Broadway Album* was more than just a return to her musical theater roots—it was a return to form. The mid 1980s saw a lot of artists who had been around for some time suffer not only commercially but artistically. Rod Stewart, Neil Diamond, Donna Summer and Elton John, among many others, had all suffered, and Barbra didn't want to go the same way.

Nothing could have been better for her at this time than to make this album. It was a critical and commercial success, bringing her once again to the top of the U.S. album charts and receiving a Grammy award. It is still regarded as one of her all-time best albums, proving that she was still a viable product in an ever-changing market.

Sondheim's "Send in the Clowns" was more sensitively read than even the hit Judy Collins version, while Barbra's exuberant "Somewhere" from *West Side Story* is magnificent, even with the synthesized sound effects swirling all around her. The accompanying promo video for this was filmed with a lone Streisand standing on an old theater stage, a single light on her making her appear almost otherworldly. She had never looked so beautiful, nor sounded so great. On "Can't Help Lovin' That Man" she's accompanied by Stevie Wonder on harmonica, once again infusing a little soul into the song. Once again, Barbra proved that she still had it.

# Nuts

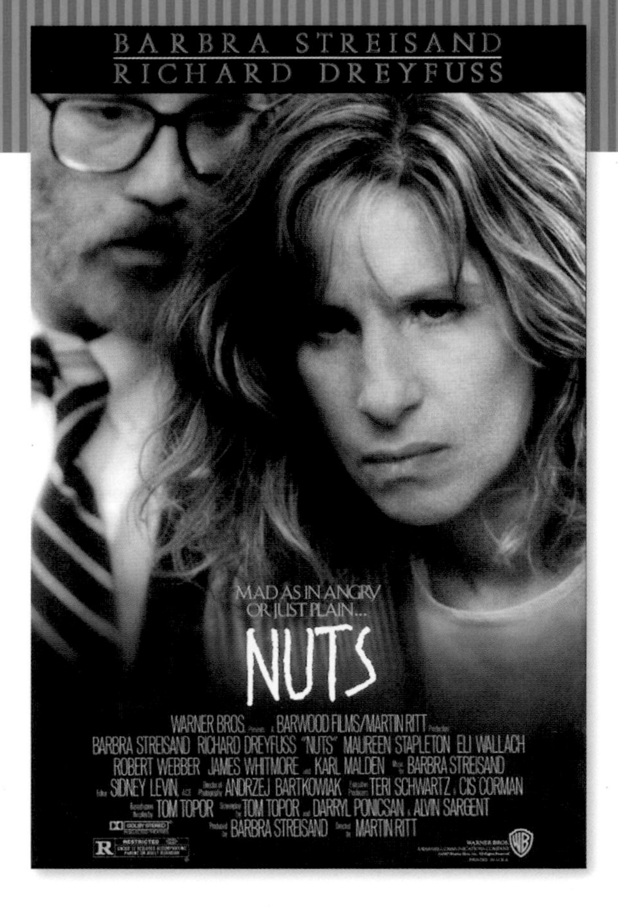


Opposite: Barbra in an unglamorous role, on set.

**Running Time** 116 mins
**Studio** Warner Bros. Pictures, Barwood Films
**Year** 1987
**Director** Martin Ritt
**Screenplay** Tom Topor, Darryl Ponicsan and Alvin Sargent
**Cast** Barbra as Claudia Draper, Richard Dreyfuss

Her last film of the decade was a departure for Barbra: a courtroom drama directed by Martin Ritt that put her opposite Richard Dreyfuss. The role was originally to be played by Debra Winger, who pulled out before filming began. This is also the last noncomedy film made by Leslie Nielsen, of whom Barbra was in awe. Finally, she met an actor who scared her but who was about to launch a completely different career in comedy. It was also Karl Malden's final film.

Barbra committed to the film after reading the play and liking it. She portrays Claudia, a prostitute (the third time for Barbra in that occupation) with a better than average background (her parents are Karl Malden and Maureen Stapleton) who is charged with the murder of one of her customers. Eli Wallach appears as a psychiatrist who tells her parents to commit her for the good of herself and society at large. Of course, Claudia says it was an act of self-defense, and so the film hinges on her fight for the truth to be known and for her sentence to be reduced. It doesn't help when she assaults her parents' lawyer, thus ending up with the public defender, played by Richard Dreyfuss, representing her. The story's ending may be predictable, but the way it unfolds was not at the time: Could the middle-class couple have ulterior motives for getting their daughter put away?

Told via flashbacks, *Nuts* was a prime vehicle for any actress because it had drama, brilliance and range—and considering how few serious dramatic roles there were for women at the time, everyone wanted to do it. Dustin Hoffman had been in the running to play Claudia's public defender, but Warner Brothers, which had set the budget at $25 million, wouldn't pay his price.

Interestingly, the photos used within the film—which needed to be as sexy as possible—were taken by Mario Casilli, a legendary photographer of women for *Playboy.* He had taken cover shots of her for her LPs *Wet* and *Guilty*. Casilli made Barbra look completely different, almost unrecognisable, in some of the poses.

Despite some less–than–flattering remarks from the late Herb Ritts and Dreyfuss, who said he would comment on the film after everyone involved was dead, the film was nominated for Best Motion Picture at the Golden Globes and Barbra was nominated as Best Actress at the Oscars. Dreyfuss was nominated as Best Actor. Both lost out—to Sally Kirkland in *Anna* and to Sean Connery in *The Untouchables*, respectively—but the nominations vindicated Barbra's lasting skill as a filmmaker. She had approval of the final cut on the film, which was her right as executive producer. Overall, critics found the performances terrific and credible.

"Claudia is honest, sometimes, shockingly honest, but the truth is all she has and she refuses to give up."

# Till I Loved You

**Released**
1988
**Label**
Columbia Records
**Producer**
Quincy Jones, Barbra Streisand, Phil Ramone, Burt Bacharach, Carole Bayer Sager and Denny Diante
**Associate Producer**
Glen Ballard and Clif Magness

**Tracks**
• The Places You Find Love • On My Way To You • Till I Loved You • Love Light • All I Ask of You • You And Me For Always • Why Let It Go?• Two People • What Were We Thinking Of • Some Good Things Never Last • One More Time Around

Barbra was in heavyweight company on this album, even more than usual, with help from legendary songwriters Burt Bacharach and Carole Bayer Sager, multi-award winning producer Quincy Jones and fabulous singers Dionne Warwick and Luther Vandross. Then there was Don Johnson, of television's *Miami Vice*. He was her new love interest, and like others from her past, she chose to have him involved in her new album. Going further than before, she dueted with him on the title track, which was an unusually (for her) very bad move, as he is no singer. She sounds incredible on this mostly forgettable track, making his dreadful performance stand out even more. It remains one of the most dated Streisand cuts because of it.

Sadly the enormous press attention over her affair with Johnson overshadowed the release of the album (which included a huge photo of them together on the inside sleeve). The cover photo was of a newly styled Barbra, the one that we still know today, her public image having remained pretty much the same ever since. "All I Ask of You" from *The Phantom of the Opera*, produced by Phil Ramone, is the album's best cut, followed closely by "The Places You Find Love," the album's opening number. Still, the record made number 10 on the *Billboard* chart and went platinum within a month of release. Barbra's success was clearly unstoppable.

# TILL I LOVED YOU

## *Five: The Nineties*

# All of My Life

THE decade kicked off well for Barbra with *The Prince of Tides* proving to be a commercial and critical success. In 1991 her fans were delighted to hear that she had, at last, finished compiling a unique, four-CD boxed set that gathered together some fantastic rare recordings, along with great best-selling song recordings from the previous twenty years of her career. *Just for the Record* (see page 227) proved to be an enduring, well-loved and enlightening compilation. Because Barbra oversaw its production, it looked, sounded and read—via some witty sleeve notes in the accompanying booklet—like a personal message from the singer.

By the beginning of 1992, Barbra had achieved a goal that had previously eluded her: She won a Directors' Guild of America award as Best Director for *The Prince of Tides*. Traditional thinking meant that she was in line for an Oscar nomination—or at least a Golden Globe—for her intensive work on the movie of which she was also star and producer. She did get a Golden Globe nomination, but only Nick Nolte, won for a truly worthy performance. It seemed that *The Prince of Tides* was being deliberately snubbed, although the competition was fierce, with the film going up against *Silence of the Lambs*, *Cape Fear* and *JFK*, among others.

> "Directing was for me a total experience. It calls upon everything you've ever seen or felt or known or heard. It was really the highlight of my… professional life."

Opposite: Barbra and Nick Nolte meeting Princess Diana at the London premiere of *The Prince of Tides*, 1991.

When the Oscars rolled around, though, *The Prince of Tides* received a stellar seven nominations. At least an Oscar nomination is a kind of award in itself, one that permanently stays with the recipient. Having missed out on the Globes, however, Barbra's expectations were modest, and so she wasn't disappointed when the award went to Jonathan Demme for *Silence of the Lambs*, as did the Best Picture award, for which *Prince* was nominated.

## Like Buttah

That year the Grammys proved to be more fruitful for Barbra. She was given the prestigious (and expected) Living Legend prize, and it was presented to her by Stephen Sondheim. That gave Barbra an enormous boost, and she went on an unprecedented public charm offensive. On February 22, 1992, the normally extremely private star popped up on the popular TV show *Saturday Night Live* in the spoof "Coffee Talk with Linda Richman". Mike Myers (as Linda Richman) dedicated the show to Barbra, commenting that she was the greatest actress in all of history and say she was "like *buttah.*" (The phrase stuck and became the title of a fanzine as well as something well-meaning fans would yell at Barbra in public.)

Opposite: On set of *Prince of Tides* with co-star Nick Nolte, 1991.

Above: With her Grammy Living Legend Award, 1991.

By June, Barbra was inducted into the Women in Film Hall of Fame. Bolstered by the recognition of her film work, she also felt confident enough to write a rebuttal to an article that critiqued her version—as opposed to Pat Conroy's novel—of *The Prince of Tides* in *Newsweek* magazine. Unfortunately,

EAGLE
CHS

Just a few of the personal items sold for Barbra by Christie's, New York, 1994.

a contractual clash prevented a laser disc version of the film from being released at the time, which would have featured her own commentary along with other extras from the film; the commentary probably would have explained many criticisms away. (The disc did finally get a release at the end of 1994.)

Never one to take too much notice of what anyone said about her personal life, Barbra went to watch "friend" Andre Agassi play at the U.S. Open. She also headed over to the United Kingdom the next year to watch him play in the quarterfinals at Wimbledon. This provoked a feeding frenzy in the British press, in which they reported her words about Agassi playing like a "zen master." By the end of the year, however, Barbra's head was back to business, having signed a long and much more lucrative contract with Sony, who had recently acquired Columbia Records.

Her subsequently released fiftieth LP and twenty-sixth studio album, *Back to Broadway* (see pages 202–203), came out on June 19, 1993. It went straight to number 1—which was, suprisingly, a first for one of her LPs. It also made her the first performer to have number 1 LPs across the sixties, seventies, eighties and nineties. At a party celebrating the LP's domination of the charts, she told her guests that she was going to perform—to much gasping—and then trotted out Barbra impersonator Jim Bailey, who is very much *not* Barbra Streisand, even with the right wig and nail extensions. Despite her reputation as a hard-nosed businesswoman, Barbra knew when to make a joke at her own expense.

## Entr'acte

Barbra's fans found more reason to celebrate in 1993, when she announced a return to making live appearances in concert. She had reportedly accepted a fee of $20 million to perform in two shows at the MGM in Las Vegas, on December 31, 1993, and January 1, 1994. The tickets sold out in hours. Clearly Barbra was feeling the need for change as she approached her fiftieth birthday. She donated her ranch to the state of California and sold off many of her art and decorative object purchases via New York's Christie's auction house. It was time, obviously, for Barbra to make her life a lot less complicated. It didn't hurt that her objects sold for $6.2 million, making it the most lucrative garage sale in history. Fans were thrilled to have any item from their idol, of course, and the sale allowed many of them to realize a dream or two.

> "Yes, my ego is big, but it's also very small in some areas. My ego is responsible for my doing what I do—bad or good."

The New Year shows went so well that in March 1994 Barbra announced that she would undertake a world tour, beginning in London at the end of April. The official stampede for her American concert dates began—and ended—on March 27. Tickets sold out for her shows in five different cities—beginning in Landover, Maryland, on May 10—in less than sixty minutes.

Above: a relaxed Barbra out and about in LA in 1992.
Following: *George* magazine, 1996.

The intensity of the fans grew greater when, later that year, Barbra had to cancel some of the dates because she lost her voice. But, knowing how loyal her admirers are, she rescheduled the dates and honored all the tickets purchased—much to the chagrin of critics who had said that she was not sick, but suffering from stage fright. To prove them wrong, Barbra sneaked onto

*The David Letterman Show* on June 28, in the middle of her Madison Square Garden dates, and caused utter pandemonium. Her popularity was at a new high; her HBO special in August became the highest-rated HBO broadcast ever. The broadcast had been edited by Barbra from footage taken at her opening and closing American dates.

With two Grammy nominations for 1995—Best Traditional Pop Vocalist (for her *Barbra: The Concert*, which also won a Peabody Award for her later in the year) and Best Female Pop Vocalist for "Ordinary Miracles"—Barbra was also presented with a Grammy Lifetime Achievement award, by Stephen Sondheim, no less. *Barbra: The Concert*, the VHS tape of the HBO special, became the highest-selling home video for the year and the recipient of ten Emmy nominations. It won two.

## A House Is Not a Home

After apparently looking for years, Barbra finally found her dream home in 1995. She bought a house on an acre in the Queen's Necklace area of Malibu, California, for $2 million. The same year Barbra became a "doctor" when she was awarded an honorary doctorate from Brandeis University. It was typical of Barbra: She may not have married a doctor, but she became one.

By early 1996, Barbra's next directorial outing, *The Mirror Has Two Faces* (see page 236–37), had wrapped. It had an amazing cast, with Jeff Bridges, Lauren Bacall and George Segal, who replaced the ailing Dudley Moore. However, after the protracted problems with *The Normal Heart,* Barbra's production company, Barwood, decided to let the rights to Kramer's play lapse. This meant that the project was now free to go to other producers. Some have criticized Barbra for sitting on the project for so long, but she had always said that she tried to make it and that in an always changing film climate, financing it wasn't easy.

On the fateful night of July 1, 1996, Barbra went to a dinner party at the home of Christine Forsyth-Peters, the ex-wife of her ex-lover Jon Peters. There, just before she was about to get back to a late-night editing session on *The Mirror Has Two Faces*, she met a handsome man by the name of James Brolin. An actor, he was well known from American TV series like *Marcus Welby, M.D.* and *Hotel* and movies such as *Capricorn One*. Brolin had auditioned to play James Bond in the early 1980s, but Roger Moore decided to continue with the role, until being replaced by another Brit, Timothy Dalton. Brolin was a respected actor, a buddy of Ryan O'Neal's, and a relaxed, good-looking guy who knew his way around Hollywood.

In the cozy sitting room of her sprawling, antique-filled Los Angeles home, Barbra Streisand and I are arguing about the Republican-drafted welfare reform bill that President Clinton signed. We're entering the fifth round. "It creates no jobs and hurts the poor," I say. Clinton will add a job component later, she retaliates, forever defending the President. We're both trying to stay polite, respecting the conventions of the muckraker-meets-diva interview. (As a self-described Robert Kennedy–Bruce Springsteen populist, I was one of the few journalists Streisand would agree to talk with.) "This bill will create a million new poor people," I insist. Exasperated, the superstar gets up and disappears into another room. She returns with a thick folder, which I notice contains faxes from the White House. This is Barbra Streisand's "welfare bill" file. So it's true: Funny Girl has become Serious Woman. Yentl has turned policy wonk.

But as Streisand has learned, the notion of a female superstar with outspoken politics is still hard for some to accept. Even before her 1995 Harvard University address on the role of the artist as citizen, critics lampooned Streisand's activism, calling her a "dilettante" and a "bubblehead." Typical of the criticism was *Washington Post* columnist Jonathan Yardley's dismissive review of the speech, in which Streisand asserted—a touch defensively—the right of the artist to be politically engaged: "Like a great many other people who have done very well in show business," Yardley wrote, "Streisand has fallen into the trap of mistaking emotion for ideas, of assuming that because she feels something, she must think it as well.... She can feel any old thing she wants to feel, and she can even pretend her feelings are thoughts, but none of this entitles her to be taken seriously as anything except an entertainer."

# diva democracy!

**Bill Clinton takes her calls. So isn't it time to take her politics seriously? Fresh from the set of her new movie, *The Mirror Has Two Faces*, Barbra Streisand tells Jack Newfield about her political journey—from a close encounter with her late father to her intimate bond with the first family**

FIROOZ ZAHEDI

FOR STYLING CREDITS SEE PAGE 11

Barbra and James hit it off that first night and ended up going home together. For maybe the first time, Barbra let work go and let herself be herself, relaxing with a man she hardly new and yet felt so comfortable with. She stressed later they didn't sleep with each other on the first date. The next month, she and James attended previews of *The Mirror Has Two Faces* together. Obviously, Barbra had a new beau, and the public approved. Barbra, knowing that the paparazzi would want photos, preempted them by releasing her own set, just to get some privacy. As for *Mirror*, her duet with Bryan Adams for the film

("I Finally Found Someone") received some airplay, and its romantic topic made everyone think it was the theme song not only for the film, but also for Barbra and James.

In November 1996, *The Mirror Has Two Faces* received its red carpet premiere at the Ziegfield Theater. To promote the film and to "talk girl talk," Barbra guested on *The Oprah Winfrey Show* as the only guest. The chat touched on affairs of the heart, as Oprah liked to do. Barbra came out of it well, earning even more fans, as if that were posssible.

After a long hard slog with the film, Barbra was happy that *The Mirror Has Two Faces* earned four Golden Globe nominations in the lead-up to the Academy Awards. Barbra was nominated for Best Actress, Bacall for Best Supporting Actress, and Marvin Hamlisch for Best Score and Best Song for the duet. Bacall was the only one of those nominees to win her Globe. Again, the competition was fierce.

Above: Starring in *The Mirror Has Two Faces*, 1996.

Opposite: With her son, Jason Gould, 1992.

At the Oscars, it came as a bit of a shock that *The Mirror Has Two Faces* received only two nominations: one for Bacall in the Best Supporting Actress category and the other for Best Song for "I Finally Found Someone." Bacall again won her award. Barbra had declined an invitation to sing her nominated song, so the honor went to Natalie Cole. On the night of the awards, however, Cole became ill. Instead of taking to the stage to sing the song herself, Barbra decided to spend the song's duration in the ladies' room while Celine Dion belted out the tune to the audience. It wasn't a snub. Barbra wasn't ready to perform, and she was with James that night. Being in the audience is a very different situation than being on the Oscar stage. Barbra couldn't have stepped in as a performer at such shot notice; she has always needed plenty of preparation before singing in front of an audience, and the pressure of appearing in front of such an august audience can only have made any nervousness far geater.

Just as 1997 was the year of love—true love, it seems—for Barbra, it was fitting that she and James announced their engagement. At the same time, Barbra's *Higher Ground* LP (see page 235) zoomed onto the charts at number 1 on the *Billboard* Top 200, which meant that she had released number 1 LPs over the course of four decades. It's no surprise that at the Grammys, Barbra was nominated twice, for Best Collaboration with Vocals for "I Finally Found Someone" and for "Tell Him," a duet recorded with Celine Dion.

## Finally Found Someone

On July 1, 1998, Barbra and James were married in Malibu and honeymooned in the Channel Islands. When James got his star on the Hollywood Walk of Fame, Barbra was there with him, even though she hadn't attended her own Walk of Fame star unveiling. The music of love played on, with a new rose being announced for next year called Barbra Streisand. The mauve flower liked a lot of water, according to some rose enthusiasts, who praised its lavish shade. On September 21, 1999, Barbra released a CD of love songs dedicated to James, naturally. The CD called *A Love Like Ours* (see pages 240–41) hit the charts at number 6, eventually going gold and platinum.

Around Thanksgiving 1999, Barbra decided to give her fans something to be very thankful for: She put tickets for her millennium concerts on sale. And right before Christmas, we were treated to a special edition DVD of *The Way We Were*. It was Streisand heaven.

Barbra celebrated the dawn of the millennium by appearing in concert in Las Vegas, on December 31, 1999, and New Years Day, 2000.

Opposite: A happy Mr. and Mrs. Brolin at the unveiling of a Hollywood Walk of Fame star in his name, 1998.

# The Prince of Tides

**Running Time** 132 mins
**Studio** Columbia Pictures Corp., Barwood Films, Longfellow Pictures
**Year** 1991
**Director** Barbra Streisand
**Screenplay** Pat Conroy and Becky Johnston
**Cast** Barbra as Susan Lowenstein, Nick Nolte

The script for *The Prince of Tides* was sent to Barbra by Michael Ovitz, who thought she may be interested in directing, producing or acting in it—or indeed all three. She says that she had loved the book before she'd read the script and had writer Becky Johnston move into her home for a few weeks in order to work on a script. Barbra also spent some weeks with Pat Conroy, the author of the novel, working on the script. Everyone liked Robert Redford for the part of Tom Wingo but, despite his wanting to work with Barbra again, his concerns about the book prevented another collaboration. With Nick Nolte on board, Barbra committed herself to directing (for the second time) and acting in the film.

The powerful story concerns a man who has repressed a terrible, unspeakable childhood event that has ruined his relationship with his family. *The Prince of Tides* treads dangerous territory but weaves in a tale of redemption. The public isn't always ready to accept drama that is too real, deep or disturbing, of course, and although *The Prince of Tides* had been a best-selling book, it was considered by many to be too complicated and vivid to fit into even 120 minutes of film. It ended up being 132 minutes long.

As often happens when books are made into movies, the story was necessarily compressed and altered for the different medium. This involved getting rid of certain flashback sequences and allowing the character of psychiatrist Susan Lowenstein to appear only in the present. Inevitably, the lonely, damaged man whose marriage is on the rocks finds comfort and understanding with a woman who appears to be in the same situation and willing to risk her professional life for him.

Above: Barbra with Nick Nolte in *Prince of Tides*.

As with all of Barbra's films, the cinematography, this time by Stephen Goldblatt, is sumptuous. Strong supporting performances from Nick Nolte, Kate Nelligan, Blythe Danner, Jeroen Krabbé and George Carlin make for a strong story. It wasn't an easy production, needing nine child actors for the three Wingo children roles, for instance. However, the movie's success made Barbra's reputation as a player in the industry. It also showed that not only could she handle emotional stories well, but that she understood the underdog, the quirky and misunderstood. Perhaps this was as since she knew what it is like to be so different, and to be judged.

The movie received accolades from the toughest critics and garnered seven Oscar nominations, including one for Best Picture. There were also three Golden Globe nominations (Nick Nolte won Best Actor). Barbra was nominated for a Golden Globe for Best Director, and the film was also nominated as Best Motion Picture, Drama. Most impressively, Barbra won Outstanding Directorial Achievement at the Directors Guild of America Awards.

"As an actress, I was intrigued by the concept of the wounded healer."

# The Prince of Tides

**ORIGINAL MOTION PICTURE SOUNDTRACK**

**Released**
1991
**Label**
Columbia Records
**Producer**
Barbra Streisand and James Newton Howard
**Musical Arrangement**
Marty Paich, Hummie Mann, Brad Dechter and Johnny Mandel

**Tracks**
▪ Teddy Bears ▪ To New York ▪ The Bloodstain ▪ The Fishmarket ▪ The New York Willies ▪ The Village Walk ▪ Lila's Theme ▪ Home Movies ▪ Daddy's Home ▪ The Hallway ▪ They Love You Dad ▪ So Cruel ▪ Savannah Awakes ▪ Love Montage ▪ Tom Comes Home ▪ The Outdoors ▪ Tom's Breakdown ▪ The Street ▪ For All We Know ▪ The Reunion ▪ End Credits ▪ For All We Know ▪ Places That Belong to You

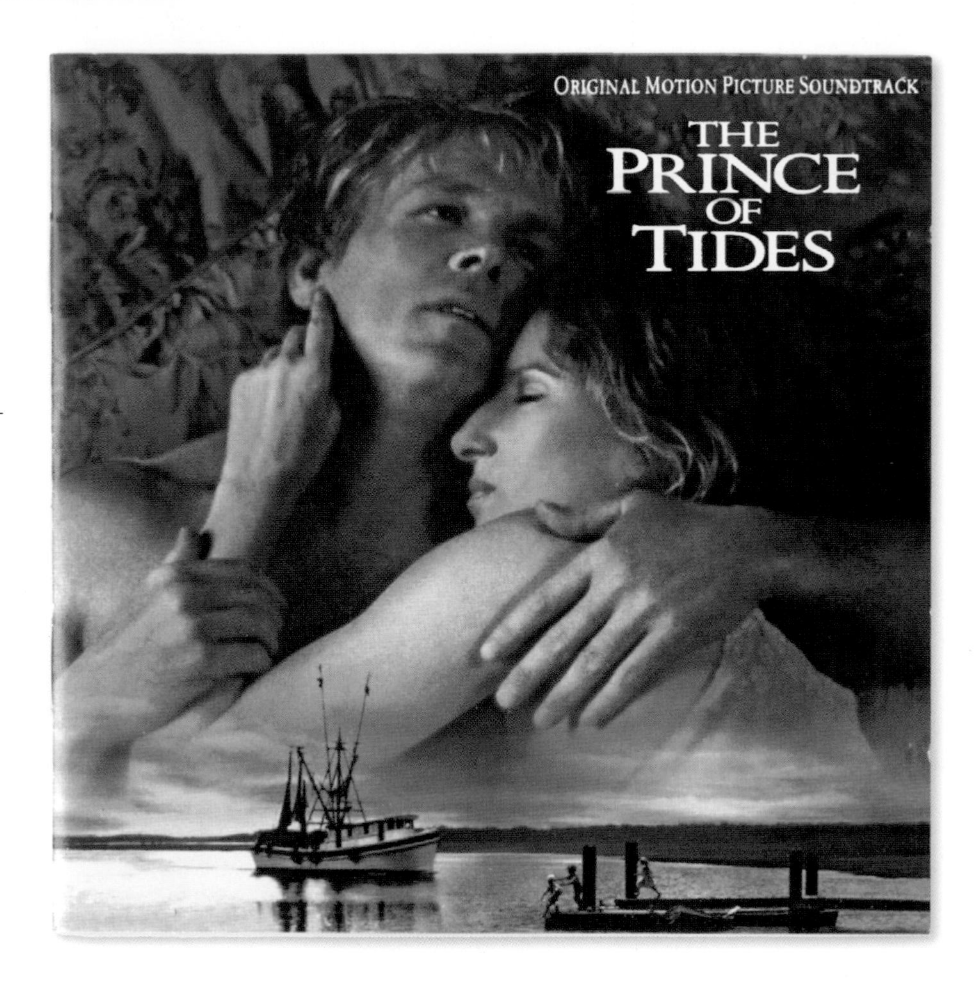


John Barry was supposed to write this soundtrack, but Barbra and his styles didn't mesh. The liner notes state that the vocals here were recorded for this LP and are not heard in the film. "For All We Know," a song that Barbra knew as performed by Billie Holiday, was reminded of it by her son, Jason, who gave his mom a copy of Holiday's *Lady in Satin* for her birthday. That, and the stellar tune "Places That Belong to You," with its wonderful melody by Howard, are sumptuous ballads made spectacular. Barbra didn't feel that the song fit into the film but she really liked it, which is why it's here. The other tracks on the original release are instrumentals written by Howard for the movie. The album wasn't a great seller, but it's worth seeking out the two Barbra vocal tracks.

# Just For the Record

**Released**
1991
**Label**
Columbia Records
**Producer**
Barbra Streisand and
Martin Erlichman
**Project Coordinator**
Karen Swenson

**Four disc box set**
The 60's (Part I)
The 60's (Part II)
The 70's
The 80's

There have been several compilation albums of Barbra's greatest hits (plus some that were not even hits) released over the years. Many were big sellers, as befit her reputation and catalog of recordings. However, Just for the Record is arguably by far the most loved and respected of all Streisand compilations to date. It's a deluxe four-CD box set of rarities, outtakes, and spoken parts, as well as the hits. This was a rare glimpse into the professional world of Streisand, a behind-the-scenes journey through her entire career—including (for the very first time) her 1955 recording, at only thirteen, of "You'll Never Know." As well as including many songs that had been in the vault for so many years, she wisely included songs sung on those very early TV shows she often appeared on back in New York City during her rise to fame.

Everything you'd want to hear is on one of the four discs, plus a lot of things you didn't know existed too. It not only shows off her incredible musical talent, but it also highlights her knack of choosing the greatest songwriters, producers, arrangers and players in the business to work with. Any other artist releasing a set like this would most likely be wrapping up her career before finally bowing out, but for Barbra it was simply a matter of encapsulating the first thirty-year phase of her career. Twenty years later there was room for another box set—there's seemingly no end to this woman's talents and no sign of her ever slowing down. *Just for the Record* is not only Streisand's finest compilation release, but also possibly the best retrospective of anyone's career that has ever been released.

VANITY FAIR
SEPTEMBER 1991/$2.50
EROTOMANIA
The Haunting
of Dr. Brennan
by Marie Brenner
BEN BRADLEE
BOWS OUT
by Peter J. Boyer
THE STRANGE PATTERNS
IN HALSTON'S LIFE
by Steven Gaines
THE KISS-AND-KILL
SPREE
by Mark MacNamara
EXIT JON PETERS
Hollywood vs. Japan
by Edward Klein
STREISAND NOW
by Kevin Sessums
09
38020
0 751174 3

# Queen of Tides

*She spent most of the last decade working only when she wanted to, which wasn't very often. After all, in her thirty years of stardom Barbra Streisand has already done everything, and now, at only forty-nine, she's a show-biz grande dame—just like Fanny Brice. KEVIN SESSUMS meets the most commanding woman in Hollywood as she directs herself in a new movie, The Prince of Tides*

174 Photographs by HERB RITTS • Styled by MARINA SCHIANO

The cover and feature pages of *Vanity Fair*, 1991.

I *vant* sea gulls . . ." Barbra Streisand dramatically whispers, then giggles at the *Yiddischer* élan with which she still enhances her every desire. Her distinct Brooklyn accent fills the Cary Grant Theater here on the Columbia Studios lot with such outlandish longing that she could easily be a Chekhov heroine in a spoof by Mel Brooks.

Streisand stands with her back to me and works on the sound editing for her upcoming motion picture, *The Prince of Tides*. In front of us, on the giant screen, South Carolinian gulls are soaring to recorded orchestral strings as she conducts the sound levels with her outstretched arms, her expressive hands and famously attended fingernails fluttering with the instinct of the coastal birds. At the control board, seated around her, are the film's sound men and assistant editors. One of them looks back at the editor Don Zimmerman and good-naturedly rolls his eyes behind Streisand's back. As director, producer, and actress, she has spent the last three years putting together the much-anticipated film version of Pat Conroy's best-seller, and she's allowing no detail to go unnoticed, not even the sound of sea gulls behind the film's lush opening music. *The Prince of Tides* is the story of one southern family's summer of healing. It stars Nick Nolte as Tom Wingo, the cracker who migrates north ostensibly to rescue his cracked sister from yet another suicide attempt and unexpectedly rescues himself from his own shattered past with the help of her psychiatrist, a woman called Lowenstein, portrayed by Streisand.

One of the technicians punches a button and the film magically rewinds, the gulls flapping a retreat. This woman who can make birds fly backward walks to the rear of the theater, where I am sitting. "This is a great image for your story," she instructs me. "Me standing there with my back to you. All the guys around me. My arms conducting it all. The screen filling up with . . . with . . . with all this *childhood stuff*."

There is only one way to deal with Barbra Streisand: tell her the truth," says Jule Styne, who met Streisand when she was still a child herself. "If you don't tell her the truth, then you're going to have problems."

Styne, the composer of *Funny Girl*, was instrumental in securing the role of Fanny Brice for Streisand after she submitted to seven grueling auditions. She was only twenty years old, and the show's creators had been searching for a woman who could convincingly portray a mother in Act Two. They talked to Anne Bancroft, but she didn't like the idea of being called Fanny onstage. At one point Mary Martin was slated for the role; at another, Carol Burnett. It was the latter who advised Styne that someone with "her Jewishness born in her" was needed, and Streisand was finally given the coveted role that thirty years ago thrust her permanently into the cultural consciousness.

FUNNY GIRL AND FUNNY LADY
Streisand, hamming it up in Beverly Hills, says she plans to spend more time in her hometown of New York.

Styne: "Barbra's all about *the work*. After we cast her, I even flew to Las Vegas, where she had already been booked as the opening act for Liberace, and taught her the score between shows—that is, when I could drag her away from the gambling tables. When we were finally in rehearsals for Broadway—now, this was before the girl was a star, she was just this strange little creature who walked out at her first audition looking like a Russian Cossack—she had her manager write me a note telling me that there were two songs that she didn't like, 'People' and 'Don't Rain on My Parade.' She didn't think she wanted to sing them. I called her right up and said, 'Barbra, if you don't sing "People," you don't sing my score.' You've got to be straight with her. This reputation about being difficult comes from untalented people misunderstanding truly talented ones. Because she's so talented she had a tendency—maybe she still does—to show off a bit. She was always shoving shovelsful of her talent in your face. Jerry Robbins summed her up. He said she does everything wrong, but it comes out right."

If not always right, it at least comes out the way she wants it. "I always had *extraordinary* willpower," Streisand tells me, noting that she has supported herself since she was ten years old, when she worked as a cashier in a local Chinese restaurant. "My grandmother used to call me '*farbrent*,' which means 'on fire.' I just couldn't accept no for an answer. I still can't."

In the early days, Streisand's ambition was so naked that New York's Mayor Wagner could have had her arrested for indecent exposure. There had never been a creature quite like her; audiences became voyeurs, discovering her as she discovered herself. "Back then she certainly wasn't the actress she later became," remembers Styne. "But our greatest stage performances have come from some of our worst actresses. Merman, for example. To this day, I've never seen a performance to rival Barbra's in *Funny Girl*."

Which is exactly what many people miss about *(Continued on page 228)*

178

# Barwood

That Barbra Streisand would want to take the reins on projects in which she wasn't the performer shouldn't come as a surprise. Always as canny with money as with ownership, Barbra's creative genius took in any number of productions—films, albums, TV movies, you name it.

Of course, as a celebrity, she's also been attached to more than her fair share of projects that never came to fruition. In order to get a production financed, a headline name is usually required, and hers is one of the biggest. Hollywood knows who can open a film, and they're loath to take risks on someone who can't.

In the early 1970s, there were reports that prestigious Swedish director Ingmar Bergman was in talks with Barbra to star in his version of Franz Lehár's 1861 operetta, *The Merry Widow*. Although Stephen Sondheim and Dino DeLaurentiis were also approached, as composer-writer and producer, the pieces did not come together. Bergman went on several years later to create his filmic take on Mozart's *The Magic Flute* instead and without any Hollywood involvement.

Big talk about who is connected with what project is typical in Hollywood circles, where names are bandied about without a shred of evidence that the talks mentioned ever happened. For instance, back in the late 1970s, John Travolta was said to be teamed with Barbra in a musical called *Fancy Hardware*. This project had been shunted from Steve McQueen and Ali MacGraw in 1972 and and wasn't made until 2011.

By the early eighties, projects were still coming in for Barbra that involved her singing. For example, *The White Hotel*, based on the popular Freudian novel of the same name by D. M. Thomas, was discussed. Evita, yet another singing role, was also mentioned, but was eventually made instead with Madonna. Barbra's attachment to that project was all media hype.

### Presenting Barwood

Barbra liked to work, and unlike other actors and performers who need to work, she could always pick and choose her projects. The days of scraping to pay the bills were over by the time of her second movie. That didn't stop her name being mentioned in connection to numerous lame projects, such as a remake of *Strictly Ballroom*, *the All About Eve*–based musical called *Applause*, *Sunset Boulevard*, and *Mame*, among many other titles and concepts.

The rumor mill will keep grinding, even resulting at times with headlines in trade papers like *The Hollywood Reporter* or *Variety* announcing Streisand projects that didn't exist, nor ever would. But just because some information appears in those publications doesn't make it true.

By the end of the 1970s Barbra decided that she should have more say in how and what movies her name was attached to, so she set up Barwood with her best friend, Cis Corman. They began production with a "making of" documentary during the filming of The Main Event in 1979. Barwood went on to produce TV movies and feature films—including, of course, *Yentl*, *Nuts*, *The Prince of Tides* and *The Mirror Has Two Faces* (1996).

Barwood also offered Barbra the opportunity make other forms of broadcast media too, specifically documentaries. Barwood enabled her to be actively involved in some of the causes and issues she wanted to aid in any way possible. So in the 1990s particularly her production company made socially aware television such as *The Long Island Incident* (1995), two documentaries in the *Rescuers: Stories of Courage* series (1997–98) and the PBS shows *The Living Century* (2001) and *What Makes a Family* (2001).

Barbra felt passionately about Barwood's involvement with Larry Kramer's pivotal HIV/AIDS drama *The Normal Heart*. A very popular theatrical piece in the eighties, when the disease was rife, Kramer's work seemed to be the perfect vehicle for Barwood. The protagonist was gay, Jewish and vocal. This would check off several boxes in what Streisand seemed to like most in projects: socially relevant, ethnically pertinent, and serious but with touches of humor. It was also a project that would attract a large segment of her fan base. It's no wonder, then, that Barwood bought the rights to the work in 1986, with Dustin Hoffman attached.

There were problems with Larry Kramer and the Barwood plans, however. Barbra, as most producers would, wanted another writer for the screenplay, which was something Kramer was not keen to agree with. The next year, *Nuts* took precedence at Barwood over and above *The Normal Heart*, which again was a typical thing to

Barbra in costume, on camera, *Nuts*, 1987, a Barwood film.

J.L. Fisher

"Directing was for me a total experience. It calls upon everything you've ever seen or felt or known or heard. It was really the highlight of my professional life."

happen in Hollywood where sometimes books, plays or screenplays are optioned and produced right away and, as in this case, sometimes they are purchased and left to simmer awhile. Often diary clashes make it impossible to get the right team together to make the movie swiftly. By 1991, the film had not been produced, and the woman upon whom one of its main characters was based died. Kramer gave up trying to write the screenplay.

## Green Light

In 1993, the project looked ready to go, this time with Ralph Fiennes—the year of *Schindler's List* and three years before Fiennes hit it even bigger with *The English Patient*. The next year was the turning point for the project, though, with commentators saying that the time had passed for The Normal Heart and that any production would now have to be a period piece. In 1996, it was budgeted and Kenneth Branagh was discussed for the leading role. The project went to another director with other actors involved, but then, as nothing was produced, bounced back to Barwood in 2001. There was mention of it again in 2008 and 2009, but still no production was listed as current for it by Barwood.

Ryan Murphy, director of TV's high school singing series *Glee*, had *The Normal Heart* in development as a producer with Oscar-nominated actor Mark Ruffalo (2010, for *The Kids Are All Right*) starring as Ned Weeks, with Larry Kramer writing the script. The stage version is still being performed all over the world and has been considered as one of the one hundred most important plays ever staged.

Barwood Films—with Barbra as executive producer—developed the feature film of *Mendel's Dwarf*, based on Simon Mawer's book of the same name. It had been in development with Barwood since 2005 and was scheduled to be released in 2011.

When Barbra moved agencies from ICM to Endeavor in 2008, Barwood also went with her, bringing all of Streisand's interests under one umbrella company. It suggested that she was getting her legacy set up with plenty of time to spare.

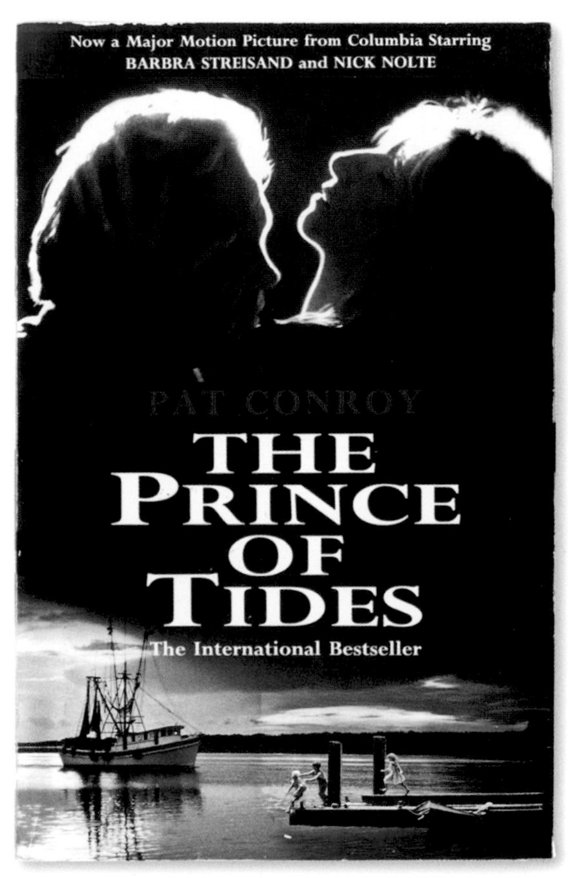


Left: Directing *The Prince of Tides*, 1990 (book cover above)

# Back to Broadway

**Released**
1993
**Label**
Columbia Records
**Producer**
David Foster, Andrew Lloyd Webber, Nigel Wright and Barbra Streisand
**Musical Arrangement**
Johnny Mandel, David Foster, Bill Ross, Barbra Streisand, Andrew Pryce Jackman, Jonathan Tunick, Billy Byers, Jeremy Lubbock and Michael Starobin

**Tracks**
▪ Some Enchanted Evening ▪ Everybody Says Don't ▪ The Music of the Night—Duet with Michael Crawford ▪ Speak Low ▪ As If We Never Said Goodbye ▪ Children Will Listen ▪ I Have a Love/One Hand, One Heart—Duet with Johnny Mathis ▪ I've Never Been in Love Before ▪ Luck Be a Lady ▪ With One Look ▪ The Man I Love ▪ Move On

This, Barbra's twenty-sixth studio album, was another return to very fine form. Proving yet again that Barbra Streisand was not only most comfortable but supremely confident with Broadway, film and show tunes. This album pretty much picks up where *The Broadway Album* left off, and the two sets fit seamlessly together. Casual listeners most likely would have no idea they were recorded eight years apart.

"Some Enchanted Evening" immediately sets the tone for the rest of the album: lush arrangements, a superb choice of material and Streisand, now just over fifty years old, sounding better than ever. The only awkward (but still very good) cut here is "The Music of the Night," a duet with Michael Crawford. "As If We Never Said Goodbye" from *Sunset Boulevard* became the opening number for her much anticipated return to the live stage in 1994. As she belts out the line "Now I'm standing center stage, I've come home at last," everyone knows exactly what she means. Her reading of that particular song couldn't have been more fitting for someone who had avoided performing publicly for so long. She could not have done a finer job with *Back to Broadway* and the subsequent live shows.

The album entered the *Billboard* album chart at number 1 in June 1993, thirty years after her debut record release. This album went on to be certified double platinum.

**Released**
1997
**Label**
Columbia Records
**Executive Producer**
Barbra Streisand and Jay Landers
**Producer**
Arif Mardin, Walter Afanasieff, David Foster, Mervyn Warren and Jeremy Lubbock
**Musical Arrangement**
Jeremy Lubbock, William Ross, Mervyn Warren, Arif Mardin, Marvin Hamlisch and William David Brohn

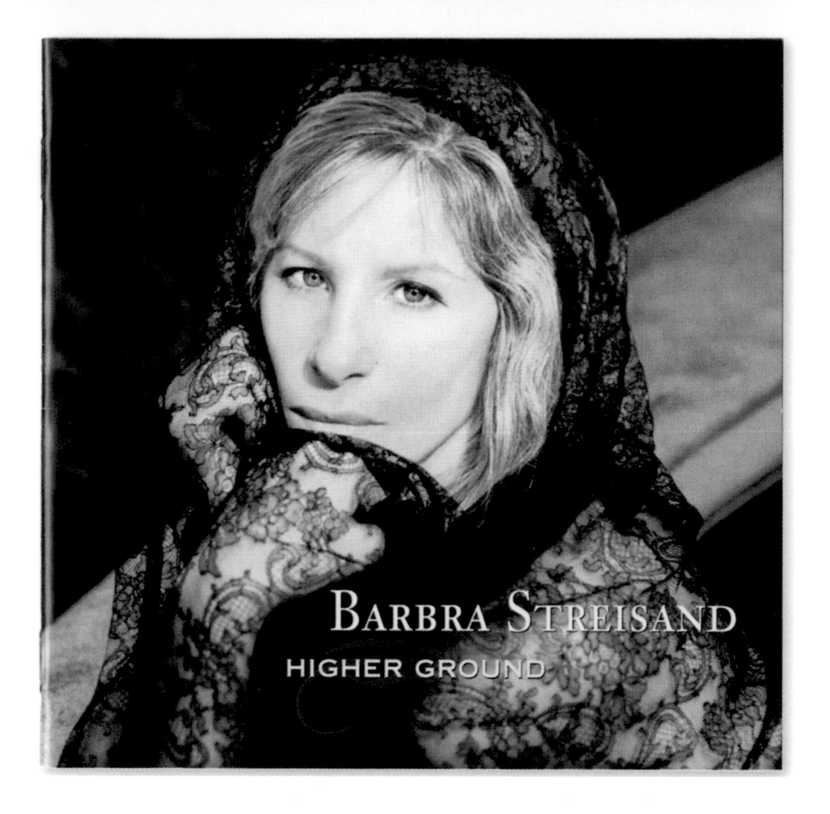


**Tracks**
• I Believe/You'll Never Walk Alone • Higher Ground • At the Same Time • Tell Him • On Holy Ground • If I Could • Circle • The Water Is Wide/Deep River • Leading with Your Heart • Lessons to Be Learned • Everything Must Change • Avinu Malkeinu

Over the years, Ms. Streisand had become very good friends with U.S. president Bill Clinton and his family, most notably his mother, Virginia Kelley. This album of mostly inspirational, uplifting songs was dedicated to her memory, after Barbra had been inspired by the music played and sung at her funeral, early in 1994.

There are some fine moments here, "If I Could" in particular, but also "Leading with Your Heart," which was the title of Kelley's autobiography. However, the album suffers from overproduction, especially on cuts like the duet with singer Celine Dion, "Tell Him"—which nevertheless became a huge hit single. Other casualties are the medley "I Believe/You'll Never Walk Alone," which is totally overblown and somewhat cloying, despite her amazing vocal performance. Another, "Avinu Malkeinu," sounds like something that was left off the *Yentl* soundtrack; it's a great song, but not for consumption on a general release album.

The whole set is far too keyboard laden and not unique-sounding, or originally produced enough; as each cut opens it feels as if you could easily be hearing an intro to a song that is about to be performed by any other female artist, and it's only when Barbra opens her mouth that one realizes that this is actually her. On most of her previous albums, the music was equally compelling, impeccably written and played, and finely produced. Rarely, if ever, has Barbra been so poorly served in those areas as she is here, and it's hard to fathom why that should be.

Having said all this, it still managed to debut on the *Billboard* album chart at number 1, and in the process making her the only female artist in history to have number 1 albums across four different decades. That's a feat unlikely to be repeated.

BARBRA STREISAND JEFF BRIDGES

A story about just how wrong two people can be before they can be right...

# THE MIRROR HAS TWO FACES

15

SOUNDTRACK AVAILABLE ON COLUMBIA RECORDS

A FILM BY BARBRA STREISAND

TRISTAR PICTURES PRESENTS IN ASSOCIATION WITH PHOENIX PICTURES AN ARNON MILCHAN/BARWOOD FILMS PRODUCTION 'THE MIRROR HAS TWO FACES' BARBRA STREISAND JEFF BRIDGES PIERCE BROSNAN GEORGE SEGAL MIMI ROGERS BRENDA VACCARO AND LAUREN BACALL MUSIC COMPOSED AND ADAPTED BY MARVIN HAMLISCH 'LOVE THEME' COMPOSED BY BARBRA STREISAND COSTUMES BY THEONI V. ALDREDGE EDITED BY JEFF WERNER DIRECTOR OF PHOTOGRAPHY DANTE SPINOTTI, A.I.C. ANDRZEJ BARTKOWIAK EXECUTIVE PRODUCER CIS CORMAN PRODUCED BY BARBRA STREISAND AND ARNON MILCHAN SCREENSTORY AND SCREENPLAY BY RICHARD LaGRAVENESE DIRECTED BY BARBRA STREISAND 'I FINALLY FOUND SOMEONE' PERFORMED BY BARBRA STREISAND AND BRYAN ADAMS

http://www.sony.com

SDDS Sony Dynamic Digital Sound. IN SELECTED THEATRES

DOLBY IN SELECTED THEATRES

RELEASED BY COLUMBIA TRISTAR FILMS (UK)

# The Mirror Has Two Faces

**Running Time** 126 mins
**Studio** Tristar Pictures, Phoenix Pictures, Barwood Films
**Year** 1996
**Director** Barbra Streisand
**Screenplay** André Cayatte, Gérard Oury and Richard LaGravenese
**Cast** Barbra as Rose Morgan, Jeff Bridges, Lauren Bacall and George Segal

Above: Barbra attempts to look "frumpy" for her role as an English professor.

This is the movie that confirmed Barbra's skill at commercial moviemaking. It was designed to show that she could take a property, develop it and create box office magic. She'd made hits before, but had not set out to deliberately create an obviously commercial, mainstream movie as she did with this.

A frothy yet thoughtful romance, it was written by Richard LaGravenese, based on a French movie from 1958 with the same name, *Le Miroir à Deux Faces*. It pivots on the notion that beauty, or the lack thereof, can cause problems in a marriage in the most unlikely manner.

The ensemble cast was astonishing; Barbra took on a (surprising) lead role as a frumpy woman who marries a mathematician who doesn't want to have sex with her (Jeff Bridges). She also has a powerhouse of a mother (Lauren Bacall) and a terrific job, as an adored professor of English literature. George Segal stepped in for Dudley Moore as Henry Fine when Moore's health sadly declined. Pierce Brosnan also appears as a smarmy brother-in-law who loves himself a bit too much, and there's a catty turn by Mimi Rogers as his disillusioned wife.

Like many women, the mysteries of what men find attractive fascinated Barbra as a person and a moviemaker. In her transformation from unsexy teacher to hard-bodied sexy lady, Barbra goes from looking very dowdy to basically looking as she did in real life—long blonde hair, fringey bangs and a fabulously svelte figure. Of course, her virtually autistic husband can't help but sit up and take notice and realize that he does in fact love her for her mind *and* her body.

Credited with being a smart movie about sex and love, one that doesn't stray from inherent complications, the film is a bit of a fantasy, but it also comes with lessons of self-acceptance, self-awareness and denial built in. It sports the moral that sometimes you have to make yourself into someone else, but someone you respect, in order to get the love you want.

Barbra teases us with snippets of the wonderful romance *A Brief Encounter* at the same time Bridges is doing his sit-ups. The performances from Bridges and Bacall were universally praised while Barbra attracted some harsh criticism for, as one critic put it, "not realizing she wasn't Michelle Pfeiffer" or that she had to be. *The Mirror Has Two Faces* is a strong and simple fantasy that speaks to the reality of love, in an uplifting and enjoyable way.

"I like to make films that make people feel. I like to make films about positive transformations."

ebok

# The Mirror Has Two Faces

**Released**
1996
**Label**
Columbia Records
**Producer**
Barbra Streisand, Marvin Hamlisch and Jay Landers
**Musical Arrangement**
Jack Hayes, Torrie Zito and Brad Dechter



**Tracks**
• Main Title/In Questa Reggia • Got Any Scotch? • An Ad? • In a Sentimental Mood • Rose Sees Greg • Alex Hurts Rose • The Dating Montage • My Intentions? • You Picked Me! • A Funny Kind of Proposal • Picnic in the Park • Greg Falls For Rose • Try a Little Tenderness —David Sanborn • The Mirror • Going Back to Mom • Rocking in the Chair • The Power Inside of Me • Rose Leaves Greg • Ruby • Rose Dumps Alex • Greg Claims Rose • The Apology / Nessun Dorma—Luciano Pavarotti • I Finally Found Someone • All of My Life

Most of the tracks here were scored by Marvin Hamlisch, and there are only two vocal ballads performed by Barbra on the album. "All of My Life" is a pretty good Streisand slow number, full of strings and plaintive piano. The album's breakout hit single, though, "I Finally Found Someone," a duet with Bryan Adams is a big power ballad of the kind that the Canadian had made his name writing and performing ("Everything I Do, I Do for You"). There's also the wonderful uber–power ballad "Nessun Dorma" (from Puccini's *Turandot*) sung by the great Italian tenor Luciano Pavarotti. Adding to the power ballad list is Richard Marx, the Chicagoan who'd scored a big hit with "Satisfied" and "Right Here Waiting" in 1989, and who sings here his own song "The Power Inside of Me." There's one other guest star on the album: David Sanborn, the alto tenor saxophonist who contributes a laid-back rendition of "Try a Little Tenderness." It's a patchy ccollection, but it made number 16 on the LP chart mainly because of the success of Barbra and Adams's duet.

# A Love Like Ours

**Released**
1999
**Label**
Columbia Records
**Executive Producer**
Barbra Streisand and Jay Landers
**Producer**
Barbra Streisand, Walter Afanasieff, David Foster, Richard Marx, Tony Brown, and Arif Mardin
**Musical Arrangement**
William Ross, Jorge Calandrelli, Arif Mardin, David Foster, Bruce Roberts and Jeremy Lubbock

**Tracks**
▪ I've Dreamed of You ▪ Isn't It a Pity? ▪ The Island ▪ Love Like Ours ▪ If You Ever Leave Me (Duet with Vince Gill) ▪ We Must Be Loving Right ▪ If I Never Met You ▪ It Must Be You ▪ Just One Lifetime ▪ If I Didn't Love You ▪ Wait ▪ The Music That Makes Me Dance

Choosing to feature her love interest on her new album sleeve was a daring move by Streisand at this point. By now Don Johnson, a recent co-cover star and paramour, was very much a part of her past. Fortunately, at the time of writing, James Brolin is still in her life and has proven to be her longest relationship thus far.

The inside sleeve featured several photographs of the happy couple together on a beach, entwined, getting married even (see opposite); clearly, she was hopelessly in love. The notion of the newly-weds sharing their personal photographs to possibly seduce and entice back any romantic followers of Barbra who might have strayed in recent years, was largely successful. Plus, it was a great marketing ploy—as if it were needed.

Musically the album didn't quite catch fire, except perhaps on "If You Ever Leave Me," a duet with country music's velvet-voiced Vince Gill. It's a beautiful song, and both singers nail it with impassioned fervor. "The Music That Makes Me Dance" also stands out—an old tune from *Funny Girl*, it's impressively reworked here.

The album is all very easy on the ear, and while there's nothing spectacular to be heard on it, like Barbra perhaps, even the most ardent followers will no doubt have mellowed with age, so this more comfortable setting serves well—the album made the *Billboard* top ten with platinum sales certified within a month of release. There were still so many Barbra fans out there that anything she released would be certified a best-seller.

*4. Love Like Ours*

*Written by Alan & Marilyn Bergman and Dave Grusin*
*Published by WB Music Corp./Threesome Music (ASCAP)*

***Produced by Barbra Streisand***

*Arranged & Conducted by William Ross*
*Original Arrangement by Jorg Keller*

*Drums: J.R. Robinson*
*Bass: Nathan East*
*Keyboards: Randy Waldman*
*Guitar: Dean Parks*

*Engineered by Frank Wolf & David Reitzas*
*Mixed by Al Schmitt*

*5. If You Ever Leave Me*
*(Duet with Vince Gill)*

*Written by Richard Marx*
*Published by Chi-Boy Music (ASCAP)*

***Produced & Arranged by David Foster & Richard Marx***

*Orchestra Arranged & Conducted by William Ross*

*Keyboards: Richard Marx, David Foster*
*Programming: Felipe Elgueta*
*Drums: J.R. Robinson*
*Bass: Nathan East*
*Acoustic Guitars: Vince Gill, Donald Kirkpatrick, Kamil Rustam*
*Electric Guitars: Donald Kirkpatrick, Vince Gill*

*Engineered by Felipe Elgueta & Humberto Gatica*
*Mixed by Mick Guzauski*

*Six: The Twenty–first Century*

# The Way We Were

HAVING said that she'd be spending less time working and more time traveling with her husband in 2000, Barbra combined both that year when in March she traveled to Australia. While "down under" she performed in Sydney and Melbourne on what she called her *Timeless* tour, and earned rave reviews. After five months off, Barbra played the Staples Center in Los Angeles. Her final concert was at Madison Square Garden in New York in typically spectacular fashion, with fans saying that it was "addictive" and "Barbra at her best."

Following the tour's end, Barbra was soon busy with preparing footage and recordings from the tour for the commercial release of *Timeless*. But somehow she still found time to receive a Cecil B. DeMille award for lifetime achievement in movies, given by the Hollywood Foreign Press Association at the Golden Globes—presented to her by Shirley MacLaine—and to receive the American Film Institute 2001 award. Both were significant in that they marked her recognition as an artist and a filmmaker.

The Grammy nominations of January 2002 saw *Timeless: Live in Concert* get a nomination for Best Traditional Vocal Pop Album. Interest in her previous films was also spurred by the first DVD release of *For Pete's Sake*, one of her most underrated comedies. The next year, *Funny Girl* was also given a revamp to DVD for the first time, along with other Barbra films such as *The Prince of Tides* and *The Owl and the Pussycat*. By the second year of the new millennium, Barbra's fan base was growing. In January 2002, *The Essential Barbra* and five remastered LPs, mainly soundtracks from her movies, were released. The following month, *Funny Lady* appeared for the first time on DVD, just a day before Christie's New York held an auction of Barbra's belongings. But all that paled into insignificance in March, when Barbra's ninety-three-year-old mother, Diana, passed away. Barbra, ever private, didn't say much to the public about her mother's passing, save for a paid notice in *The New York Times* on April 2, 2002, which read, "Diana had a beautiful singing voice—a legacy passed on to Barbra and Roslyn. May the music still go on."

Opposite: Barbra and James Brolin arriving at the White House in 2000 for the National Medal of Arts presentation, where she received an award from President Clinton.

Barbra did go on, and in November, Columbia released *Duets*, a compilation collection made up with song collaborations from past years, plus a couple of new ones. Barry Manilow and Barbra dueted on a Manilow/Marx song titled "I Won't Be the One to Let Go," and Josh Groban joined her for "All I Know of Love." The album became Barbra's fifty-ninth foray into the charts (it peaked at number 38). On December 12, 2002, she called into Seattle's Radio Delilah for an interview about *Duets*; she returned to the same show in January 2003 to talk specifically about the duet with Manilow.

Barbra hugs Robert Redford as he holds his honorary Oscar in 2002.

The same month, Barbra's *Christmas Memories* LP earned a Grammy nomination. Mid-month, Barbra and James attended the premiere of *A Guy Thing* in Los Angeles and were swamped by the media and fans. At the Oscars in March, Barbra presented the golden statuette for Best Original Song to Eminem. In midsummer, *The Barbra Streisand Collection* came out on DVD, and included *Up the Sandbox, The Main Event, Nuts,* and *What's Up, Doc?* Barbra also showed her domestic and Democratic side by contributing a recipe to Bill Clinton's cookbook.

## Second Time Around

In August 2003, *Entertainment Tonight* and *The New York Daily News* reported that Barbra had a small procedure to tighten her jawline, which came as something of a shock to fans, who were concerned for her health. The gossip pages were kept busy when Barbra reportedly went over the Canadian border to visit her husband on the set of his TV movie, in which he played Ronald Reagan. It was rumored that Barbra, as is her style, convinced the director to reshoot a scene while she was there.

In October, the auction website eBay held a Streisand auction. Linked to her personal website, she sold off the famous see-through pantsuit she wore when she won her first Oscar. It was a momentous sale. *The Movie Album* (see page 265) was released in October, debuting at number 5 on the *Billboard* charts. It contained some great performances by Barbra of songs such as "Smile," the gorgeous "Moon River", and "Wild Is the Wind." A DVD accompanied a special edition of the CD. By the end of the year, a lawsuit that Barbra had initiated regarding photos that had been taken of her home that had been published in several magazines was dismissed.

> "Everyone has a right to love and be loved, and nobody on this earth has the right to tell anyone that their love for another human being is morally wrong."

*The Movie Album* was nominated for Best Traditional Pop Vocal Album at the 2004 Grammys. It didn't win, but fans were treated to the long-awaited and wonderful appearance of Barbra on TV's high-profile actors' chat show *Inside the Actors Studio*. Barbra, having been spurned by the Actors Studio early in her career (for being too young), was awarded an honorary membership. In front of a live audience, Barbra recorded five hours of discussion, with subjects ranging from her beginnings to her aspirations. Host James Lipton shared a running joke with her that he too sang at the fabled Bon Soir. While on set, she asked for food and received an enormous selection of cookies and a candy bar. (She noticed the Oreos in particular.) Her appearance broke all viewing records for the TV series, which was watched by more than one million people.  Later in the year, Barbra carried out another purge of her belongings. She held yet another auction of her personal goods, and this time the proceeds went to benefit various charities. Eyeglasses, gowns and items worn in her films were included, along with a Ford mobile home.

With the stripping away of so much of her past in the form of physical belongings, it was rumored that Barbra was evolving spiritually and emotionally. It was as if she had decided to reinvent herself again. When in 2005 she made a triumphant return to the big screen, it was as if she was ready for the world to see the new Streisand. This time she wasn't desperate to be the star of the screen or to have control over every aspect of the movie's production. A more laid-back, warm, almost hippie Barbra who appeared as Roz Focker in *Meet the Fockers* (see pages 270–71). A hilarious slapstick comedy released just after the holidays, it was a big hit commercially and critically. Everyone was happy to have Barbra back on screen after her eight-year hiatus. In February 2005, Barbra and her *Fockers* co-star Dustin Hoffman presented the Best Picture Oscar to Clint Eastwood as producer of *Million Dollar Baby* at the Academy Awards. Dustin and Barbra had terrific chemistry, as recordings of the show reveal: Barbra said she forgot her glasses, so Dustin read the result of the award and then whispered it into her ear.

## Smile

During 2005, in what was a first for her, Barbra recorded a sequel album. It was follow-up to 1980's hugely successful *Guilty*, and like the first album this too would be made with singer Barry Gibb of The Bee Gees. The resultant release, titled *Guilty Pleasures* (see page 272) debuted on October 10 and reached number 5 on the U.S. album charts. It stayed there for nineteen weeks, going gold on October 21. It sold more than 100,000 copies in its first week on the charts. Hailed as being "refreshing" by reviewers, fans loved the smooth sound of the two artists as they duetted together. To promote the release, Barbra appeared on Diane Sawyer's *PrimeTime* television show on September 22 and 26. She also appeared on the UK's *Good Morning TV* and *The Ellen DeGeneres Show*. A twelve-inch dance single taken from the album titled "Night of My Life" reached second place on the *Billboard* Dance charts—all of which was not bad considering that the two artists had a combined age of 123!

In January 2006, her debut recording, *The Barbra Streisand Album*, was inducted into the Grammy Hall of Fame, forty-three years after its initial release. It was an award given to recordings of "lasting significance." Furthering the cult of Barbra, five of her classic TV specials became available for the first time on DVD on November 22. *My Name is Barbra* (1965), *Color Me Barbra* (1966), *The Belle of 14th Street* (1967), *A Happening in Central Park* (1967) and *Barbra Streisand . . . and Other Musical Instruments* (1973) proved to be revelations for fans and newcomers alike. The TV specials looked fresh and crisp in their digital form.

Barbra performing at Andre Agassi's Tenth Grand Slam for Children benefit, 2005.

With son Jason, husband James and Samantha, in Paris, 2007.

In March 2006, Barbra appeared at a fundraiser for Hillary Clinton; raising more than $2.6 million, it was more successful than that of David Geffen's celebrity party for Barack Obama held at the same time. By June, she'd set her fall concert tour schedule, and great excitement was generated when it was announced that Barbra would come back to the stage with the dishy quartet Il Divo, an international group of classical singers, as her guests. She set a series of dates across America, starting in Philadelphia on October 4 ending up in LA by November 20.

Barbra combined forces with Tony Bennett to record a version of "Smile," the song co-written by Charlie Chaplin, for inclusion on an album of duets to mark Bennett's eightieth birthday. Recorded in her Malibu home in August, the legendary violinist Pinchas Zukerman also played on the track, which was released in September. They sang the song together in November during an NBC TV special for Bennett. On October 4, Barbra's North American concert tour began in Philadelphia, and over the next two months it traveled to fourteen different locations. She had a special set built for the show, which was split into two acts and during which she sang almost thirty songs drawn from her back catalog. The guest stars for the tour, Il Divo, opened the shows, and then returned during the headline act performance in order to sing with Barbra on "I Finally Found Someone" and "Somewhere." The shows sold out on announcement and reviews were ecstatic.

Before Barbra's first-ever European tour (and her first UK dates for thirteen years) began in June 2007, a very rare acetate recording—one of the few Barbra did early in her career—went to auction. It was one of only ten known to exist from the early sixties and is probably the only one—outside of those in Barbra's vault and one owned by one of Barbra's friends—that still exists. It contained recordings of "Come to the Supermarket (In Old Peking)" and "I Stayed Too Long at the Fair." A CD was made from it so bidders could hear it without wearing out the delicate article. The acetate, with a reserve of $5,000, surprisingly, went unsold.

In advance of the European tour, *Streisand: Live in Concert 2006* was released, and it entered the *Billboard* 200 chart at number 7. By May, more of her costumes—including the one worn while singing "Don't Rain on My Parade" in *Funny Girl*—went under the hammer at Christie's auction house. In another change to her professional life, Barbra changed her management agency to Endeavor Talent Agency, which would also represent her company Barwood Films.

The European and British dates were an enormous success, with nights being added to her London show three times. She added songs to the set list because she'd never sung them there before, and took time between dates so that she and James could see some of the scenery. It was, by all accounts, a truly rewarding trip for everyone—performer and fans.

In February 2008, financial magazine *Forbes* listed Barbra as the number 2 top earning woman performer for her previous twelve months' earnings of approximately $60 million. This showed Barbra's business acumen. Not only had she guarded her career well and protected her assets (particularly her voice), but she also respected her fans while still pursuing artistic achievement. None of that was an easy balance to keep, and few artists ever achieve her level of artistic and financial power.

In September, it was announced that Barbra was to receive a Kennedy Center Honor, America's version of a performing arts knighthood. The Honors gala, which was the highlight of the Washington cultural year, took place in December. She shared the evening with four other honorees, including actor Morgan Freeman, country singer George Jones, choreographer Twyla Tharp and musicians Peter Townshend and Roger Daltrey (of the Who).

> "I don't feel like a legend. I feel like a work in progress."

In 2009, Barbra was as busy as ever. On April 25, the ratings for a CBS-aired one-hour TV special were high, with almost five million viewers having watched *Streisand: Live in Concert*. It was in fact an edited version of her *Live in Concert 2006* DVD recording, but it helped to boost sales of other concert recordings, which were due out on DVD the following day. September saw the release of *Love Is the Answer* (see page 273) a collection of songs recorded with an orchestra and a small jazz band, produced by pianist Diana Krall (who also plays on the recordings). The deluxe edition came with an extra CD containing the songs recorded by Barbra with only the jazz band. There was a third edition, which had a mixture of orchestral and band tracks, released exclusively via Starbucks coffee shops. Three nights before *Love Is the Answer* had been released, on September 26, Barbra performed at an exceedingly rare club show in New York City—it was a free concert for one hundred of her incredibly lucky fans. Her first club date for forty-eight years, it was destined for CD and DVD release the following year.

In October, Julien's Auctions sold off more of Barbra's clothing and other items to benefit the Streisand Foundation, making $600,000. Barbra also appeared on a list of most generous celebrities, having donated $1.7 million to charity. (The previous year, she had donated $11 million.)

Opposite: On TV, 2011.

By January 2010, Barbra had finished with filming the reprise of her role as Roz Focker in *Little Fockers*. She got back to business as usual, lending her voice to a new charity song for Haiti, a follow-up to the 1985 hit "We Are the World." Barbra joined other singers, including Celine Dion, Gladys Knight, Justin Bieber, Usher, will.i.am, LL Cool J, Harry Connick Jr. and Wyclef Jean, and actors Vince Vaughn and Jeff Bridges for the recording. Barbra contributed four takes, with the producers and her agreeing that the fourth was the best. The single debuted at number 2 on the *Billboard* Hot 100.

Above: Director Kathryn Bigelow with her Best Director Oscar, received from Barbra in 2010.

Opposite: The front cover of Barbra's 2010 book.

Barbra agreed to present an award at the eighty-second Oscars, and it turned out to be a historic and perhaps bittersweet occasion. At the Academy Awards on Sunday, March 7, 2010, Barbra followed her greeting of "Hello, gorgeous," with, "Well, the time has come," as she gave the Best Director award to Kathryn Bigelow for her film *The Hurt Locker*. Bigelow became the first female ever to win the award. Barbra was never nominated in that category.

*One Night Only: Barbra Streisand and Quartet at the Village Vanguard* was released on CD and Blu-ray DVD in May, and went straight to number 1 on the DVD charts. In September, Barbra threw her agent, Marty Erlichman, an eighty-first birthday party, which also marked fifty years of their working together. The party, at Barbra's Malibu home, had been delayed because of the success of *Love Is the Answer* and the preparation of her Village Vanguard gig DVD. Marty's gift from his client? A Mercedes hybrid car, darling.

Barbra and Robert Redford's appearance on *The Oprah Winfrey Show* on November 15 made the fans go crazy—it was the first time the two stars had been seen together since filming *The Way We Were* together more than thirty years prior. Barbra also appeared in *People* magazine, *Ladies' Home Journal* and *House Beautiful* to publicize her book, *My Passion for Design*. As with everything she does, the book was a success, reaching the *New York Times* best-seller list not long after its publication on November 24, 2010. On December 8, the Recording Academy announced that Barbra had been selected as its MusiCares Person of the Year, a prestigious honor to celebrate her generosity and musical achievements. There would doubtless be many, many more such awards sent her way in the future.

## A Beacon

At the age of sixty-nine, when most people would be slowing down in their lives, Barbra Streisand embarked on a new stage in her career. She wasn't interested in simply rereleasing old material; Barbra wanted to make fresh creations. Early in 2011 rampant rumors—backed up by articles in the established press—had it that Barbra was going to star in a new movie version of *Gypsy*, as the domineering mother, Rose. The project had been kicking around for ages, but articles in *The New York Times* suggested that it could actually happen, and soon. In an interview in the *Hartford Courier*, Arthur Laurents put those rumors to death by claiming that both he and Stephen Sondheim were now against the idea. A reputable online entertainment website claimed that Universal Studios was still negotiating for the project, however. Time will tell.

Barbra headed to the White House as one of the guests of President Obama at a state dinner that honored Chinese president Hu Jintao. Asked about what she knew about China, Barbra quipped, "I worked in a Chinese restaurant." Apparently, the real reason she was there was because Hu Jintao was a big Streisand fan—and that was claimed without any irony. Other famous people at the dinner were cellist Yo-Yo Ma, film star Jackie Chan, Olympic skater Michelle Kwan and fashion designer Vera Wang.

In late January, *The Hollywood Reporter* said that Paramount had given the road-trip comedy *My Mother's Curse* the green light. The script is a hilarious take on generational clashes. Barbra plays Seth Rogen's mother, with Anne Fletcher (*The Proposal*) as director of what is a terrific two-hander about a mother and son who take a road trip across America. The only possible problem fans might have with it is that Barbra doesn't sing in the movie, not even a tiny bit.

*My Mother's Curse* is a comedy based on Dan Fogelman's well-crafted script, which lingered for years on Hollywood's famous Black List—a list of scripts so good that everyone is baffled as to why they don't get made. The director is a former choreographer who made a splash in the directing world with her debut *Step Up*, before *27 Dresses* and then *The Proposal*, an enormous hit for Sandra Bullock and Ryan Reynolds. Fletcher brings a fresh, deft touch to comedy scripts, which is exactly what *My Mother's Curse* required.

Previous pages: Dustin Hoffman and Barbra as the Fockers in *Little Fockers*.

Opposite: Singing at the 2011 Grammy Awards show.

Rogen plays Andy Brewster, an young LA businessman with a revolutionary cleaning product that you could drink if you wanted to. Although it seems to be something everyone would want, Andy can't sell it. On his way across the country, he stops in to see how his mother, Joyce (Barbra), is doing since

his father's death. She's depressed, watching TV all day long and eating junk food. So naturally she's ecstatic to see him. Wanting to help her, he finds one of her old boyfriends online and takes her with him on his business trip where he will, eventually, take her to her old love. It's a mixture of road trip and family comedy, of a tender and tough relationship between mother and child. Imagine Roz Focker and Gaylord going across the country in a car, seeing strip clubs and eating seventy-two-ounce steaks along the way.

Rogen, although the leading player, is virtually blown off the screen by Barbra. It's not his fault; it's just that she has the better part and her natural comedic timing has been honed over decades of acting and singing. In an early draft of the script, Andy and Joyce have a few awkward comedy moments that hinge on sex. Of course, throughout her career, Barbra's characters may have been "proper" women (not pushovers), but they haven't exactly shied away from sexual discussion. The material is perfect for her as a sexually aware mother who is completely confident and comfortable, while still seeing herself as a good mother. She may use the f-word quite a bit in a scene or two, but that doesn't diminish her power as a mom and independent woman. In fact, it is safe to say that Barbra's character steals the movie—and you'd never believe that she made it at age sixty-eight.

To look at her when she made a rare televised appearance at the 2011 Grammys in February (*Love Is the Answer* was nominated in the Best Traditional Pop Vocal category), you wouldn't believe that she'd collected her first such award almost forty years earlier. Barbra sang her big hit "Evergreen," and also presented a Grammy to Arcade Fire—which was a surprise win for the Canadian band—while standing alongside Kris Kristofferson, her co-star from *A Star Is Born*. Barbra seemed a little tentative during her performance

> "I'm not that ambitious anymore. I just like my privacy."

that night, when compared to her wonderful singing at the MusicCares event on February 11, only two days before. At the MusiCares gig Barbra was honored by fellow performers Tony Bennett, Jeff Beck, LeAnn Rimes, Seal, BeBe Winans, Stevie Wonder, Diana Krall, Barry Manilow, and the cast of *Glee*, who performed their interpretations of Barbra's many hits. There, in a more closed environment, Barbra's voice was soaring and clear. Prince

handed Barbra the great honor. Barbra quipped, "My niece recently watched a DVD of *Funny Girl* for the first time and asked me why I was singing songs from *Glee*!"

One of Barbra's lasting contributions to Jewish girls all over the world was summed up by actress and comedienne Fran Drescher, who attended the MusiCares event. She said, "[Barbra] did everything that at the time was the antithesis of what a woman with a large nose should do according to fashion. She embraced her nose with confidence. She's been doing that her entire career, saying to everyone, 'I am what I am and I do what I do.' It really was a beacon for all us Jewish girls from Queens with frizzy hair."

Throughout her career, whenever Barbra's been placed in front of a camera, she has shined a light for all those girls—regardless of ethnicity—who felt awkward in their bodies. Her example inspires us all.

With Kris Kristofferson at the 2011 Grammy Awards show.

## Coming Soon?

That Barbra has had such a fantastic career in the film industry, as an actress, producer and director, is testimony to her talent and persistence. After winning every award there is to win, she has very little left to prove. When she stepped forward to give Kathryn Bigelow the Oscar for Best Director in 2009 for *The Hurt Locker*, it was perhaps a nod from the industry for Barbra's own achievements in filmmaking. Many believe that honor should have come to her, if not for *The Prince of Tides* or *The Mirror Has Two Faces*, then at least for *Yentl*, where her creative power was most positively and successfully displayed.

Barbra as Joyce with her screen son Seth Rogen, on the set of *My Mother's Curse*, 2011.

Opposite: The House of Streisand meets the House of Windsor; Barbra and Prince William in LA, July 2011.

If her fans had their way, they would see the return of Barbra the actress of the 1960s—the sexy, stylish performer with the wonderful clothes and the sassy dialogue, embellished with memorable songs. When Barbra was cutting a swath through the entertainment industry back then, she was doing it in a style that can only be imagined now. She was a groundbreaker, a trendsetter, and the woman who set the bar almost impossibly high for every other performer after her. Barbra's achievements across the board cannot be denied. This is why, even now, Billy Crystal can sing a Streisand song seemingly out of context and people get the reference immediately. What Barbra may wish to do as far as her career in films goes, however, could be something very different from what her fans want; even they may not understand how her creativity ebbs and flows. It is easy to forget just how taxing and difficult the film industry is; getting a project together was always hard, but with the enormous upheavals within the industry over the past two decades and the changing nature of the role film plays in our entertainment world, what Barbra chooses to do may surprise everyone. It is possible that she might not consider doing a musical film again, mainly because of her voice which, she has said, is not always there on demand anymore. Clearly, her home, her marriage and other areas of her life can and have taken precedence over moviemaking.

However, her charisma and confidence, being the kind that old-fashioned screen goddesses used to display, make Barbra one of the last of the true Hollywood greats. That was clearly evident when in July 2011 the heir to the throne of England, Prince William, and his recent bride Catherine, were presented to her at a BAFTA-hosted dinner in Los Angeles. While other stars seemed awestruck in the presence of true royalty, the royal couple seemed in awe only of Barbra. As one quality British newspaper put it, Barbra is more regal than William and Kate. She is the queen of screen, stage and a new generation of *Glee*-inspired performers. Long may she reign.

# Christmas Memories

**Released**
2001
**Label**
Columbia Records
**Executive Producer**
Barbra Streisand and Jay Landers
**Producer**
Barbra Streisand, William Ross and Robbie Buchanan
**Musical Arrangement**
William Ross, Jorge Calandrelli, Eddie Karam, Robbie Buchanan, Chris Boardman, David Foster and Bob Esty

**Tracks**
• I'll Be Home for Christmas • A Christmas Love Song• What Are You Doing New Year's Eve? • I Remember • Snowbound • It Must Have Been the Misteltoe • Christmas Lullaby • Christmas Mem'ries • Grown up Christmas List • Ave Maria • Closer • One God

This album includes one song many always thought odd not to be included on the *Christmas Album*, namely "I'll Be Home for Christmas," this set's standout track. There were no surprises here, other than choosing to rerecord "Ave Maria."

While most Christmas albums often feature very clichéd design on their covers, this one is particularly bad. It is arguably her worst sleeve in more than fifty albums and forty years. In a sleeve note Barbra commented on the 9/11 bombing of the Twin Towers and dedicated the album to "all who grieve for those who have perished." She also dedicated it to the husband of designer and friend Donna Karan, Stephan Weiss, who had passed away during that year. This seasonal collection reached number 15 on the *Billboard* album chart and sold a million copies before the holiday.

# The Movie Album

**Released**
2003
**Label**
Columbia Records
**Executive Producer**
Barbra Streisand and Jay Landers
**Producer**
Barbra Streisand, Robbie Buchanan and Johnny Mandel
**Musical Arrangement**
Jeremy Lubbock, Robbie Buchanan, Jorge Calandrelli and Johnny Mandel

---

**Tracks**
• Smile • Moon River • I'm in the Mood for Love • Wild Is the Wind • Emily • More In Love With You • How Do You Keep the Music Playing? • Calling You • But Beautiful • The Second Time Around • Goodbye for Now • You're Gonna Hear From Me

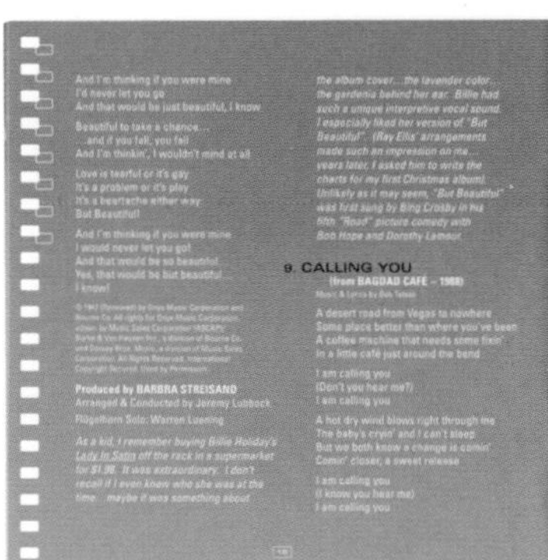

Streisand has long been a big movie fan, from her days as a teenager when she would cross the bridge to Manhattan in order to catch the latest releases on the biggest screens. It was acting, not singing, that initially drew an eager Barbra to the lights of Times Square and Broadway. Her choice of songs for this album clearly indicates her love of cinema and of the great songs made famous in movies such as *Breakfast at Tiffany's*, *Wild Is the Wind* and the much later but equally compelling *Baghdad Cafe*. Charlie Chaplin's "Smile" (lyrics by Turner/Parsons) opens this most consummate of Streisand albums and "Moon River" would bring tears to anyone's eyes.

Sumptuous strings are very much in evidence here, with Streisand sounding as sweet as a bird and forming the essential part of the whole arrangement from beginning to end. There are very few keyboards to be heard. This is Barbra at her very best, thoroughly enjoying being enveloped in the whole sound. It was yet another *Billboard* top ten.

# The Men in Her Life

In her professional life, Barbra has often had a hard time working with older men. Be they Walter Matthau, Robert Redford or Kris Kristofferson, many established actors allegedly found her impossible to work with. While French gentleman actor Yves Montand and she seemed to get along well while on the set of *On a Clear Day You Can See Forever*, it has been suggested that the language barrier helped.

Barbra's strong personality and total belief in her own judgment, right or wrong, very rarely wavered. While that can rub people the wrong way, it is also an asset when considered in the right way. Richard Dreyfuss, who played the role of the public defender in *Nuts* and who is only five years younger than Barbra, was asked what it was like to work with her during the making of that film. He quipped that he would talk about it when everyone who made the film was dead.

Over and over again, Barbra's sense of what she felt was the right thing to do clashed with that of her directors and other creatives. Strangely enough, although the professionals she worked with (and those whom she hired for her own productions) were established in their careers, only some of them complained about her creative vision. Directors working with her would find her coming behind the camera, wanting to reshoot scenes she thought

were less than great. Often, she did reshoot scenes, to a director's dismay. Only the affable Peter Yates really seemed to have found a way to get along with her, while making *For Pete's Sake* in 1974. Read any account of cinematographers or sound recordists who worked with her, however, and you'll find them praising Barbra. She may have been pushy, insistent and stubborn, but she was also invariably right.

Of course, it is easy to play pop psychiatrist and say that because her father died so young that she was bound to have father figure issues in her life. That line is too easy to take; Barbra admired her father, who was said to be accomplished and intelligent. Barbra could only have been inspired by her father's reputation as a hugely respected teacher and PhD.

Overcoming her mother's and stepfather's indifference and resistance to her chosen career path

Opposite: Barbra and Elliot Gould in 1963
Above: With Jon Peters in 1976.

could be another spur to why Barbra felt the need to succeed on her terms, rather than meekly accept the views of people, male or female, who may have had more experience and knowledge than she did but were still as fallible as anyone else. Without her sense of certainty, Barbra couldn't have come as far as she did as quickly as she did.

Barbra suffered the same disappointments in her private relationships that many strong creative people suffer. She chose to have relationships with people who were perhaps not as strong as she is, or who could not match her energy. Early on, it is fair to say Barbra was a woman on a mission to prove herself, and she could depend on nobody but herself.

Having been apparently referred to by her stepfather throughout her early life as being "ugly," it's no surprise she found the bohemian way of life in Greenwich Village not only an escape from a conformist, orthodox way of life, but also a

chance for her to flourish. In the Village she could exaggerate, magnify and enjoy all the things about herself she had been asked to repress. Interestingly, her mother was eventually granted a legal separation from Barbra's stepfather, Louis Kind, on grounds of cruelty.

Whatever the reason, Barbra endured some disastrous love affairs throughout her life. Because of who she was, some of those relationships were conducted in the full glare of the media.

In the beginning, all of Barbra's relationships were with men in the theater, the most notable of which was perhaps Barry Dennen, with whom she lived for a year in the early 1960s (he recently auctioned unique recordings he made of Barbra from that very early stage of her career). After Dennen, Barbra met, fell in love with, and married actor Elliott Gould, with whom she had a son, Jason. Sadly, their union failed in 1971. She then had a relationship with hairdresser–turned–movie producer Jon Peters in the 1970s, which affected her career in a variety of ways. Blinded by love, Peters, who had met Barbra during the filming of *For Pete's Sake* when he was brought in to give her a haircut, was given control over her subsequently much panned 1974 *ButterFly* album. A record producer he was not, though, and it showed. Conversely, his involvement with *A Star Is Born* three years later was much more successful and rewarding for both of them. That film—and its soundtrack album—remains one of the most successful screen musicals of all time. Peters has since tried to sell a tell-all book about his career as a lover of Hollywood's greatest women. Barbra responded to the news by saying that Peters's proposed book has many inaccuracies.

After her romance with Peters ended, Barbra reportedly dated former Canadian premier Pierre Trudeau, tennis star Andre Agassi, musician Richard Baskin and actor Don Johnson (*Miami Vice*). Possibly the single biggest mistake of her professional life was encouraging Johnson to duet with her on the *Til I Loved You* album in 1988. He was not a singer, and choosing to have him appear on the album sleeve with her was perhaps a step too far. Her adoring public was uncertain whether this relationship would last, and they were right to be skeptical.

Barbra was only twenty years old when she met and married Gould. She was young, naïve, in love and her career was on the rise at a rapid rate, while Gould's took a more indirect path. During their marriage, only one movie starring Gould made an impression, *Bob & Carol & Ted & Alice*, in 1969, for which he was nominated for an Oscar. After they split he enjoyed one of his career highlights in the enormously successul Robert Altman–directed

*M*A*S*H*, in 1970. During the 1963–70 period Barbra went from success to bigger success, of course, and it cannot have helped the relationship that both actors were working constantly. Barbra seemed to be disinclined toward marriage after her first experience of it.

That is, until she met actor James Brolin at a dinner party in 1996 given by Jon Peters's ex-wife. It seems she had finally met a man who was not at all fazed by her. Respectful, yes, but in awe, definitely not. A successful actor in his own right and with a colorful past, he was a man she didn't need to mother, nor did he represent a father figure for Barbra. They were married in 1998.

Gould and Brolin bookend all the love affairs and short-lived relationships she went through in between, during a time when clearly she was focusing more on her career than anything else. Being happy in her personal life has apparently made her performances, both in the studio and on stage, less edgy and more comfortable and relaxed, throughout her life. In the twenty-first century however, it seems that Barbra has accepted that her happiness can rely on the stability, trust and romance which she seems to have found with James Brolin.

Opposite: With Richard Baskin, 1984.
Above: With Don Johnson, 1986.

# Meet the Fockers

**Running Time** 115 mins
**Studio** Universal Pictures, DreamWorks SKG, Tribeca Productions
**Year** 2004
**Director** Jay Roach
**Screenplay** Jim Herzfeld and John Hamburg
**Cast** Barbra as Rozalin Focker, Robert DeNiro, Ben Stiller, Dustin Hoffman, Blythe Danner and Owen Wilson

---

The length of time between movies was getting longer for Barbra. From the ridiculously hectic schedule of two a year when she started out, she'd slowly increased rest periods between shoots. After eight years away from the big screen, Barbra made a welcome return, albeit in a supporting role, to film comedy. She joined the cast of a recent movie franchise that had begun with *Meet the Parents* in 2000, starring Robert DeNiro and Ben Stiller. Her role as Ma Focker in her seventeenth feature film was familiar to anyone who had watched her for three decades on screen. Rosalind "Roz" Focker knows a thing or two and isn't afraid to talk sex, which she does for a living as a sex therapist to senior citizens.

DeNiro and Stiller were complemented by the hiring of Streisand and Dustin Hoffman, cast as the wacky parents to Stiller's character. You believe that this couple would name their son Gaylord Focker.

She and Hoffman prefectly capture the difference between their laid-back hippie social style and that of the more uptight WASPy Byrneses (DeNiro and Danner). The Fockers touch people; they say anything that comes into their head; they eat and dance and discuss bodily functions.

Left: "Earth Mother" Barbra massages the ear lobes of WASPy Blythe Danner.

Barbra went all out to get the look for Roz Focker exactly right, including getting a fake tan and buying clothes from a mall store. Her look is that of a relaxed earth mother, with an enormous frizzy wig and too much jewelry she doesn't look like the Barbra of old, even if some critics sniped that this was the same look she had sported in *A Star Is Born* in 1976.

Throughout the movie Barbra looks as if she knows that she's made it at last and simply wants to entertain us—to make us laugh, relax and forget our troubles. She can't quite disappear into the background, but she shows she can easily "become" Roz Focker and that she is a terrific comedic actress. Perhaps for the first time on screen, Barbra's performance reflects the way she is when at home with friends.

Despite its lack of critical acclaim—something comedy sequels rarely if ever receive—*Meet the Fockers* was a huge commercial success. From a production budget estimated at between $60 and $80 million (not including marketing or promotion), it made a worldwide gross of $516 million.

> "[I] looked back at all these old movies of hers like *Owl and the Pussycat* and *What's Up, Doc?*. She's funny, and she's got great comic timing. So this is a callback to that era of Barbra Streisand."
>
> ***—John Hamburg, talking to the New Jersey Star Ledger on rewriting the script for Streisand***

# Guilty Pleasures

**Released**
2005
**Label**
Columbia Records
**Executive Producer**
Barbra Streisand and Jay Landers
**Producer**
Barry Gibb and John Merchant

**Tracks**
▪ Come Tomorrow ▪ Stranger in a Strange Land ▪ Hideaway ▪ It's Up to You ▪ Night of My Life ▪ Above the Law ▪ Without Your Love ▪ All the Children ▪ Golden Dawn ▪ (Our Love) Don't Throw It All Away ▪ Letting Go

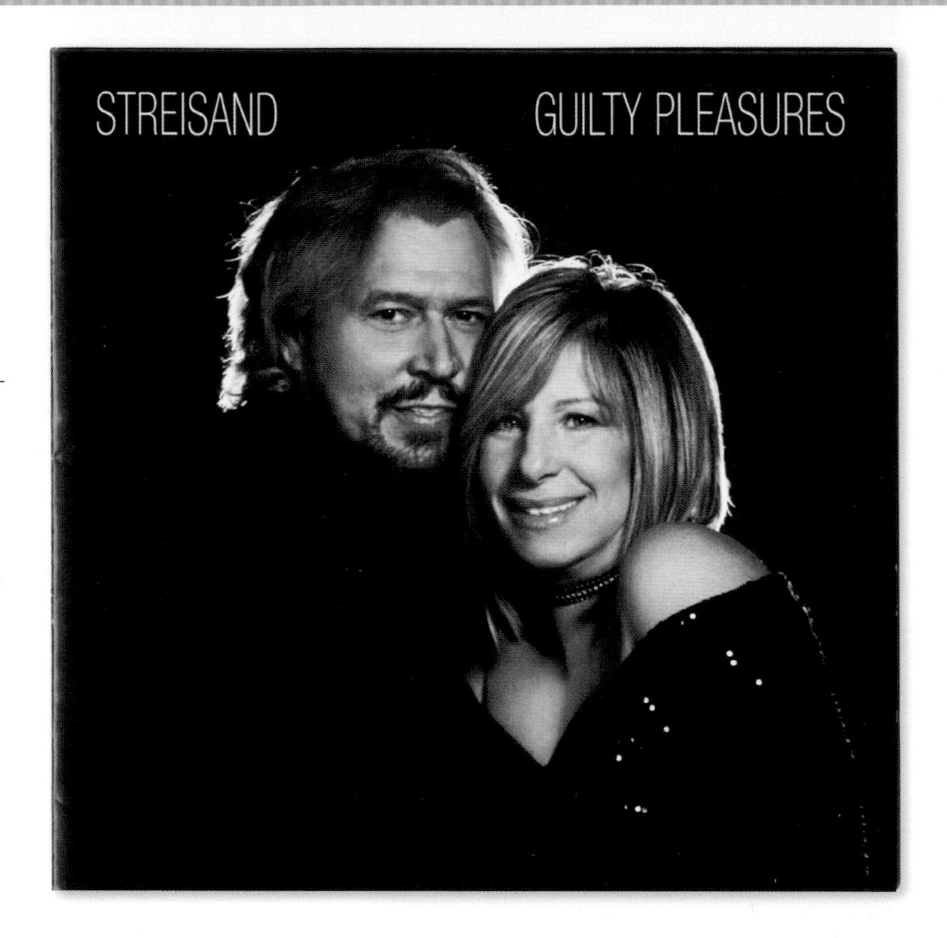


Streisand fans had long awaited a reunion with Barry Gibb, and twenty-five years after their first pairing, it happened. Time has been very good to Barbra; she's still looking and sounding fabulous—unlike Gibb, whose falsetto sounds somewhat odd coming from a man who's now past sixty. However, his production skills remain faultless, and as with Barbra's two *Broadway* albums, also recorded several years apart, these two fit seamlessly together. Deciding to remaster the original "Guilty" from 1980 was a good move, too—on random play one could almost think these tracks were all recorded during the same sessions, which is quite a testament to both talents.

"Stranger in a Strange Land" sounds as though it's pulled from a late 1970s Bee Gees album. Gibb's harmonies remain intact, and Barbra's lead voice soars. On "Golden Dawn" you are transported right back to the halcyon days of Barbra in the 1970s.

This album more than served its purpose, reaching the top five on both sides of the Atlantic when it was released in 2005, and going platinum in many countries. Clearly, Streisand and Gibb are a musical match made in heaven.

# Love Is the Answer

**Released**
2009
**Label**
Columbia Records
**Executive Producer**
Barbra Streisand
**Producer**
Diana Krall and Tommy LiPuma
**Musical Arrangement**
Johnny Mandel, Alan Broadbent, Bill Ross and Anthony Wilson

**Tracks**
• Here's to Life • In the Wee Small Hours of the Morning • Gentle Rain • If You Go Away (Ne me quitte pas) • Spring Can Really Hang You Up the Most • Make Someone Happy • Where Do You Start? • A Time for Love • Here's That Rainy Day • Love Dance • Smoke Gets in Your Eyes • Some Other Time • You Must Believe in Spring (Bonus track)

Ten years after including her husband, James Brolin, on the cover of *A Love Like Ours*, Streisand, still happily married, seems more content than ever, and this album therefore couldn't have been more fitting for her at this stage in not only her career but her life. This album sees Barbra stripped back, unplugged almost. Here her voice is center stage, not the production, albeit it is sublimely handled by Tommy LiPuma with Diana Krall on piano. This became her most critically acclaimed album in years, and she shot to the top of the *Billboard* charts yet again, making her the only artist in history to have number 1 albums over five different decades. Clearly overjoyed at this success, she wrote a note on her official website thanking "My fans and my friends, who have made this possible."

With all those accolades came some great classic American songs, played and sung with utter perfection. "In the Wee Small Hours of the Morning" (the title track of one of Frank Sinatra's best albums, recorded in 1955), Jerome Kern's "Smoke Gets in Your Eyes", (a huge hit for the Platters in 1958), and Jacques Brel's "If You Go Away" (a hit for Nina Simone in 1965) are all songs that Streisand's longtime admirers hoped she'd one day record, and here they sound as if they were written for her.

The album encapsulates everything people have come to expect from and love about Barbra. The girl whose first ever recording back in 1955 was "You'll Never Know" (written for Alice Faye in 1943) returned to great songs written during the early-to-mid period of the twentieth century, a golden time for songwriting and singing. Just like on her first recording, here she is best when accompanied by simple piano chords, played in order to highlight one of the truly great things about Barbra: her voice.

# Little Fockers

Above: Roz Focker becomes a star in her own right. Left: With screen son, Ben Stiller, on set.

**Running Time** 98 mins
**Studio** DreamWorks Pictures, Everyman Pictures, Paramount Pictures, Tribeca Productions, Universal Pictures, Relativity Media
**Year** 2010
**Director** Paul Weitz
**Screenplay** John Hamburg and Larry Huckey
**Cast** Barbra as Rozalin Focker, Robert DeNiro, Ben Stiller, Dustin Hoffman, Blythe Danner and Owen Wilson

---

Six years on, the Fockers franchise continued. To the already stellar cast was added even more top talent: Harvey Keitel, Laura Dern and Jessica Alba. Defying the critics who berated the comedy for tired plot lines, this foray into the trouble-prone Focker and Byrnes families added older children, a flirtatious coworker, and brought wayward family friend from the first movie, Owen Wilson, to the fore again, in a willful mash of farce and family fracas.

Barbra is not on screen as much she had been in *Meet the Fockers*, but she and screen husband Hoffman were once again the beating heart of the sequel that opened just in time for Christmas 2010. Although berated by critics for scraping the bottom of the *Focker* barrel (some reviewers were not even that kind), Streisand held her own in this sea of the broadest, most predictable comedy. One may question why she accepted a role in such an ill-crafted (if crudely amusing) affair, but it couldn't have been made without her.

Franchise movies do better with their essential elements untouched, which includes cast, director and writers if possible. Hoffman proved difficult to contract for this particular production and agreed to do only six scenes; it seemed he was unhappy with the script and with the replacement of Jay Roach, who had directed the first two films, with the less experienced Paul Weitz. Given that Barbra was one of the best things in *Meet the Fockers*, she really had to be in *Little Fockers* to sweeten the dubious pot.

A nomination for a Razzie was taken as a positive turn by a Barbra fan who remarked that if she did indeed win one in 2011, she would have won all of the major awards, good and bad. And anyway, the Razzies are considered to be very cool in Hollywood. In the end though, Barbra lost out on it to *Little Fockers* co-star Jessica Alba.

Her supporting turn as Roz is essential viewing for fans, of course. Indeed, it's as if the entire audience breathes a sigh of relief when she appears, dressed strikingly in red or gold and black. She's gloriously free, doling out advice on her new TV talk show. In a one-minute promotional interview for the film, Barbra said, "The times we live in are very stressful. And people want to laugh, they want to enjoy themselves and forget their worries." As Roz Focker, she certainly appeared to.

"Things are a little silly, you know.
These are people you can relate to, too."

ONE NIGHT O

BARBRA STREISAND

AND QUARTET

at the VILLAGE VANGUARD

*September 26, 2009*

# One Night Only: Barbra Streisand and Quartet at the Village Vanguard

**Released**
2010
**Label**
Columbia Records
**Executive Producer**
Barbra Streisand and Martin Erlichman
**Producer**
Richard Jay-Alexander and Scott Lochmus
**Musical Arrangement**
Jay Landers

**Tracks**
▪ Introductions ▪ Here's to Life ▪ In The Wee Small Hours of the Morning ▪ Gentle Rain ▪ Spring Can Really Hang You Up the Most ▪ If You Go Away (Ne Me Quitte Pas) ▪ Where Do You Start? ▪ Nobody's Heart (Belongs to Me) ▪ Make Someone Happy ▪ My Funny Valentine ▪ Bewitched, Bothered and Bewildered ▪ Evergreen (Love Theme from *A Star Is Born*) ▪ Exit Music ▪ Some Other Time ▪ The Way We Were

It was indisputably the hottest ticket in New York City in the whole of 2009. On September 26, Barbra Streisand, along with a four-piece jazz band comprising pianist Tamir Hendelman, guitarist Brian Koonin, drummer Ray Marchica and bassist Jeff Carney, performed at the tiny Village Vanguard. There might have been room for only her closest pals and a handful of lucky fans at the club, but the release of this album came with a DVD of the show too, allowing anyone to witness the kind of performance that stars of her stature simply don't make anymore. The evening was nostalgic and magic, with Barbra sounding confident, sultry, and probably the best club singer you have ever heard.

Side one
BEAUTIFUL (Carole King)
Arranged by Nick DeCaro/Drums: Jim Gordon/ Bass: Joe Osborn/Pianos: Larry Muhoberac and Lincoln Mayorga/Guitar: Louie Shelton
LOVE (John Lennon)
Arranged by Nick DeCaro/Clarinet and Oboe Solos: Gene Cipriano/Piano: Nick DeCaro/ Drums: Hal Blaine
WHERE YOU LEAD (Carole King)
Arranged by Fanny/Drums: Alice de Buhr/Bass: Jean Millington/Piano: Nickey Barclay/Guitar: June Millington/Organ: Billy Preston/ Tambourine: Richard Perry/ Background Singers: Clydie King, Venetta Fields, Oma Drake and Fanny
I NEVER MEANT TO HURT YOU
(Laura Nyro)
Arranged and Conducted by Dick Hazard
Medley: ONE LESS BELL TO ANSWER A HOUSE IS NOT A HOME (Burt Bacharach-Hal David)
Arranged by Kenny Welch/Orchestrated by Peter Matz
Side two
SPACE CAPTAIN (Mathew Moore)
Arranged by Fanny/Piano: Nickey Barclay/Guitar: June Millington/Drums: Alice de Buhr/Bass: Jean Millington/Organ: Billy Preston/Horns: Jim Price and Bobby Keyes/Background Singers: Clydie King, Venetta Fields, Oma Drake, Shirley Mathews/Percussion: Alice de Buhr and Richard Perry
SINCE I FELL FOR YOU
(Buddy Johnson)
Arranged and Conducted by Gene Page
MOTHER (John Lennon)
Arranged by Gene Page and Richard Perry/Organ: Billy Preston/Drums: Jim Keltner/Bass: Larry Knechtel/Guitar: Mike Deasy/Piano and Pipe Organ: Richard Perry
THE SUMMER KNOWS
(Theme From "Summer of '42")
(Michel Le Grand/Marilyn and Alan Bergman)
Arranged and Conducted by Dick Hazard
I MEAN TO SHINE
(Donald Fagen-Walter Becker)
Arranged by Head/Drums and Percussion: Alice de Buhr/Acoustic Guitar: June Millington, Hugh McCracken/Bass: John Osborn/Guitar: Eric Weissberg/Organ: Donald Fagen/Piano: Mike Rubini/Lead Guitar: John Uribe/Horns: Bobby Keyes, Jim Price/Strings Arranged by Nick DeCaro


The inside design of the *Barbra Joan Streisand* album.

KC 30792
YOU'VE GOT A FRIEND
(Carole King)
Arranged by Head/Drums: Alice de Buhr/Acoustic Guitar: June Millington/Electric Guitar: Mike Deasy/Bass: Larry Knechtel/Piano: Larry Muhoberac/Strings Arranged by Nick DeCaro/ Brass Arranged by Gene Page
PRODUCED BY RICHARD PERRY
Engineering/Sy Mitchell
Remix Engineers/Bill Schnee, Sy Mitchell
Recordists/Bill Schnee, George Beauregard, Willie "The Kid" Greer, John Fiore, Jack Andrews
A Very Special Thanks to Doug Sachs
Album Design/Virginia Team
Photography/Ed Thrasher
(courtesy of Warner/Reprise)

## Discography

**1963** *The Barbra Streisand Album*
**1963** *The Second Barbra Streisand Album*
**1964** *The Third Album*
**1964** *Funny Girl (Original Broadway Cast Recording)*
**1964** *People*
**1965** *My Name Is Barbra*
**1965** *My Name Is Barbra, Two . . .*
**1966** *Color Me Barbra*
**1966** *Je m'appelle Barbra*
**1967** *Simply Streisand*
**1967** *A Christmas Album*
**1969** *What about Today?*
**1971** *Stoney End*
**1971** *Barbra Joan Streisand*
**1973** *Barbra Streisand . . . and Other Musical Instruments*
**1974** *The Way We Were*
**1974** *ButterFly*
**1975** *Lazy Afternoon*
**1976** *Classical Barbra*
**1977** *Streisand Superman*
**1978** *Songbird*
**1979** *Wet*
**1980** *Guilty*
**1984** *Emotion*
**1985** *The Broadway Album*
**1988** *Till I Loved You*
**1993** *Back to Broadway*
**1997** *Higher Ground*
**1999** *A Love Like Ours*
**2001** *Christmas Memories*

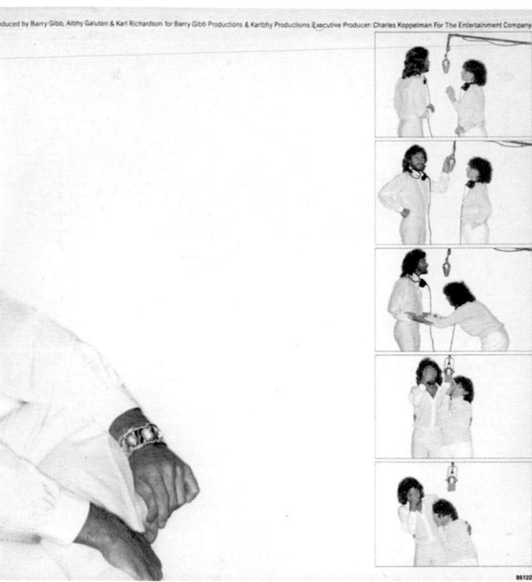

| | |
|---|---|
| 2003 | *The Movie Album* |
| 2005 | *Guilty Pleasures* |
| 2009 | *Love Is the Answer* |
| 2011 | *What Matters Most* |

**Live albums**

| | |
|---|---|
| 1968 | *A Happening in Central Park* |
| 1972 | *Live Concert at the Forum* |
| 1987 | *One Voice* |
| 1994 | *Barbra: The Concert* |
| 1995 | *Barbra: The Concert: Highlights* |
| 2000 | *Timeless: Live in Concert* |
| 2007 | *Streisand: Live in Concert 2006* |
| 2010 | *One Night Only: Barbra Streisand and Quartet at the Village Vanguard* |

**Soundtrack albums**

| | |
|---|---|
| 1962 | *I Can Get It for You Wholesale* |
| 1962 | *Pins and Needles—25th Anniversary* |
| 1968 | *Funny Girl (Original Soundtrack Recording)* |
| 1969 | *Hello, Dolly!* |
| 1970 | *On a Clear Day You Can See Forever* |
| 1971 | *The Owl and the Pussycat* |
| 1974 | *The Way We Were* |
| 1975 | *Funny Lady* |
| 1976 | *A Star Is Born* |
| 1979 | *The Main Event* |
| 1983 | *Yentl* |
| 1987 | *Nuts* |
| 1991 | *The Prince of Tides* |
| 1996 | *The Mirror Has Two Faces* |

## Filmography

**1968** *Funny Girl*
**1969** *Hello, Dolly!*
**1970** *On a Clear Day You Can See Forever*
**1970** *The Owl and the Pussycat*
**1972** *What's Up, Doc?*
**1972** *Up the Sandbox*
**1973** *The Way We Were*
**1974** *For Pete's Sake*
**1975** *Funny Lady*
**1976** *A Star Is Born*
**1979** *The Main Event*
**1981** *All Night Long*
**1983** *Yentl*
**1987** Nuts
**1991** *The Prince of Tides*
**1996** *The Mirror Has Two Faces*
**2004** *Meet the Fockers*
**2010** *Little Fockers*
**2012** *My Mother's Curse*

## DVDs

**My Name Is Barbra (1965)**
The first Barbra Streisand TV special was show soon after *Funny Girl*. This black–and–white show didn't have any guests—a step that was unusual at the time. This is the first time we get a full dose of the all-singing, all-dancing Barbra, taking us through "Alice in Wonderland" and ending up with "People," a fur coat department, and a show of "Don't Rain on My Parade." This is a staple for all fans of Barbra.

**Color Me Barbra (1966)**
The second show for Barbra was two years later, in 1966. This was filmed, of course, in color. As in Barbra's new introduction to the special, it was shot in the Philadelphia Museum of Art with one camera, as the others had broken. If you see photos of Barbra as Nefertiti, this is where they're from. There is also a baffling sequence of Barbra singing with a variety of bewildered animals. Nobody would make this kind of special now, so this is a real piece of history.

**One Voice (1986)**
An all-star audience came to see Barbra's backyard show—some say her best—paying $5,000 a seat for her

first concert in almost twenty years. Many fans consider this to be the real *Timeless*; Barbra is in perfect voice, swathed in white with sparkles on her shoulder, wearing a long white skirt slit up the side, and using a see-through Lucite stool to prop her up onstage. Robin Williams does a brief intro. A real slice of the eighties, with a guest appearance from Barry Gibb.

### Barbra: The Concert (1995)

Barbra's concert from 1993 was her well-documented comeback to the stage—and again she is in fine form. Singing "I'm in the Mood for Love" and "What Is This Thing Called Love" give this concert a unique feel, with lots of televisual extras added in postproduction.

### Timeless: Live in Concert (2001)

Although Barbra takes the safe route through a lot of tunes, this is a well-constructed concert, with lots of biographical detail and a great deal of fun. Barbra treats the crowd to global satellite hookups around the world, a chat with Shirley MacLaine, and much better hair. This is 127 minutes of pure Barbra ushering in the new millennium. Treat yourself to a superb rendition of "Cry Me a River" among its forty song highlights.

### Barbra Streisand—The Concerts (2009)

This three-disc set contains the 2006 concert with those suave classical chaps Il Divo as well as Barbra's 1994 concert that had only previously been available on VHS. In the 1994 concert she doesn't play safe but goes for all the difficult notes. (Note: the Asian release of this concert has a bonus track of "What Are You Doing the Rest of Your Life?") Also included is 1986's formerly VHS-only HBO special *Putting It Together* with the first promo video for *Somewhere*. There's also an interview with Barbra and footage of other TV specials.

### One Night Only: Barbra Streisand and Quartet at the Village Vanguard (2010)

Here, Barbra sang to only 123 fans who got their tickets via a lottery. The evening has receded into legend. This is the singer with a quartet and songs like the old days when she was singing for her supper in a cabaret. She also does eight tunes from the new album plus five standards. There's also a lot of playfulness from Barbra herself, making this a very fun night.

# Index

**PICTURE CREDITS**

*The author and publishers have made every reasonable effort to contact all copyright holders. Any errors that may have occurred are inadvertent and anyone who for any reason who has not been contacted is invited to write to the publishers so that a full acknowledgement may be made in subsequent editions of this work.*

Page © 2 SNAP/Rex Features
5 © Everett Collection/Rex Features
6 © Sunset Boulevard/Corbis
9 © Bettmann/CORBIS
10 © Bettmann/CORBIS
12 © Sunset Boulevard/Corbis
14 © WireImage
17 © Tracy Bennett / Dreamworks Pictu/Bureau L.A. Collection/ Corbis
18 © Elke Stolzenberg/CORBIS
21 © UCL Cultural Department
24 © SNAP/Rex Features
27 © Bettmann/CORBIS
29 © Bettmann/CORBIS
30 © UCL Cultural Department
33 © NY Daily News via Getty Images
35 © Graham Attwood/Rex Features
36 © The Kobal Collection
39 © UCL Cultural Department
40 © Trinity Mirror / Mirrorpix / Alamy
43 © UCL Cultural Department
47 © UCL Cultural Department
49 © UCL Cultural Department
52 © UCL Cultural Department
55 © UCL Cultural Department
91 © UCL Cultural Department
94 © NY Daily News via Getty Images
95 © AP/PA Photos
102 © SNAP/Rex Features
104 © Bettmann/CORBIS
107 © Getty Images
111 © UCL Cultural Department
114 © UCL Cultural Department
117 © Everett Collection/Rex Features
118 © Sunset Boulevard/Corbis
120 © UCL Cultural Department
122–23 © ITV/Rex Features
124–25 © UCL Cultural Department
129 © UCL Cultural Department
135 © UCL Cultural Department
137 © UCL Cultural Department
139 © Moviestore collection Ltd / Alamy
142 © UCL Cultural Department
143 © Pictorial Press Ltd / Alamy
150 © UCL Cultural Department
151 © UCL Cultural Department
153 © Everett Collection/Rex Features
154 © Bettmann/Corbis
156 © ITV/Rex Features
158 © Photos 12 / Alamy
159 © UCL Cultural Department
164 © Sunset Boulevard/Corbis
165 © UCL Cultural Department
174 © Pictorial Press Ltd / Alamy
175 UCL Cultural Department
177 © Bettmann/CORBIS
179 © Siggi Bucher/Reuters/Corbis
180 © Douglas Kirkland/CORBIS
183 © Douglas Kirkland/CORBIS
184 © Douglas Kirkland/CORBIS
186 © WireImage
187 © UCL Cultural Department
188 © UCL Cultural Department
189 © Getty Images
191 © WireImage
195 © Pictorial Press Ltd / Alamy
196 © Douglas Kirkland/CORBIS
198 © David James/Sygma/Corbis
204 © United Archives GmbH / Alamy
205 © UCL Cultural Department
208 © WireImage
211 © Richard Young/Rex Features
212 © UCL Cultural Department
213 © UCL Cultural Department
214 © Rick Maiman/Sygma/Corbis
216 © UCL Cultural Department
220 © BEI/Rex Features
221 © Photos 12 / Alamy
222 © TRAPPER FRANK/CORBIS SYGMA
224 © AF archive / Alamy
231 © UCL Cultural Department
232 © UCL Cultural Department
237 © United Archives GmbH / Alamy
238 © Photos 12 / Alamy
242 © Shaan Kokin/Julien's Auctions/Rex Features
245 © A Berliner/BEI/Rex Features
246 © AFP/Getty Images
248 © Barry Sweet/epa/Corbis
250 © Philippe Wojazer/dpa/Corbis
253 © UCL Cultural Department
254 © KPA/Zuma/Rex Features
256–57 © UCL Cultural Department
259 © WireImage
261 © UCL Cultural Department
262 © On Location News/Rex Features
263 © Rex Features
266 © Getty Images
267 © Steve Schapiro/Corbis
268 ©UCL Cultural Deptartment
270 © UCL Cultural Department
271 © UCL Cultural Department
274 © UCL Cultural Department
275 © UCL Cultural Department

**ACKNOWLEDGMENTS**

Many thanks to Mal Peachey, passionate music lover and fabulous editor, to John Conway and Nicola Hodgson for their sterling work. I also wish to thank Grant Burnside for all of his knowledge and invaluable help on this project. To steal from the best, Grant, I can only say, "Hello Gorgeous!"
*Allegra Rossi, London, 2011*